THE MAKING OF A MIND

By the same author

THE PHENOMENON OF MAN

THE DIVINE MILIEU

LETTERS FROM A TRAVELLER

THE FUTURE OF MAN

HYMN OF THE UNIVERSE

photo: Editions Bernard Grasset

Teilhard de Chardin during World War I

PIERRE TEILHARD DE CHARDIN

THE MAKING
OF A MIND

LETTERS FROM A SOLDIER-PRIEST
1914-1919

TRANSLATED FROM THE FRENCH
'GENÈSE D'UNE PENSÉE'
BY RENÉ HAGUE

HARPER & ROW, PUBLISHERS, NEW YORK

Contents

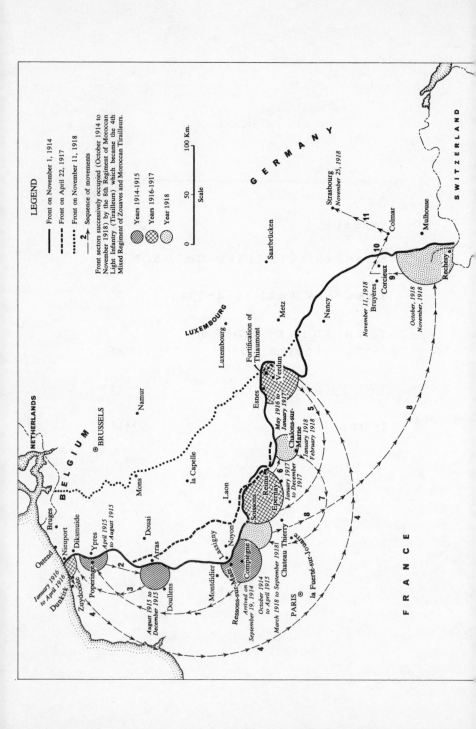

LEGEND

Front on November 1, 1914
Front on April 22, 1917
Front on November 11, 1918
Sequence of movements

Front sectors successively occupied (October 1914 to November 1918) by the 8th Regiment of Moroccan Light Infantry (Tirailleurs) which became the 4th Mixed Regiment of Zouaves and Moroccan Tirailleurs.

Years 1914-1915
Years 1916-1917
Year 1918

Scale
0   50   100 Km.

GERMANY

SWITZERLAND

NETHERLANDS

BELGIUM

⊛ BRUSSELS

LUXEMBOURG

Luxembourg

FRANCE

Ostend
Bruges
Nieuport
Zuydcoote
Dunkirk
Diksmuide
Ypres
Poperinge
Mons
la Capelle
Namur

January 1916 to April 1916

April 1915 to August 1915

August 1915 to December 1915

Douai
Arras
Doullens
Montdidier
Lassigny
Noyon
Ressons-sur-Matz
Compiègne
Laon
Soissons
Reims
Épernay
Chalons-sur-Marne
Esnes
Fortification of Thiaumont
Verdun
Metz
Saarbrücken
Nancy

Arrived on September 19, 1914
October 1914 to April 1915
March 1918 to September 1918

PARIS ⊛
la Fuerté-sur-Jouarre
Château-Thierry

May 1916 to January 1917

January 1917 to December 1917

January 1918 February 1918

November 11, 1918
Bruyères
Corcieux
Colmar
Strasbourg
November 25, 1918

October, 1918
November, 1918

Rechesy
Mulhouse

THE MAKING OF A MIND

PREFACE

At the time of her death Marguerite Teillard (Claude Aragonnès) had almost completed the draft of her study of Père Teilhard's war years; she had already taken the precaution of asking us to see to its publication should she be unable to do so herself. We were touched by her trust and have tried to carry out her wishes. How serious a responsibility was entailed became apparent as soon as we examined the material.

One thing in particular impressed us: Marguerite Teillard's self-effacement. In presenting the letters she had omitted everything that concerned herself personally and concentrated on allowing the personality of Père Teilhard to emerge.

We felt, however, that it would be impossible to understand the birth and development of Père Teilhard's thought if the part played by Marguerite were not appreciated. Her modesty and her sense of dignity caused her to withdraw into the background, but her contribution, from the very nature of her character, was of capital importance; and now that death has released her from any possible suspicion of vanity or pride we feel that her personality should no longer be left in self-imposed obscurity.

We have therefore published the full text of the letters, omitting only such passages as are of purely family interest and of too personal a nature. Similarly we have given the full names of various relations of Père Teilhard (brothers and cousins) instead of the abbreviated or familiar forms he uses. These are the only textual alterations we have thought ourselves justified in making.

It has not been possible to reproduce in print the superimposition of words or phrases that betray Père Teilhard's hesitation in choosing the phrase that best expresses his thought. It indicates an attempt to achieve a gradation between the terms or formulas used, rather as a straight line is defined by its two extreme points.

This search for exactness in phraseology is so important in following the development of Père Teilhard's thought that we have printed in parentheses the words or phrases that appear in the original as additions above the line. Abbreviations have been written out in full.

There is no doubt but that a considerable number of letters are missing. Some obviously went astray when Père Teilhard was on the move during the war, and others were mislaid by Marguerite when she was travelling in France or abroad immediately after the war. A note in her hand, found among the material for the book of war letters, shows that she could find no letters for the periods 15th April to 10th June 1917, and 16th October 1917 to 9th July 1918.

The letters that survive, however, and are now printed, make it perfectly clear that it was during the war that the real substance of Père Teilhard's thought began to emerge in its full force and vigour.

Marguerite Teillard's strong personality is studied more fully later in this volume. She and her cousin were drawn together both by the ties of kinship and by an intellectual affinity and spiritual sympathy that brought complete and unreserved confidence. In reading Père Teilhard's letters one sees how large a part Marguerite played in the development of his thought and one can appreciate the moving tribute he pays her in the letter written at the signing of the armistice.

On the other hand, Marguerite drew great strength from her cousin's spiritual direction. Highly strung and with a passion to advance along the road of Christian perfection, she suffered intensely when every sort of obstacle hampered her progress. It seemed to her impossible to emulate the example of her cousins, Père Teilhard's sisters (Françoise, a Little Sister of the

Poor, who died in Shanghai, and Marguerite-Marie (Guiguite) who retained her serenity of spirit even when broken by ill-health). Although Marguerite longed to devote herself to the service of Christ, she felt no vocation for the religious life. Père Teilhard's letters show how he made her understand that her taste for the things of the spirit could be cultivated through devotion to her educational work. One is moved as one watches her advancing along her road, helped also, as the letters again show, by M. Verdier, later Cardinal and Archbishop of Paris, and one develops a great respect for Marguerite.

The vows referred to by Père Teilhard and his cousin throughout their correspondence take on a deep spiritual and human significance when one realises that on 26th May 1918 the former made his perpetual vows as a Jesuit at Sainte-Foy-lès-Lyon, and that on 21st November of the same year Marguerite made a solemn promise to God to devote her life to education.[1] It is worth noting, too, that Père Teilhard suggested certain modifications in the wording of the promise, a wise precaution that was soon to be justified when Marguerite fell ill in 1922 and was obliged to give up her work as head of the Institut Notre-Dame-des-Champs and recuperate in the South of France and in Rome before going back to teaching.

The text of the letters seldom calls for elucidation. We have not thought it necessary to include more than a few notes to explain an occasional reference or detail. All the letters are addressed to Marguerite. They may be seen as one side of a conversation that appeared on paper only because the writers were unable to speak directly to one another; the reader can get to the heart of a thought that struggles to find exact expression and at the same time he can witness the unfolding of a profoundly human story.

Père Teilhard went to the war at the age of 34, with no previous military experience. It did not take him long to understand the nature and meaning of war. His letters from the front have a striking appositeness for us today, for the war of 1914–18

[1] cf. letter dated 4th November 1918.

foreshadowed the second world conflict when two civilizations confronted one another and all the nations of the world were involved in the complex mixture of nobility and baseness, suffering and joy, self-sacrifice and selfishness that such a conflict produces.

At no time was he ever lost in or crushed by the events in which he took part. He had the gift of sharing an experience and at the same time remaining detached from it. When one notes the times and places at which he was writing, one can appreciate the extraordinary serenity of mind that could be produced only by Père Teilhard's vision of an all-embracing unity in the universe. It was this that enabled him both to be one with warring humanity and at the same time to understand that the chaos in which human cells were struggling was only apparent and that beneath these shattering events there was an underlying order. He saw beyond the horizons of this world so that the field of battle, where death seemed to triumph, was to him the living crucible or mould in which a new world was being fashioned. The ancient home-lands might be so torn by the horrors of war that the traditional seeds could no longer take root, but a new seed-bed would be formed, rich with blood and tears, with the very flesh of men who had given their lives, and in this would be nourished another seed, new, and yet essentially eternal.

As Père Teilhard became increasingly conscious of his vocation he could write:

' So far as my powers allow me, *because I am a priest*, I am determined in future to be the first to realize what the world loves, what it seeks for, what it suffers; the first to join in the search, to feel with the world, to know suffering; the first to fulfil myself and to sacrifice myself,—more widely human and more nobly of this earth than any man who serves the world. I wish on the one hand, to immerse myself in things, and as I enter into them to make them my own and so extract from them the very last particle they hold of eternal life,—so that nothing is lost—. I am determined at the same time, by following the counsels of perfection, to retrieve through renunciation all that our three-fold concupiscence contains of the heavenly fire; through chastity, poverty, and obedience to sanctify the power enclosed in love, in riches, in autonomy.

' That is why I have taken my vows and assumed my priest-hood (the only source of my strength and happiness) in a spirit that accepts the powers of this earth and sees God in them . . .'[1]

It was in the light of his faith that from the ruins that covered the land Père Teilhard saw an unusual and delicate plant spring up in which he recognized the seed of the expected harvest. From that moment he made up his mind to do all that he could to bring that plant to maturity.

There were very few at that time who understood what lay behind the constant, eager, effort that Père Teilhard was to devote throughout his whole life to the advancement of this conviction. Very few understood that his thought flowered from roots that reached back to the origin of the world, as though it were the channel through which flowed the vital sap of all past years reaching up to master the future.

For the force that purifies and sublimates all the riches of the world and all men's aspirations, that transforms the fluid essence in all matter into vital sap, this force is none other than the love of the incarnate Christ. The face of the earth may be rent and the plants it bears may perish, but until the end of time the unseen network of spiritual forces will continue to nourish the flower of hope. Today's flower comes to maturity; its seed ripens. When the grain is harvested and ground we shall eat the bread by which man liv·s, in which the vital germ of matter, kneaded with the leaven of immolated love, becomes both gift and food.

Those whose lives have been given to bringing this time closer have died to the earth, to live again from the undying sap of life.

We may, indeed, say in the words of the parable, ' Unless the seed dies, it cannot bear fruit,' and add the verse of the Magnificat, ' *Et exaltavit humiles.*'

[1] from *Le Prêtre* (written at the front in 1918).

MARGUERITE TEILLARD-CHAMBON
(1880–1959)

(who wrote under the name Claude Aragonnès)

Implicit in the very word 'correspondence' is the notion of a dialogue, of question and answer, of two alternate speakers. In the correspondence printed here only one speaker is heard, for the letters written by Marguerite Teillard-Chambon to Pierre Teilhard de Chardin have been lost. We should, however, try to understand what sort of person it was to whom he opened his mind so unreservedly and how worthy she was of the trust he placed in her and of the confidences she received from him. Nothing can compensate for the loss of Marguerite Teillard's letters but we will try to describe Père Teilhard's cousin.

Marguerite Teillard-Chambon was born in 13th December 1880 at Clermont-Ferrand, in a grim old house that is now the Pascal Museum. Pierre and Marguerite belonged to two branches of a family that had always been closely connected. The Teillard-Chambon children used to go from Clermont to Sarcenat, where they would meet their Teilhard de Chardin cousins.[1] There were numerous children on both sides, of much the same age, and they must have enjoyed together many long walks over the mountains and shared the joy of exploring a countryside that was among the most beautiful and varied in France. It was thus that Pierre and Marguerite came, in childhood and youth, to know their common heritage. They shared, however, more than the beauties of Auvergne, for they knew the same spiritual awakening.

Marguerite was no ordinary woman, and the career she had

[1] The slight difference in spelling (Teillard, Teilhard) will be noted.

13

chosen for herself was, at least in its initial stages, more uncertain and daring than that followed by her cousin, who went practically straight from school to the novitiate. Her father was a man of wide reading and culture, and deeply interested in his daughter's studies. He sent her first to the Good Shepherd nuns at Clermont. In those days, however, at the close of the last century, there was little future in following the normal curriculum for girls; all it led to was a certificate that counted for very little. Marguerite had much more ambitious plans for herself. It was still less than twenty years since Camille Sée had started the first Lycées for girls. Until that time their education had been confined entirely to the religious orders. When Jules Ferry set about secularizing the educational system, one of his most important measures was the introduction of state secondary education for girls. This had provoked a strong reaction in Catholic circles, and given the atmosphere of those days it was inevitable that feeling should run high and lead to bitter rivalry between public and private girls' schools, with Church and state fighting for control over the children's minds. This background explains much violence and some unfair views.

It was in this polemical atmosphere that Marguerite Teillard completed her secondary education. She made up her mind to play an important part in the struggle. She saw that if private education was to hold its own it must be completely reorganized. It would no longer be sufficient to educate good mothers and housewives by teaching them no more than a modicum of useful knowledge with, in addition, some ladylike accomplishments. Women in future were to find a more important place in society and they had as much need as their brothers to be prepared for it; and this meant that the standard of education, in private as well as in state schools, must be equal to the new demands.

The most talented girls, therefore, of Marguerite's age were setting about obtaining the same university qualifications as teachers in the state schools, but were doing so in order to work in private establishments. Marguerite, feeling that this was her

14

vocation, decided to work for a degree in Arts and Philosophy. First, however, she had to obtain her *Certificat*, which corresponded more or less to the present CAPES.[1] She did this by correspondence, working at home at Clermont. After passing the examination, however, she had to go to Paris, which was practically the only place at which she could study for her *agrégation*.[2]

The move to Paris must have been a tremendous wrench for Marguerite. She was separated from her family, was living poorly in a modest hostel for young women, and had to face the formidable university and win from it the intellectual equipment with which to fight it. At that time 'scientism' reigned supreme at the Sorbonne, with such stars as Durkheim, Lévy-Bruhl, Rauh and Lanson, whose rigorous and exact scholarship was matched only by their intransigent secularism. Not long ago, writing about his own early days, M. Etienne Gilson gave a picture of the university that is appropriate in this connection:

'Anyone who, round about 1905, left this little self-contained world for the Faculty of Arts at Paris would not feel lost or find himself on strange ground. It was a new world, but he knew what was in store for him. He had been brought up to respect the scholars who would direct his higher studies; his attitude was one of trust, and he was eager to accept their control. There was only one reservation in this acceptance. The young student of philosophy who was learning a discipline that was new to him did not expect it to tell him what he should think and believe. On that point his mind was already made up; what he wanted to do was to reinforce his convictions and deepen the basis of his belief, and he had to carry out this double task in the midst of influences that were either indifferent or hostile. He had, if possible, to grow, and so continue to develop his own personality. This was the problem before him, and this he could solve only by himself and on his own responsibility.'[3]

[1] *Certificat d'Aptitude au Professorat dans l'Enseignement Secondaire.*

[2] A competitive examination conducted by the state for admission to posts on the teaching staff of the Lycées (state schools).

[3] *Le Philosophe et la Théologie*, p. 27.

The case of Gilson, who was to have a brilliant university career, is not of course quite the same as that of Marguerite Teillard, who was to devote herself to non-state education. While he felt quite at home, she was certainly in a strange land. In spite, however, of her fundamental opposition to the metaphysical attitude of her professors, she gained from them an intellectual discipline that is independent of faith and can even strengthen it and give it greater solidity and substance. Moreover, these were the days when Henri Bergson was the David who boldly faced the Goliath of the University. Already he had launched two fine smooth stones from the brook in *Time and Free Will* and *Matter and Memory*. Marguerite had probably read these before she took her *agrégation* in 1904.

At this point Marguerite could have taken up a university career, but her vocation lay elsewhere, and such a choice never even entered her mind. Especially in non-state schools, women who had graduated as *agrégée* were so few that, although she was only 24, she was immediately offered work of a highly responsible nature, being asked to take over the boarding school that had been run by the Sion nuns at 61 bis rue Notre-Dame-des-Champs.[1] Marguerite accepted the charge, and in taking over the running of the school, for which her purely intellectual training was in no way a preparation, she showed great self-sacrifice. It meant that she gave up not only the security of academic life but also the exercise of her literary talent, which, as the future was amply to demonstrate, was outstanding. She accepted a rigorous and demanding task which was to fill her life for years and keep her to some extent cut off from the intellectual movements of the time, even though her wide and receptive intelligence gave her an uncommon insight into them.

However, in spite of the difficulties that can well be imagined, Marguerite's work as principal was eminently successful. For administrative reasons, the parents' association built at 20 Rue du Montparnasse the buildings that are now the Institut Notre-

[1] Under the *Séparation* (disestablishment) the Sion nuns were no longer allowed to teach.

Dame-des-Champs. Marguerite was quite ready to face, on behalf of the Institute, material difficulties that she had not been frightened of for herself, and boldly aimed at preparing girls for the *baccalauréat*[1] instead of simply for the usual leaving certificate. This called for a large number of specialized teachers with the necessary university qualifications. At the same time it enabled many girls to go on to higher studies and so provide replacements for older teachers and create a class of women whose influence would be felt in advanced fields of scholarship.

Marguerite Teillard's courage and intelligence as a pioneer in such work can readily be appreciated. When, in the years immediately before the 1914 war, she met her cousin Pierre again after he had finished his long studies as a Jesuit, they were no longer the boy and girl who had walked, full of hopeful dreams, over their native hills in Auvergne, but mature people whom years of work and trial had prepared to make their mark in life. No one was better qualified than Marguerite to be the trusted friend who assisted at the flowering of one of the greatest minds of our century. The letters printed here are a record, from day to day, of their mutual trust. They bring out, too, all the difficulties that Marguerite had to face as principal of the Institute while her cousin was risking his life at the front on behalf of his fellow men and was becoming conscious of his mind's first intuitive progress towards what was to be his life work.

Unfortunately, Marguerite had over-estimated her own powers of endurance. Her work proved too much for her; in May 1922 she became seriously ill and had to give up her position at the Institute. She spent the winter of 1922-3 in Italy. Her discovery of this new and beautiful world found expression in her first book, a novel, *La Loi du faible;* and thus Claude Aragonnès (the pseudonym she borrowed from one of her ancestors, who had been a friend of Mademoiselle de Scudéry) was at last able, thanks to this illness, to follow her vocation as a writer, a profession for which she was as well equipped as for teaching.

[1] School leaving certificate giving access to the university and essential for all liberal and civil service careers.

Even so, right until the end, education was still to make as many demands as literature upon her time and energy. Although, when she recovered her health, she did not again take on the direction of the Institute, in October 1924 she taught literature to senior and junior forms and continued to do so for the next thirty years—until 1953. In addition she was until her death the active and vigorous general secretary of the Association of Girls' Secondary Schools; she was the power behind the annual conferences, and wrote for the association's review countless articles and notes on the cinema, the theatre and the books of the day. Her enduring concern was to keep Catholic teachers abreast of cultural development.

This left Claude Aragonnès little leisure to devote to her own original work; even so, everything she wrote was of permanent value, and showed uncommon talent and sensibility, combined with forceful intelligence. She contributed to a number of reviews and periodicals, and in 1934 brought out her second book, *Mademoiselle de Scudéry, reine du tendre*.

Her choice of another subject, Marie d'Agoult, celebrated for her liaison with the composer Liszt, may seem surprising, but what attracted her in the Comtesse d'Agoult was not only her love affairs but also her work as a writer (under the pseudonym of Daniel Stern) fully involved in the controversies of her day. What Claude Aragonnès liked in her was that she made her mark on the literature of her time, as Mademoiselle de Scudéry had in hers.

For this book she was awarded the Femina Vacaresco prize, and this brought her to the notice of the Femina Committee who later asked her to join them. Since the committee's proceedings are secret, it would be out of place to do more than refer to Marguerite's valuable contributions; until her death her great gifts of balanced and temperate judgment were always at their service.

Marguerite Teillard was deeply convinced that women were called upon to play their own part in the cultural life of humanity, that they should be encouraged to do so and should receive the necessary training. It was this basic conviction that integrated her life as a great educationalist and an accomplished, though unfortunately not a prolific, author.

In the summer of 1939, and until the second world war broke out, Marguerite stayed for some time in the U.S.A. Oddly enough, the purpose of her journey had been to renew some childhood memories. She writes in the foreword to her *Lincoln, héros d'un peuple* (1955), ' Two years ago a very old American lady died in Virginia, at the age of 94. In her childhood she had known Lincoln. Her father, Ward Hill Lamon, had been a close friend of the President, had worked with him as a lawyer in Illinois, and had followed him to the White House, where Lincoln had employed him in a number of responsible posts and assignments. Later, Lamon's daughter came to France and married into our family, and, as Dorothy Lamon-Teillard, was our neighbour for some years. I used to listen to her stories . . .'

It was thus that Lincoln became a familiar figure to Marguerite, and it was to envisage him against his own background that in 1935 she crossed the Atlantic. There she had the pleasure of meeting Père Teilhard de Chardin again, who had long been familiar with the U.S.A. The first fruit of her visit was a little book, *Prises de vues américaines*, published in 1945, just after the end of the war, when anything connected with the U.S.A. aroused intense interest in European countries. With charm of style and clarity of expression, Claude Aragonnès gave the French public her impressions both of the older America, which she had made it her business to rediscover, and of the U.S.A. on the eve of the war.

This was only the prelude to an important book on Lincoln, a masterly work, well worthy of its subject. It is astonishing to see with what a penetrating historical sense Claude Aragonnès understood the U.S.A. of a century ago and what psychological insight she brought to bear on the life of a great man so different from any we are used to finding in European history. In a man like Lincoln there was some quality of ancient simplicity that gives him a kinship to Plutarch's heroes; and this is the man who is found at the head of a state in full process of development, passing through the throes of adolescence. Just, and wise, and a true democrat, cut off by a tragic death, Lincoln rightly shares with Washington and Jefferson the title of father of his country, and the United States of today are largely his handiwork. A simple truth, indeed, and yet I know of no French writer who has given it such exact and forthright expression as Claude Aragonnès. To achieve this called for the same forthrightness of thought in herself and the same nobility of character. Our concern, however, is not with Lincoln but with Marguerite Teillard, and we may safely say that in this biography she displayed the qualities of mind and character that made her an incomparable editor of Père Teilhard de Chardin's letters from the front.

She had in fact hardly finished her *Lincoln*, which was published in the autumn of 1955, when Père Teilhard died in New York. A new duty now awaited her, for she had received a great many letters from her cousin and felt that so rich a store should not be hidden under a bushel. The result was the two volumes of letters written during his travels. Some words she used in her introduction may equally well be applied to the present collection:

' My links with Père Teilhard as cousin, and our friendship which was rather that of a brother and sister, put me in the privileged position of receiving many notes and letters from him on his travels, over a particularly important and productive period of his life. As they seemed to me to form a document of exceptional value, I felt they should be published for the benefit of everyone wishing for a deeper acquaintance with one of the noblest and most attractive figures of our epoch.'

At the time of her death, Marguerite Teillard was preparing for publication the letters her cousin wrote to her from the front during the first world war. She had already written an excellent introduction, included in this volume. It brings out the wide range of her mind, her fine sensibility, and her power of exact expression in a way that makes one understand why

Père Teilhard was so ready to confide in her. In Marguerite one finds qualities that are seldom met together, for her intelligence was matched by her strength of character, and this in turn by her sensibility. She had had to face great, if hidden, trials. She held firm to what she knew to be true, and at the same time was open to receive from the minds of others; and, herself a wonderful teacher and trainer, she was peculiarly fitted to understand the astonishing unfolding of an intelligence that amounted to genius.

All her life Marguerite was to bear the marks of her cousin's influence. The conclusion, for example, of her introduction to *Lincoln* is completely 'Teilhardian': she writes, 'He (Lincoln) would have agreed that those whose exacting profession he followed (she is speaking of statesmen) should turn their eyes towards the "vast future" he envisaged as awaiting mankind, the fruit of a common effort exerted by all men working in harmony.' Similarly, at the very end of her life, when Marguerite Teillard introduced some of her friends to Sarcenat, the house that had meant so much in Père Teilhard's life and in her own, she used to do so with a simplicity and sureness of touch that were all her own. Her very reticence was in itself most moving, and anyone who has had this experience, or been introduced by Marguerite into the intimate circle of a great family of the past, or has stood with her and looked out over the grand country you see from Sarcenat, will know how irreplaceable is her loss.

We pray that those who in life were so close to one another, may have been brought together again in death; for ever. In men's memories, we know, they will not be divided. There seems to be some mysterious law in our nature which almost invariably ordains that by the side of a great man there shall always stand, slightly in the shadows, the figure of a great woman. Once again this law is demonstrated in Pierre Teilhard de Chardin and Marguerite Teillard-Chambon.

Alice Teillard-Chambon
Max Henri Bégouën

THE GREAT WAR
1914–1919

Of the outside events in Pierre Teilhard's life the war was probably the most decisive of all. It had a profound effect on his whole being. It would not be too much to say (in fact he thought so himself, and said as much) that it enabled him to see himself. In any case, it hastened an interior development that would have occurred less rapidly and, maybe, less inexorably had it not been for circumstances that greatly increased his experience of men, that provided him with an intellectual impetus, and gave a fine temper to his personality.

Like so many others, he was flung into a medley in which all types of men, differing in race, in social position, and in mentality, were thrown together; he was brought up against all that was most real and terrible in life and death, from the depths of atrocity to superhuman feats of heroism; he shared the agonizing effort, prolonged almost to breaking-point, of his own generation flung into the crucible; and he emerged from it a new man, ready to face with moral courage, so much more demanding than physical courage, the battle for truth, for the integrity of his own mind, and for the fulfilment of the personal task whose nature had become apparent to him during those terrible and yet fruitful years.

This happened when Pierre Teilhard was thirty-three years old. He had had no physical or spiritual training to prepare him for a soldier's life. His health was robust, and he still retained from childhood and youth his taste for walking and an open-air life. During his novitiate in Jersey and later in

England he had been able to enjoy a healthier and more athletic life than he would have found at a French Seminary in those days (in particular there were geological expeditions and swimming in the sea). On the other hand there was the fatigue and nervous exhaustion of long hours of exacting study. Certainly he had not met with any equivalent to the hardships of life at the front, or the physical effort and suffering that awaited him there. He had never done his military service, so that this was his first experience of soldiering.

For twelve years, moreover, he had been away from France, and was thus completely unfamiliar with the ferment of ideas and political passions that, on the eve of the war, was boiling up in the minds of young people between twenty and thirty years of age. He was untouched by the patriotic enthusiasm that carried them along as war between France and Germany appeared imminent. When his class was called up in December 1914 it seemed to him simply a matter of unavoidable duty.

He loved life, and he loved his own life. As it opened out before him, he saw a double vocation: God called him to serve him in a scientific career that he found attractive and full of promise. By following it he would be able to make the best use of his talents and gifts 'for the greater glory of God'. It was in the ranks of the Society that he had been mobilized since his nineteenth year, and, since the Society continues the preparation and training of its recruits until they are thirty, his active service had only just begun.

Now he had to drop it: the call to war was inconvenient, but it would, one hoped, be a short war—a current illusion shared even by 'well-informed circles' in the rear—no more than an interlude in one's life. Like the others, Pierre would have to leave his chosen path for a time. 'Like the others . . .'—this was to be his motto throughout his four years of war, serving in the humblest rank; with a corporal's stripes on his arm and a pack on his back, he shared the fate of those conscripted. Moreover, two of his brothers were already at the front, as lieutenants in the artillery, two more were training in the rear to join them, and the youngest but one of the six sons serving in the forces had just been killed in action. Many of his fellow-Jesuits had been called up and he had already heard that several had fallen. Now it was his turn, and that was as it should be. The only thing he was afraid of was that he might have to hang about in barracks. The front line attracted him, for there he would at least be in action. Already we find in him the deep conviction, to harden in his mind as he faced life's trials, that everything that happens must be accepted in a spirit of welcome. Moreover, for a young man there was a flavour of adventure about it, and there was always something youthful in Pierre. Both his external circumstances and his own interior reflexion had matured him, and he was ready to accept what seemed simply an event as possibly an advent, no matter what unknown destiny the future might hold, even should it be life's greatest mystery, death itself. Now was the time, he felt, and here the place, at which God awaited him.

The outbreak of the first world war was very different from that of the second. The latter had haunted our minds for more than twenty years; during that time war had been endemic in one part of the world or another, poisoning the atmosphere with its grim memories and casting a shadow over the future. In 1914 war fell upon the world like a thunderbolt. Civilized nations felt that it was something that could never really happen, even though some years earlier a distant but unmistakable warning note had been sounded.[1] The handful of politicians who were to make a decision that affected millions of human beings, and even the professional soldiers whose business it was to see it coming and prepare for it, found that they could only fling themselves with a blind fatalism and even a sort of shocking lightheartedness into the unfathomed abyss of war.

Today that war seems so far away that it has taken on another sort of unreality, especially in the eyes of those who never fought or lived through it; it has been relegated to the past, and the

[1] No doubt a reference to the Agadir incident of 1905 which brought Germany and France so close to war.

literature it gave birth to has been pushed into the background by memories of more recent horrors.

One of the most interesting things in Pierre Teilhard's correspondence is his attitude towards a phenomenon in which one of the great turning-points of history is recognizable. He found himself suddenly both actor and spectator in the foreground of the conflict; he brought to it an eager curiosity and a penetrating eye; he gave his whole being to it, with all his courage as a man and all his faith as a Christian. His letters are a timely reminder of what one generation accomplished and suffered and preserved. All he had in mind was to record, for himself and some intimate friends, his own life and thoughts from day to day, and he never suspected that he was leaving behind him a document of the first importance for its objectivity, its clear-sightedness, and its openhearted and all-embracing humanity.

' For us soldier-priests,' he said, ' war was a baptism into reality.'

It is as well to realise just what it was like for Père Teilhard to arrive as a new regimental stretcher-bearer at the headquarters of a mixed regiment of Zouaves and Moroccan light infantry (Tirailleurs). The medical orderlies are the humblest branch of the army. Looked down on by the combatant troops, theirs is a thankless role. Their work is dangerous and yet it is looked on as a ' soft number ', fit only for weaklings. They are made to feel this but in an attack it is they who have to bring in the wounded, get them down to the aid-post, bandage them, give them first aid, and at the same time be responsible for all the most onerous fatigues that are kept for the non-combatants. In the trenches, they have to face the same deluge of shells. In his first letters from the Yser front, during the Flanders campaign in which his regiment held the same ground for almost a whole year, Père Teilhard writes with pride that he has already made the acquaintance of every sort of projectile sent over by the Germans at short range, and returned with interest.

In these, as later in very different circumstances, he quickly adapted himself to unfamiliar conditions, partly, no doubt, because he used his intelligence and had plenty of ' guts ', but also because he knew how to handle men. It was soon recognized that he was the most fitted to be in charge of a section, and he was promoted to corporal. While machine-guns were still sweeping the ground he would dash out with his men, and then advance himself as close as he possibly could to the enemy lines to find a wounded man, pick him up on his back and carry him to the rear. The men he led would complain that he went too far—' let him get on with it himself . . .'

He was serving with a picked regiment of assault troops, and from January 1915 until the armistice of 11th November 1918 they were moved from one end of the front to another, from Flanders to Verdun, brought back to Champagne, and then sent north again. They were in action with Mangin's army, in the great battles of the Oise in July 1918, and in the big counter-attack that shook and finally broke the German line and drove them back to the frontier. Their own division (under Guyot de Salins) was held in readiness to deliver the final blow in Lorraine, when the internal collapse of the Reich disorganized and demoralized the German troops. The sudden capitulation of the enemy and the armistice found them in Alsace, and until March 1919 they were with the occupying forces in Germany.

Pierre Teilhard then returned to Auvergne for demobilization. After four years at the front, broken by only a few brief periods of leave, he came out, unscathed, without a wound or a day's illness. If anything, his excellent constitution was even strengthened by his experiences. In the often wearisome fatigues of war, in the physical and spiritual shocks of that hell into which men were so continually flung, he acquired the powers of endurance he was later to display as a traveller and explorer.

When he describes the fighting, however, he never exaggerates its awfulness and horror. His disregard for effect governs the whole tone of his writing. With an earnest simplicity and compassion he puts down what he saw, and what he went

27

through, in the darkest and saddest days. There is nothing of Barbusse's realism in his letters. Moreover, since he was writing to those who were near and dear to him, he deliberately minimized his own danger and makes no mention of his own courageous deeds, for which he was three times mentioned in Army and Divisional Orders, and was awarded the Croix de Guerre, the Médaille Militaire and the Légion d'Honneur.

He sank deeper into the quagmire of war than many other writers or novelists, but there is no striving for literary effect in his letters; nevertheless, and indeed for that very reason, they strike the reader as the work of an important witness and one of the great writers of the war.

Pierre Teilhard did more than live the war. He reflected upon it with a sharp awareness of its different aspects, of what he used to call its ' dimension '. It typified Pascal's reconciliation of opposites: the combined wretchedness and grandeur of man emerged for him in the dazzling light of truth, and provided the theme for one of the essays he wrote at that time, charged with all the emotions aroused by his most harrowing experiences.[1]

There may be some who, on re-reading his letters today, fail to understand or who even misunderstand the fascination of the trenches. Père Teilhard well knew, from his own experience, that it was here that man sometimes reached a peak of his own being and felt that there was a tremendous grandeur and significance in his actions. Some people have found this shocking. Pierre Teilhard's soldiering was whole-hearted. He shared fully in the collective tension from which an army derives its strength. (Discipline is simply the mechanism that the engine sets in motion.) Everyone knows that if the tension slackens, the war begins to fold up; it comes to an end when men no longer believe in it, for every worth-while action depends upon some faith. If German Imperialism had to be destroyed, then the war was a just war at the time. For Pierre Teilhard there was no problem of conscientious objection. Someone has commented that fortunately he did not himself have to take life. It is true that

[1] La Nostalgie du front.

his duties were pacific, to pour oil into the wounds inflicted by war, but this argument would have seemed to him a piece of empty casuistry. In war, everyone kills, from the commander-in-chief to the worker in the munition factory, and Pierre Teilhard felt acute distress because he never went over the top with the others when the attack was launched. He 'compensated', therefore, by acts of personal bravery. He had an intense feeling of participating in the tragedy of war, but he examined it more deeply as a phenomenon, and learnt to see beyond the immediate aspect of the conflict and what was immediately at stake. In it he saw a crisis of evolution which had to be gone through. Civilized nations, at grips with one another in a merciless struggle, were moving against the great life-current, which he already saw as an irresistible progress towards unification of the human race.

During the second world war, when Pierre Teilhard was marooned in Pekin, he reflected even more deeply on this terrible internal cleavage and on the senselessness of freedom in a state of chaos that holds back the progress all men are looking for. The only earthly task worthy of us is 'to build the earth'.

For Père Teilhard the war was also a great human experience, a chance to act as a person in his relation with men whose life he was sharing. He refused ever to look for or to accept anything that would distinguish him from his comrades, and turned down the amenities his superiors would have been willing to obtain for him. 'No mark of rank, no special consideration, no comfort.' He must, he felt, stay in the ranks. Rubbing shoulders day and night and in times of great stress, with his fellows was a reef on which a priest's dignity might well have foundered, exposed as he was to their watchful eyes and to their unspoken but often by no means friendly thoughts. Père Teilhard's natural dignity and comradely simplicity enabled him to avoid these rocks. His men had taken him to their hearts. To the Zouaves he was 'Monsieur Teilhard', to the African troops the 'Sidi Marabout'. He shared out all his family sent him for the men, the parcels of food, the rugby footballs to keep them amused when out of the line, the warm clothing in winter and the tobacco in all seasons, but this would not have been enough without the equable temper and accessibility which made him a person you could always count on, especially when things went badly.

Out of regard for Corporal Teilhard the men used to improvise an altar and decorate it for Sunday mass—sometimes with two or three inopportune shells to take the place of the bell. In front there might be a ' three-star ' veteran with some N.C.O.'s who had come to hear him preach. Speaking to such a mixed audience, he learnt to adapt himself to their different mentalities. Here circumstances were in his favour. These men, lost in a no man's land, were in daily peril of their lives, their souls were hardened by the wearisome old routine, but war's terrifying demands moved them, and deep down there was a substratum ready to receive the seed. And yet, speaking to them as a priest, he never tried to work upon them emotionally or to appeal to a feeling for the magical or to superstitious fetishism: he had so much respect for even the humblest minds that he was able to appeal to their intelligence as men and try to arouse in it a worthy idea of God.

It was rather different when he was speaking with the officers. Various conversations disclosed illuminating points of contact on both sides. He used to weigh up what obstacles separated most of them from the Christian idea as it had been presented to them and which they had rejected or left on one side. He would feel his way, looking for an opportunity to drop in a telling thought, or at any rate something that would raise a question in the minds even of those who seemed the least worried by religious problems. In any case, the human qualities of the priest ensured respect for his faith.

Père Teilhard, quite spontaneously, performed another type of ministry at the front, by his assistance in the parish work that had more or less gone to pieces in the fighting areas. Some parishes had no one to serve them, the parish priest having been called up or sent to the rear; the church might have been damaged by shell-fire or be abandoned, but there would still be people living there with no form of public worship. Père Teilhard would open up the presbytery again, go there every day from his billet, say mass and hold services. If the *curé* was still living in the village, he would be put up by him: an attic and a palliasse was all he wanted. It gave him a quiet corner where he could retire for a few hours every day to recollect himself and work. In return the *curé* would get him to sing high mass, preach, and instruct his flock. Père Teilhard gave himself to this work ungrudgingly; and what a delight it was to him when some hospitable and warmhearted *curé* was inspired to invite to a meal some of his fellow-priests who had been called up. Then for a brief hour it was an escape from the spiritual solitude that was the soldier-priest's normal lot.

During his four years at the front, Père Teilhard carried on this ministry whenever circumstances made it possible, for he was, as he would be all his life, a priest first and foremost.

At the same time a certain amount of solitude was a refuge to him. From time to time he had to escape from the crowded jungle of humanity which everyone, but most of all the strong personalities, felt stifling. When he was not on duty, he used to find escape in the freedom of the open fields, in long walks. If he could not do so in the day time, he would go out at night, on what he called his ' noctambulations '. More than ever he found release and refreshment in nature.

Among the dunes of Flanders, the sea was a great joy to him, maybe because an ancient legacy from his seafaring ancestors in Picardy came to the surface again. Here the boundless horizons, with their shifting outlines and colours, entranced him. Later it was the heights of the Meuse, the ridges of Champagne, the forests of the Oise, all the aspects of the French provinces he was traversing, nearly always for the first time. He learnt a great deal from this long and sometimes tragic contact between the soldiers on active service and the strange countryside of the front, where he lived huddled in the valley bottoms, on the banks of rivers, billeted with the local inhabitants, side by side with the peasants, conscious always of the danger and dire poverty in which they lived and seeing how their ravaged fields, abandoned to the armies, had reverted to wildness.

With the eye of a geologist he could read the bone-structure of the country and reconstruct its visible appearance from within; as a naturalist he could people it with its own fauna and flora, collecting and examining anything that caught his eye. An anemone that was new to him would be described and drawn for his father, who would be able to put a name to it for him, as he would for various aquatic birds that resembled some familiar species to be seen flying over the Allier. On the eve of the attack launched by Mangin's army, when the tanks had already rumbled into the forest of Villers-Cotterets, ready for the grim encounters that awaited them, Pierre Teilhard could note for his family: 'We're picking lilies-of-the-valley and mushrooms, and gathering snails—what a rustic life!'

This contact with simple, unspoilt things was a brief interlude of peace. Once, however, he was back among the things of war and the men who fought it he found himself again, in one whole section of his being, completely and utterly, from the very nature of his make-up, alone.

There were just the odd few who could, with a little tact and sensibility, get closer to him and realise a little that they were dealing with an exceptional personality. It might be a passing remark in conversation or an occasional glimpse of his innermost reactions. They could understand at least that he was too ' busy inside ' to be fully part of their world. His thoughts were not their thoughts. It was impossible to label him as everybody who shares a common life is ultimately labelled.

He was, in fact, living through a fascinating interior adventure. For the first time he was discovering himself. He was finding that the most secret depths of his soul had come to the surface: the remarkable gifts, the innate tendencies that since his distant childhood had been associated with, but not assimilated to all that his education, the intellectual equipment he had acquired, and the self-cultivation of a man trained to exercise the spirit, had made of him—to all the potentialities and desires that these had accumulated within him.

The fading of his past into the background, the temporary break with his habits of life and the general pattern of his twofold environment, religious and scientific, gave him a great independence of mind. He was beginning to discern ' the look that God,' he used to say, ' wished to give his soul '; for it was always with the feeling that the eyes of God were upon him that he looked into himself to learn what he was.

He felt that he had reached a milestone in his life. While his fellow-Jesuits and scientific colleagues were sympathizing with him for the time wasted in the war, he himself knew that this breathing-space would stand him in good stead. He would at last be able to give form to a rich store of visions and enthusiasms that were now clamouring for expression; and this must be done before death overtook him; which again meant that it must be done immediately, for death might well be round the corner.

The dazzling Presence that had become manifest to him ' before the age of ten ' as running through the immensity of creation, was now summoning him. If he was to make men see this God hidden in the world—and how hidden he realized more every day—he must see him more vividly himself. All that made life worth living, if life should still be granted to him, was to be God's man in this new world.

When, in 1916, he sent me his first writing, *La Vie cosmique*, he described it as ' my intellectual testament '. He thought that this, his first piece, might be his only one, and wished it to be kept safe; and throughout the four years of war it was with the same idea in mind that he sent back the later essays. There was no pride of authorship or self-conceit in this anxiety; it was simply that he was convinced that such light as had been given to him should be passed on to others, and that conviction remained with him throughout his whole life.

The transformation that was to lead him to full maturity could only be brought about by the conformity of his own will to the divine grace, and on this point he was ever watchful. War was for him an urgent invitation to prayer. In some dug-out or rickety billet, his natural gift for concentration enabled him to find, paradoxically, a monastic cell: by cutting himself off from his surroundings he achieved an intense purity of interior atmosphere. Between offensives he managed to preserve some regularity of religious exercise even in the irregular life of active service. Here his daily mass was the central point. He would go miles on foot, fasting, to the church at which he could say it. If that were impossible, he would say it wherever he might be, using his portable altar: a bag, like a surgeon's, holding a miniature set of the sacred vessels. On forced marches and during attacks he was deprived of mass, and felt it deeply.

On the day after a most murderous battle, where he had seen so many fall whom he knew and loved, and which he himself survived only by a miracle, he said mass for his dead comrades and wrote, 'I believe that on that day I said the most fervent mass of my life.' One sees him, too, literally overcome by the priest's privilege of carrying the Eucharist upon his person, during those bloody days. The presence of Christ in the most sacred mystery of faith was to be the theme of two essays[1] instinct with passionate fervour. If he could not openly celebrate the Christian feasts that mark the progress of the liturgical year, he would ponder over them with his breviary, each one raising a personal echo in his soul. The joy of Easter, its inexhaustible fund of glorious hope, was to entrance him until his very last days. Here he found the whole Christian mystery that nourished him with a constant flow of life-giving sap.[2]

---

[1] *Christ in the World of Matter*, three mystical tales (1916), (published in *Hymn of the Universe*, Eng. trans. Harper, 1965) and *Le Prêtre* (1918).

[2] As was his duty as a religious, he kept in close contact with his superiors, and sent them whatever he wrote. His interior dispositions were so well known to them that before the end of the war (in May 1918) he was allowed to take his final vows in the Society of Jesus.

' To whom that hath, more shall be given '.

From half-disguised allusions in his letters and still more from his mystical essays of that time, one may surmise that during these days passed in the shadow of death he had some experience of mounting to the sister peaks of Faith, Hope and Charity, and that there he found some of those flashes of illumination which make what he wrote pulsate with a warm glow of light. In a short biographical sketch such as this, serving only to introduce the text of the letters, there is no room to study in detail, step by step, the development of Père Teilhard's thought. Some day, such a study must be made. All I wish to do here is to indicate, as they occurred, the external circumstances and, if possible, the personal frames of mind (so far as they were expressed in letters or conversation) that may serve to illuminate the progress of Père Teilhard's thought, what animated it, its general trend, and its overall orientation, during these four years.

His writings fall into three groups: philosophical essays, mystical meditations and aspirations, thoughts on apostolic work, followed one another in no apparent order but in very rapid sequence, when one considers how loaded with thought they were, and that the author was at the same time living a life full of tragic events and ceaseless activity.

Fortunately, Père Teilhard was always careful to add the exact date and place to his letters and even his most trifling compositions, thereby greatly simplifying the work of a biographer or bibliographer. We can accordingly fix the precise date for the completion of each of the essays, of which, between 1916 and the beginning of 1919, he produced not less than sixteen. Often, too, the letters enable us to determine even the interval between the conception of the idea and the completion of the essay.

The word ' project ' has become popular since Sartre,[1] and it may be appropriate to use it here, and adapt it in a special

---

[1] cf. ' A free intention, a free initial project is fundamental to my being; indeed it is my being itself. There exists in every one of us an initial project, which can be laid bare by the appropriate phenomenological process of exisential psychoanalysis.' (Gabriel Marcel on Sartre.)

precise sense to Pierre Teilhard, who said of himself, 'So far as I can remember my own self, I have always lived in a forward-looking tension.' He was perfectly conscious of this tension, and if he felt it slacken, he would become uneasy as though he were losing his foothold. Something more, he felt, was always to be achieved; he was constantly seeking and expecting the best, always reaching out still further, always full of hope, always in a state of perpetual 'newness', as Gide was fond of saying (though he, indeed, was deeply entrenched in his own hedonism); and so he was always spreading his sails to the wind of adventure, ready for the greatest of all voyages, the only one that fired his enthusiasm, the search for and meeting with God.

Once the first intuition had been conceived in his mind, its full expression was a rapid process. 'There's something I'm trying to focus in my mind,' he might write, and a few days later one would be surprised to find, if he had happened to have a quiet interval, that he had completed it.

He had been struck by a passage in Balzac, where the novelist explains that a writer finds himself compelled to write as though he were carried away by a landslide. The flood of ideas (a whole world trembling about his ears) and the need to preserve the original freshness of inspiration, impose an urgent haste. Pierre Teilhard had the same experience: it is impossible to retrace one's steps along the road of intuition, for the nascent idea fades a little as soon as it is incarnated in words and transposed into dialectic. It may be necessary to chain down truths, but truth itself must never be chained. Even when the form of Pierre Teilhard's writing is most finished, its power of emphasis, its impact, one might say, comes from the first spark that kindled the whole. The 'happiness' of the thought gives birth to the happiness of expression; and that is why in a couple of lines one can immediately recognize his style. They are his mind in action, the man himself is in the words. There is a passionate sharing of confidence with the invisible partner in the dialogue; and the dialogue is with God: 'He and I,' in Newman's words. All he wrote came to fruit in prayer.

The work he produced during the war, in which his thought, always in the presence of God, and always combining so much honesty and reverence with its boldness, seeks out and feels its way along new roads, does more than give promise of maturity; it is its magnificent emergence. We cannot fail to recognize its immense value, and yet we should note that Père Teilhard himself took a different view of it. This was not simply a matter of modesty, but of intellectual standards.

'My war papers may be interesting psychologically for studying the ontogenesis of an idea, but there is nothing in them that I have not expressed more clearly at a later date.' (Letter to Marguerite Teillard, New York, 1952.)

As a scientist and philosopher, constantly striving to get a more exact grip on the truths he had arrived at and to express the latest form his thought had taken with ever greater and greater concentration and compression, these war-time compositions seemed to him altogether 'too young', rather as though they belonged to his own 'pre-history'. And yet who was better fitted than he was to appreciate the importance of every form of prehistory and ontogenesis?

This view that he took of his early work may profitably be applied by us now, and we may well conclude that we have his own authority to ensure for it the survival that he himself did not claim for it.[1]

In the first essay, *La Vie cosmique*, we find his initial awakening to an astonished awareness of the world, a pantheistic vision and its urgent temptation, already overcome by his demand for unity in a transcendant.

In the *Lutte contre la multitude* he goes deep into the problem of the one and the many, a theme to which he returns in *L'Union*

[1] *La Vie cosmique* (1916); *Christ in the World of Matter* (1916); *La Maîtrise du monde et le règne de Dieu* (1916); *La Lutte contre la multitude* (1917); *Le Milieu mystique* (1917); *L'Union créatrice* (1917); *La Nostalgie du front* (1917); *L'Ame du monde* (1918); *Le Prêtre* (1918); *La Grande Monade* (1918); *Mon Univers* (1918); *La Foi qui opère* (1918); *Forma Christi* (1918); *Note pour servir à l'Evangélisation des temps nouveaux* (1919); *Terre promise* (1919); *L'Elément universel* (1919).

créatrice. In *Mon Univers* he outlines a synthesis of the relations between God and the world, and a similar search for some ' centration' of the universe is to be found at the same time in *L'Ame du monde* and *La Grande Monade.* The christic theme had appeared in 1916, in *Christ in the World of Matter.* It is rounded off and completed in the *Milieu mystique* and *Le Prêtre,* which herald *La Messe sur le monde* (1923) just as the *Milieu mystique* does the *Milieu divin* of 1927. In *Maîtrise du monde et le règne de Dieu* and *Note pour servir à l'évangélisation des temps nouveaux* Pierre Teilhard examines the meaning and conditions of the apostolate that the Church will have to adapt to the needs of the modern world.

There is no need to add that there is no sign of haste in either the form or substance of these first writings. The progress of the thought, like that of the writing, is deliberate and controlled. There is nothing of the dilettante in his work, for he had too much respect for the subjects he treated. Everything he wrote is really *written.* The very appearance of his manuscripts has such a neatness of writing and arrangement that they might have been produced in a quiet study, even though his hand still shook from tiredness and nervous strain after a spell in the trenches.

If the assured tone he writes in seems bold, tense with ' prophetic impatience', with an undercurrent of youthful vivacity when he attacks various ways of thinking opposed to his own, it should be attributed to his anxiety to bring out some important aspects of Christianity that were obscured for his contemporaries by other writers at that time. His ' lucid and intrepid spirit'[1] never shrank from the startling. It must be remembered, too, that he was writing primarily for himself. He was drawing up a testimony, almost, as we have seen, a testament. He communicated his work to a restricted circle, with no hope of having it published. He had tried to do so with two articles on current problems; one was refused, and the other accepted after cutting.

[1] The phrase is Sir Julian Huxley's, writing of *The Phenomenon of Man.*

He asked himself whether he would ever be able to disclose all that he had seen and felt and thought during this amazing period of transformation. Just before his demobilization he wondered anxiously, ' Will they ever listen to me? '

Claude Aragonnès
July 1959   *(Marguerite Teillard-Chambon)*

PIERRE TEILHARD DE CHARDIN, registered for non-combatant duties in 1902 and again in 1904, had never done his military service. In December 1914 a recruiting board passed him as 'fit for active service'. He was called up almost immediately and posted as a medical orderly to the 13th infantry section of a unit stationed first at Vichy and later at Clermont-Ferrand. He left for the front on 20th January 1915, as a stretcher-bearer, 2nd class, in the 8th regiment of Moroccan light infantry (Tirailleurs), which on 23rd June 1915 became the 4th mixed regiment of Zouaves and Moroccan Tirailleurs. On 13th May 1915 he was promoted to corporal.

CITATIONS

29th August 1915. *Cited in Divisional Orders.* 'Volunteered to leave the aid-post in order to serve in the front-line trenches. Displayed the greatest self-sacrifice and contempt for danger.'

17th September 1916. *Cited in Army Orders.* 'A model of bravery, self-sacrifice, and coolness. From the 15th to the 19th August he directed the teams of stretcher-bearers over ground torn by shell-fire and swept by machine-guns. On the 18th August he went out to within 20 yards of the enemy lines to retrieve the body of a fallen officer and brought it back to the trenches.'

20th June 1917. *Médaille Militaire.* 'A first-rate N.C.O. His sterling character has won him confidence and respect. On 20th May 1917 he deliberately entered a trench under heavy bombardment to bring back a casualty.'

21st May 1921. *At the request of his old regiment he was made Chevalier of the Légion d'Honneur.* 'An outstanding stretcher-bearer, who during four years of active service, was in every battle and engagement the regiment took part in, applying to remain in the ranks in order that he might be with the men, whose dangers and hardships he constantly shared.'

The Letters

I'm writing to you, not from the front, but from Uncle Joseph's[1] chimney-corner—symbolic, indeed, of the absence of any heroism in my present existence. There was no difficulty in changing my first assignment (private in the 105th) for a posting to the 13th section of stretcher-bearers (Gribeauval barracks, otherwise known as ' Paulines '), and it is there that for the last two days I have been vegetating, wearing a brown suit—three parts civilian —with a *képi*, without much hope of getting up to the front line for some weeks. As stretcher-bearers in a combatant unit we are barred from the hospitals, and have nothing to occupy us but some rather boring exercises. I can see that I'll be hard put to it if I am to avoid mental and spiritual ossification.— Nothing could be less romantic than the stretcher-bearers' *milieu* in the depot; what is more, all individual characteristics seem to be completely lost to view. It's the supreme example of the commonplace, obscure, life I've so often recommended to you.

Pray that I may be able to benefit from it, and that it may prepare me for better things . . .

At Sarcenat, things are going as well as could be. There's good news from those in the forces.

Goodbye—keep right on, relying on our Lord alone. Kind regards to Mme Parion.[2]

PIERRE

Moulins-gare, Wednesday morning [*20th January 1915*]

It has happened, at last—and with as little notice as last time— I am posted to ' No. 2 ambulance, 4th Moroccan brigade, sector 98 '—I have an idea it's not far from Gabriel.

[1] Joseph Teilhard de Chardin, his father's brother.
[2] Madame Parion, assistant head of the Institut Notre-Dame-des-Champs, and an intimate friend of Marguerite Teillard.

We're off in an hour's time for Creil—Pray for me.

Ever yours,

PIERRE

[*Cuvilly*] *22nd January* [*1915*]

I'm writing to you from a hut 10 km. from the Boche. It's still too far, and I'm still not sure that I'll be able to get out of the job of medical orderly (instead of stretcher-bearer). There are no wounded here. We can hear a lot of gunfire from Gabriel's direction, whom I hope to see. I must be very close to Marcel. We're sleeping, comfortably enough, on straw.

Altogether, my position is still unsettled, and it's a *very* humble one: you feel very insignificant alongside the combatant troops, and they make you feel it . . . If I stay here, I shall probably have no difficulty in saying mass, but for the last five days it hasn't been possible—and that I miss. Still, I pray for you and the others. Remember me kindly to everyone. My respects to Mme Parion.

PIERRE

Address: 4th Moroccan Ambulance—sector 98

[*Cuvilly*] *23rd January 1915*

I've received your postcard. Thank you. Marcel very kindly came to see me this morning; you saw him recently, so there's no need for me to tell you that he's very well. It was a real joy to us to see one another again. It won't, I think, be the last time.

A moment later, Gabriel turned up, plump and bearded.— No special news of my own. It's cold but fine. We watch the trenches being bombarded in the distance, and cut firewood.

I said mass this morning, and no doubt shall be able to say it here regularly. Always remembering you.

PIERRE

[*Cuvilly*] *Sunday 30th January 1915*

No. 1 hut, 4th section, 2nd Moroccan ambulance, has just gleefully shared the contents of the parcel so generously sent by Mme Parion and you. I kept in particular for myself the friendship with which, at least as much as with woollen comforts, it was filled. Wait until my position is definitely settled before sending another. I have a chance of being posted to the 8th Tirailleurs as chaplain-stretcher-bearer, which would be infinitely better than my present job.

There's still gunfire here all the time, but I see no shells or wounded. And it is still the same humble life. I try to apply myself to it, in order, if it please God, to gain more merit. Marcel has very kindly been to see me twice again. Wherever I go, I land among the family!

Did you get my letter of the beginning of January, in answer to your poem? Keep it up, won't you? Tomorrow my mass will be offered chiefly for those who sent and filled the parcel. This card is half, of course, for Mme Parion. May our Lord keep her brother, and bless you all at the Institute.

My love to all of you, and most particularly to your parents.

PIERRE

[*Marest, Oise*] *5th February* [*1915*]

Now I am part of the glorious 8th Tirailleurs, and this morning, during a short move, I felt proud to march behind a regiment of *chéchias*.[1] I'm rather, of course, *in partibus infidelium*, but there's no lack of Christians, and I'm the *only* priest in the

[1] Referring to the cap worn by French North African troops.

regiment. We're still resting. When we go into the trenches I'll call on you for what I find will be useful. Yesterday I saw Marcel who was extremely nice to me and took me to his 'home'. But I've missed Gabriel and fear that it will be a long time before I see him again.—I forgot to tell you that here I am with *real*, and excellent officers. It can't but hearten one to work with such M.O.'s as these.—This morning, the first Friday, I was unable to say mass and had to content myself with offering up to our Lord the humping of my kit on a 15 km. march.—One way and another, things are pretty easy.—Tomorrow I'll be able to say mass. I shall pray for all of you at the Institute.— Thanks for your last letter: I'm glad to hear what you tell me of Le Chambon.[1]

As to separations, we may be sure that our hearts will always bleed for them; but that is the price we must pay for our Lord's entering into us a little further.

Ever yours,

PIERRE

[*Marest, Oise*] *9th February 1915*

This is to ask you for . . . a football (association, not rugby, i.e. round, not oval). No doubt you don't keep such things in stock at the Institute, but perhaps you won't have far to look for some generous person who'll put up the 15 francs which will buy an afternoon occupation for the 8th Tirailleurs during our present (over-long) rest period. A football is very badly wanted here, since the only one we had came seriously to grief yesterday. That's when I thought of you. But just do what you can, *without* putting yourself out—this I absolutely insist on.

I feel increasingly happy at having been posted to a regiment in which, as I told you, I am the only priest, and where there is a large number of men who, when the time comes, will turn to me for help. I hope really to have found my right place.

[1] The Teillard-Chambons' property in the Cantal.

Camp life is pretty monotonous. The great business of the day is the soup-making ... Thanks to the powerful voices of the Bordelais, of whom there are many in my section, our evening Benediction is quite impressive. At the moment, a little talent for music or cooking would serve me better than all my palaeontology ...

Good news from Sarcenat: Olivier has had a rough time of it in the Argonne. How long shall I have to wait for my own baptism of fire? Your idea of going to Sarcenat for a rest is an excellent one, and most kind. Do your best to go through with it. I'm not mentioning it to Guiguite.[1]

Goodbye. I pray for you, and I ask our Lord to associate our activities, however far from one another they may seem, so that they may ' render ' more to his service. Every sort of kind message to your family and to Mme Parion.

PIERRE

[L'Ecouvillon] *Monday, 15th February 1915*

The football has arrived, at the same time as your card. On behalf of the 8th Tirailleurs, thank you! I'll let you know if it's put to good use.—We're no longer resting but in billets 4 or 5 kilometres from the trenches, close to which we go on duty in shifts. They're very well-kept trenches in some woods. The only aid-post I've yet seen is a small dug-out, very warm, picturesquely hollowed out in the middle of the forest. I have a feeling of the Boche being very close, but haven't seen any yet.—At the moment there's no danger at all.—I think I shall become more and more a chaplain; I manage to tour the whole length of the lines held by the regiment. There's little fighting; even so, a captain got himself killed just half an hour after I'd left the aid-post; happily (from my point of view) he was killed outright, otherwise I'd have been very upset at not having been there. So long as there's not more fighting, I shall have little

[1] Marguerite-Marie, Père Teilhard's younger sister.

to do as a 'minister' at war; but I'm gradually getting to know people.—Pray that I may have zeal, and with it pluck and tact, and above all holiness; your own work, often so trying, can do a great deal for me, and so the two of us will be working together —or rather the three of us, if Mme Parion will be good enough to add her acts of patience in her role of bursar.—If you're sending me anything, could you include a pair of braces and two or three sweaters?

Ever yours,

PIERRE

[Montigny] 24–25th February 1915

I've just received your lavish parcel of woollies; the cap was spotted straight away by my corporal, an excellent youngster who is rather badly off: the braces were seized upon, and with the rest I shall make happy men of some of the Tirailleurs whom I have got to know in the trenches during the last few days—for, at last, I've had a spell in the trenches; not yet in the heroic trenches where your feet get frozen and bullets rain down, but still in real front-line trenches, right next door to the Boche, where you hear the whistle of shells and the crack of bullets if a head shows over the parapet for too long.—I can't quite remember how much I have told you about the sequence of my various moves during the last fortnight. This, briefly, is what they amount to: when the regiment, after a rest period, took over a sector, I began by working a shift in a dug-out, like the other stretcher-bearers. Then the colonel sent me back to the billets so that I could be in a more central position. When I came to consider it, I decided that that was not really my place, and that it would be better for me to be seen as much as possible all along the line. Last week's experience has convinced me, I think, that that is the right way to go about it.—The aid-post I have been in for the last five days is in the cellar of a farmhouse, magnificently situated on the spur of a hill from which you can see the enemy line right from Lassigny to Soissons. You reach it by crossing a wood with trees mown down by shell-fire, then a meadow thick with graves (from the fighting in September) and pitted with shell-holes. All that's left of the farm, which must have been very prosperous, is the bare walls, and skeletons of agricultural machines. It would be a dismal sight if the view weren't so grand and the hidden life of the great war so intensely felt. In the evenings, I never tire of looking at the wide expanse of hills, gently rounded and wooded, in all of which the enemy is lurking, though there is nothing to hear but a distant rifle-shot and the cry of the owls ... but all that is the romantic side. From my point of view, what is really interesting has been to find that in my cellar and its vicinity the men were very approachable. I haven't, of course, made any conversions, nor given anyone absolution (the dangers we encounter are, at the moment, too trifling: not one man has been wounded during the past ten days); but I have made contact with many fine lads, the more easily because in a regiment of native troops the French are eager to seize a chance of talking with one of their own sort. On Sunday I said mass in the colonel's cellar, and dined with the officers:—on Monday I shared the machine-gun sergeant-major's stew; and so on ... All this, I hope, will gradually establish me as the priest-comrade to whom a man can turn when things go wrong. Pray hard that this may come about; I work, in part, with your prayers (and cares) and those of the Institute. You understand what I mean, don't you?—I'm back on duty on Saturday evening or Sunday morning.—What the men lack most of all, even more than warm clothing, is some means of distraction, games and books. There are great drawbacks to cards, and they're not very desirable. Perhaps some small draught-boards (cardboard) or something of the sort would do as well. Books (historical stories or novels, paper-backed) would be eagerly competed for. But such things, the books at any rate, are difficult to get hold of. However, should you have the chance ...—the football is in use whenever there's a free afternoon.—Will you thank Mme Parion for her letter of the

16th,—and for the parcel in which she shared? Ask her, please, to take this letter as being partly for herself. Did you know that I had written to Guiguite about your idea of going to Sarcenat? You'll be the only friend she'll have been able to have there this winter.—Good news from the boys; Victor is still away; Olivier is blasting the Germans ' *in high spirits* ';—Gabriel is rather bored in the second line, where, however, the shells still look him out; it's a month since I was able to see him!

Goodbye: every kind message to my uncle and aunt, and to your sisters. I pray for you and your two families.[1]

PIERRE

[Boesinghe, near Ypres] 17th May 1915

This is in answer to your last card and to Mme Parion's good long letter. I'm writing to both of you from the entrance to my lair, which you can only get into today by skidding down the terribly slippery clay. Well, we're still in the Yser sector, uncomfortably close to the Boche guns, who give us little rest; in spite of something of a lull (although yesterday we put on a pretty big attack) shelling is still pretty general, though the 390 and 420 mm. that come over with a noise like a tram seem to have closed down. Thus, the day before yesterday, one of our best captains was badly hit; it was then more than at any other time perhaps that I felt the power of the priest ... During this last week, I have been through two or three terribly moving experiences ... I'll tell you about them later, if God preserves us. Since the Ascension I've begun to say mass again, in a ruined inn, on a sideboard often shaken by the explosion of shells. As I wrote to Guiguite, I ought to be happy every morning at thinking that I have a chance, at some time during the day, of appearing before our Lord and of finally possessing him .. And yet I still haven't quite reached that point. Nature is always

[1] The Institut Notre-Dame-des-Champs, of which Marguerite Teillard was head, and her own family.

the stronger. Gradually, however, I am finding that out here a man comes in the end to think less of his own skin and to look on death as an ordinary event that may occur to anyone.

I don't forget to pray for you and the Institute.

One thing I regret is that I haven't time to collect my impressions a little and put them down on paper: there would be so much of interest to say about this death-struggle through which the Yperlée countryside is going. But to do this I should have to get about more than I do. Still, if we go back to rest I might try to do so. I must tell you, too, that two days ago I was made a corporal. This will perhaps make my job as chaplain easier.

Ever yours,

PIERRE

Every sort of good wish and remembrance to Robert, and of encouragement to Mme Parion for the lectures.

[Rexpoede] 28th May 1915

It's a long time since I had a pen in my hand, and now that I have, I am writing on a packing-case in a field of beet: already however, this is a step towards comfort, and you will be right in guessing that we're resting. One fine night we silently left our lairs, and I must humbly admit that we began to blossom out again as we left the area of shelling and became people who could look at the crops growing untouched and towns full of life, without any burden of danger to weigh down our spirits. In a week's time, if they leave us idle for so long, I shall no doubt feel a nostalgia for the firing line, but for the moment I am allowing myself to relax.—On the whole, the last part of our time at Ypres was quieter than the beginning, but then one found that the spacing out of deaths and hazards enabled one to ' savour ' all the bitterness more fully; moreover, we had all more or less come to detest the sector, so that life at the end was hardly more cheerful than at the beginning.

Two shells that landed in our cookhouse (without killing anyone) and many others whose explosions shook our dug-outs ended by making our quarters an unpleasant place to live in. I haven't been leading quite the life you may perhaps think I have, entirely occupied in bandaging and comforting. Except when there's an attack—pretty seldom, on the whole—when work piles up and has to be done in a hurry, and necessarily, I fear, in a very mechanical way—the occasions when one has to bring in the badly wounded are comparatively rare, and I missed many;—moreover, I am quite helpless when it comes to dealing with the native troops, because of the difference in language and the gulf that separates the two mentalities. In the end, accordingly, it has only been with occasional individuals, officers particularly, that I have been able to act as a priest; it is true that a single minute of such occasions, when you feel as needed and, through his help, as strong as our Lord, makes you forget the long periods of inactivity and justifies weeks of waiting and of life apparently turned to no account.—I am greatly struck by this double fact: the very small number of souls in whom the need for religion has awoken, and the extraordinary vulgarity that goes with this atrophy. The Christian souls in my circle are very few in number, but it is as clear as daylight that they are, with rare exceptions, the only ones that are ' fulfilled ', the only ones that are truly human. And so the apparent failure of religion is in reality a triumphant vindication of the need of it and of its effectiveness. May I confess, just to your ears, that at times I feel terribly tired of the selfish, bourgeois (to put it no worse) surroundings I am imprisoned in? At such moments I long to dismiss all this world to its bottles or its bunk and build myself an ivory tower. But, from the Christian angle, that would be shameful. Did our Lord do anything but step down and teach us? I must remain on good terms with the 'common herd' and keep in contact with it. Pray that God may help me to do so.

It's largely because of my being in a section of non-combatants that I find so little moral beauty in my surroundings. In some units (French) where I have friends,[1] there's a finer bloom, and all they say about front-line virtues is true, I believe. Still, there it is: where I am it's difficult to see them clearly, or at any rate often. All the more reason to stay where I am, don't you think?

I'm telling you all this because I feel the need to bring it out into the open a little, but not at all to let you see any despondency in me, which could be rather contagious and which, I hope, is non-existent. One mustn't close one's eyes to difficulty and to shortcomings; the more one recognizes them, the less they upset one.—If there is one thing of which I have become convinced just recently, it is that in relations with others you can never be too kind and gentle in your manner; gentleness is our first source of strength, the first also, perhaps, of the visible virtues. I have always repented when I have allowed harshness or contempt to show—and yet it is so agreeable a temptation.

But to come back to outside news—I was saying that this last fortnight, so far as we have been concerned, has not been distinguished by any major activity: only isolated casualties to be picked up now and again. I can't remember if it was to you that I told the story of a particularly eventful tour in the front-line trenches. That night the Boche was plastering the slope that separates us from them even more heavily than on other nights, and there was a continual crack of machine-gun bullets on the earth parapet above our heads, mingled with the dull explosion of grenades. Every minute, flares lit up the line, followed by salvoes of gun-fire. To crown our misfortunes, it was raining, and one had to make one's way, with a casualty on one's back, along a muddy winding communication trench, in which we could move only in single file. A dozen times I thought we'd never reach the end and would have to give up. Finally, however, plastered with mud, we managed to get our man out: but I can assure you that we were relieved to pass

[1] i.e. some of his Jesuit colleagues serving in the army.

him on to some of our fellows in the support line. This episode made me appreciate the courage shown by the troops who spend days and nights under this hail of fire, which I have never more than passed through, and who charge into the thick of it.—I know that on the other hand they have the excitement of battle; but all the same I felt very small compared with those men. At the moment, I'm pretty comfortably billeted in the barn of a Flemish farm; my only complaint is that the weather is rather too chilly. Everything is quiet, and the country lush with vegetation.—Yesterday I received Mme Parion's long letter. I shall think of myself, on the 3rd, as being at the Institute's first communion day, but when I've reached the door of number 20 Rue Montparnasse, I shall need to take myself to 61 bis Rue Notre-Dame-des-Champs to see the chapel again and ceremonies at which I was present last year and the year before. When shall I see your new home?—Your parcel hasn't arrived yet: when it comes I shall obediently, to please you, take to the kola[1] —just to please you. I do hardly any dressings myself; but your bandages may come in useful, perhaps. I'll let you know.

Goodbye. Just as I'm finishing this letter, I'm rather disturbed in case you may conclude that I've got the ' blues ', and that this feeling may, no matter how slightly, dishearten you. Mind that doesn't happen. Fundamentally I'm glad to have been at Ypres. I hope to emerge more of a man and more of a priest. And more than ever I believe that life is beautiful, in the grimmest circumstances—when you look around God is always there. All I ask you once again is to unite your ' effort to live ' with mine, so that, each supporting the other, we may work more effectively in the service of our Lord.—Be *fundamentally* at peace and happy, won't you? If we believe that this struggle between two civilizations is worth men sacrificing to it their individual lives, why should we wonder that the safeguarding of Christian education (even in perhaps imperfect forms) should be obtained at the cost of some people's existence,

[1] Referring, presumably, to the stimulant (caffeine) obtained from chewing kola nuts.

among which your own may perhaps be included? If, in some part of yourself, you are 'wounded' or 'killed' in order that men's right to mould the souls of their children in Christ and in freedom may finally triumph—if you are wounded, even by a ricochet or a spent bullet, in that great battle, why should you grieve?—Our Lord does not forget those who suffer in his service.

Ever yours—I'll answer Mme Parion's letter soon.

PIERRE

[*Zuydcoote*] 4th July 1915

This is in answer to your two letters of the 24th and 28th. The latter caught up with me in the sand-dunes east of Dunkirk, where we were on manœuvres for two days; you'll see, then, that we are still, and perhaps for a long time to come, in the rear of the firing line. The only chance we have of hearing from the Boche is a message—very infrequent—from some long-range howitzer.—So I've been able to think over at leisure what you say about the difficulties you find in 'living in the world as though not being of the world'. This is what I have to say. Above all, trust in the *slow* work of God. We are, quite naturally, impatient in everything to reach the end without delay. We should like to skip the intermediate stages. We are impatient of being *on the way to* something *unknown*, something *new*. And yet it is the law of all progress that it is made by passing through some stages of instability—and that may take a very long time. Thus, we have been through a whole year's suspense, not knowing what the future holds for civilization. And so, I think, it is with you. Your ideas mature gradually—let them grow, let them shape themselves, without undue haste. Don't try to 'force' them on, as though you could be today what time (that is to say, grace and circumstances acting on your own good will) will make you tomorrow. Only God could say what this new spirit gradually forming within you will be. Give our Lord the benefit of believing that his hand is leading you surely through the obscurity and the 'becoming', and accept, for love of him, the anxiety of feeling yourself in suspense and incomplete.—Until the day comes when at last you feel that you're on firm ground, remember that for you this ' firm ground ' may well consist in a way of life that is lay and ' individualist '. It is quite true that a certain logic and a certain necessity brings it about that the majority of souls convinced that only God is worth giving oneself to, group themselves into a unit. Happily, however, that is not a universal rule. *All* ways of living can be sanctified, and for each individual the ideal way is that to which our Lord leads him through the natural development of his tastes and the pressure of circumstances.

I don't think it's quite right to say, as you do, that in the religious life men look for more security by *reducing* their activity: it would be a great pity if they believed that, and a poor compliment to Providence. No, to canalize [direct] is not to reduce. Take as your principle, and never tire of repeating it to those around you, this: one of the surest marks of the truth of religion, in itself and in an individual soul, is to note to what extent it brings into action, that is, causes to rise up from sources deep within each one of us, a certain maximum of energy and effort. Action and sanctification go hand in hand, each supporting the other.—You want to feel yourself more balanced in the hurly-burly of a free life: strive to increase your own personal impetus, your thrust towards the good to be achieved in your own circle. When your moral ' vital force ' has thus been increased, the contrary winds that might make you waver or hesitate if you were *at rest* will hardly divert you from your course, for you will be *under way*.—You don't know how to practise ' renunciation in the midst of activity '. But you answer this for yourself: by action! The greatest sacrifice we can make, the greatest victory we can win over ourselves, is to surmount inertia, the tendency to follow the line of least resistance. Christian action, by its nature, both detaches one and unites one to our Lord. Without bothering yourself about theoretical renunciations, begin by devoting yourself to the fulfilment of the task, often thankless, assigned to you *by God*. He himself will help you, he will give you (by his unseen approval, and, if he so wishes, by a guide in whom you may have the consolation of being aware of him) the firm base you need to work from. Allow yourself to be formed by God. You shed tears of envy when you see people who make eternity part of their lives. But I assure you, your own, too, is filled with eternity.—Eternity comes into our conscious existence from the day when we ' set course' for God; and in your case, that means from now;—you will never be able to get rid of the countless waverings that alarm you because they still make you zig-zag; only action, more and more intense, along the line of God's will—distasteful though it may be—will reduce them.

Thank you for the press cuttings about Latapie.[1] You must suffer at feeling humiliated in front of Emm. de M.[2] Blessed are those who suffer at not seeing the Church so fair as they would wish and who are only the more submissive and prayerful for it. It is a profound grief, but of high spiritual value. It can never be repeated too often: the Catholic is the man who is sure of the existence of Jesus Christ.—There are motives that God is master of, and *in spite of* many stumbling-blocks. Why is it that so many minds see nothing but the stumbling-blocks and wait until they have removed them before they look at the motives? We must be patient.—*Kultur* is an exceedingly complex thing. Who knows but that the Holy Father's reserve, which we feel so painfully, is not the touch of the brake needed to save us from a sectarian absolutism . . .

God bless you. My love to Mme Parion. And every kind message to all of you.

PIERRE

Splendid about the work for the bursaries. You are one of the few able to get on with it,—and that's the compensation

---

[1] A French journalist, best known for an inquiry that appeared in *Liberté* in 1905: *Are we ready?*

[2] Emmanuel de Margerie, the geologist, of the Institut de France.

for the worries of being Principal—one makes up for the other.
P.S. Add to my address ' 1st Battalion ' (see envelope).

[*Zuydcoote*] *27th July 1915*

Just a word, today, to let you know that I am still vegetating
in the green fields of my Flemish farm,—and to tell you that
I am praying to our Lord to grant you a restful and invigorating
holiday.—Abandon yourself without reserve to the familiar
grandeur of old Cantal, and let the silent peace of your native
mountains enter into you and live in you. You need this rest
if you are to take up again the activities that call you and await
you, so that they may sanctify you. Looked at in one way,
nature is a drug, lulling us to sleep in the cradle of nirvana and
all the ancient pantheism; in a more real way, she is a penetrating
summons to the slow efforts, patient and unseen, by which the
individual, himself borne along by a whole past, humbly prepares
a world he will never know. Just now I too wish that I could,
morally speaking, strengthen myself in the giving of my whole
self to my present task, by serene contemplation of the work
of life that God pursues with the help of his creatures. But
service as a soldier in a company that has been resting for the
last two months (which means being caught up again in the rigid
network of barrack-square routine) makes it impossible for me
to pray properly, or think properly, or look at things properly.
And yet there is no lack of pleasant sights to look at here. Leaning
on the heavy railing that runs round our farm, I can see a regular
sea of corn, rolling away to the horizon at the edge of the
Flemish ' flats '; like clusters of islands, farms emerge from the
midst of the corn, invariably set in a ring of tall greenery; here
and there lofty steeples rise, conjuring up peculiar-looking
names (Rexpoede, Hondschoote, etc.) or bringing to mind a
whole lovely distant past (Le-Pont-aux-Cerfs).—Some days ago
I was sitting in the dunes facing the great green sea in which
submarines glide and mines drift; to the east, over Ostend and

Dixmude, huge clouds, catching the full light of the setting sun, were piling up in fantastically moulded fleecy masses, dotted with little ink-spots (Boche anti-aircraft shells). It was most beautiful, and it gave one's heart a great urge to live. Why should one have to allow all these draughts of inspiration to enter one without having the time to make them produce anything, without even having anyone with whom to share something of them . . . Once again, no doubt, because in the present struggle each of us must forget what he might acquire of selfish personal improvement to become just part of the single effort devoted to the common task. Providence, too, has been kind enough to send me, in the form of an *aspirant*,[1] a charming White Father (a deacon) who serves my mass every morning in the house we live in. You may be sure that at that time I do not forget you or your two families.

Ever yours,

PIERRE

[*Dunes de Zuydcoote*] *5–6th August 1915*

This is in answer to your very welcome letter of August 1st; and in return for the whiff of mountain air it brought me, I want this letter of mine to carry with it a little of the great sea breeze. That is why, to write it, I have come and sat down at the edge of the dune, from which you can overlook the great green (today almost blue) sea and the long strip of sand that stretches away from Dunkirk on my left, to the positions, now a legend for all time, from which, last November, the *goums* and *cipayes*[2] held off the assault on Calais.

Yes, you're quite right, it's by its mask of imperturbability that Nature gives repose to our restless activities; the rhythm of her changes, too slow for the brief span of our human lives, makes us think that she is motionless; the limitless series of

[1] officer-cadet.
[2] French North African troops: *cipaye*, cf. the British Indian *sepoy*.

vibrations by which matter builds itself up appears to our senses as a synthesis of stable qualities; life itself seems to be clothed in forms that are handed out ready made, acquired and preserved without effort. This immobility, this stability, this order, delights us and relaxes us in contrast with the arduous, inde-cipherable future that we feel is working itself out within us.— Yet are they anything more than an appearance in which we ' incarnate ', more or less mistakenly, our dreams of the ultimate and the divine?—When you take a really close look at Nature, she may not always appear as inexorable and cruel as the face she shows to Taine and Vigny, but she lets us discern in her an almost heart-rending effort towards light and consciousness.

It was this aspect of Nature that Bergson, that great man, saw so clearly, and it is thus that she reveals herself to us (as to St Augustine), not as divine and worthy of adoration, but as humble and suppliant. ' No, I am not thy God.'—That's what I am saying to myself at this very moment, as I look at the sea. That's what I want you to read in the contours of your own countryside and the up-thrust of your great firs. ' *Natura ingemiscit et parturit*,' says St Paul, more or less.[1] When you suffer and toil, what you are doing is simply to attach your own small effort to him who is the soul of all creation.—If you understand this language of the souls that make their way up towards heaven, you will go back to your duties and cares as Principal with renewed strength. Believe me: throughout all your long internal battle with worry and uncertainty God has, slowly and surely, been taking you for himself. Part of this work of divine ' annexation ' is without any doubt at all the disappointment you feel about the Xaviers [2] (on whom your family affection rested such hopes) and the other experiences, so wounding to your heart, which you refer to without specifying them explicitly. For souls that do not make up their minds to look beyond their visible environment for some base on which to found their

[1] ' *Omnis creatura ingemiscit, et parturit usque ad huc,*' Romans 8.22: ' The whole of nature groans in a common travail all the while.'

[2] Marguerite Teillard's uncle and aunt.

efforts, some interest in their lives, there is a danger that such setbacks may make them shut themselves in and become embittered; in your case they can and should *release* you.

Now, thanks to these setbacks, you are a little more thrown back on God, a little more made one with him,—a little stronger, too, to spread goodness around you: charity, if it is to be inexhaustibly serene and loving, must have made the sacrifice of every reward to be looked for in human gratitude and affection.

Writing to you from the dunes means that I'm still in Flanders—and still resting. There's nothing, therefore, of much interest to tell you—except, perhaps, that the brigade was reviewed recently by Lyautey, and the regiment had the honour of receiving colours from Poincaré himself. Unfortunately I wasn't present myself at the second of these two functions, which must have been well worth seeing, for it turned into one of the classic ' scenes at the front ': ' Under a protective umbrella of aircraft, the troops paraded near the little town of X ... Suddenly a car drives up. A brisk figure gets out, wearing a peaked cap—the President of the Republic ... etc.' That's how it went. The place chosen for the review had recently been under fire from the German 380's, but they missed the opportunity of having another try.—Thanks to my new friend, the White Father, I am able now to enjoy an exchange of ideas: I've been using him to try out just how sound and exact are certain ideas that have managed to take shape in my mind during the disturbed months we've just been through.

For example, at the request of a friend of mine, I am trying to straighten out some ideas on the problem of evil.[1] ' If there were a good God, he would never allow this war.' Many minds, and not all of them mediocre, are just now greatly exercised by that question. When I have two or three pages ready, I'll let you see them. Even more than war-*scenes* I ought to fix the *impressions* it arouses, the *lights* it throws on the world.—I've just been reading Mgr Baudrillart's[2] *Catholicisme et la Guerre*

[1] No trace survives of this attempt.
[2] Rector of the Institut Catholique in Paris.

Allemande. I liked Goyau's[1] (and even Gaudeau's)[2] articles. But who is ever going to define the relations of the individual and society, lay the foundations of a moral philosophy of collective associations? It seems to me that once you pass from individual consciousness to collective phenomena you fall back into the inevitable, into blindness—as though the agglomeration of human societies ended by causing a new matter to crystallize around us . . . one thing at any rate I can see more clearly, that one of dogma's most precious properties is that it forces us to maintain the primacy and priority over everything of souls, that is, of individual centres.

One way and another, at this distance from the firing line, I am going back to leading a pretty normal little life; I'm becoming accustomed again to living with a far distant horizon of life stretching before me—it's time to get back to the trenches.

Thank you for giving me news of your brothers: I'm glad to hear of Robert's activities and hope XIII Corps will make a move. You know that Gabriel, as a last resource, is trying to go up as an observer in a ' sausage balloon '? Victor has had his baptism of fire,—a glorious one, too, it seems, though I've heard no details. You'll be told all about this at Sarcenat in a couple of weeks' time. I don't expect to get leave before the end of September. Yes, I too wish we could meet but I fear that the way I'll have to travel won't allow me to stop off at Paris. We'll see when the time comes.

Goodbye. I say mass ' *at home* ', always. But tomorrow, the first Friday, we'll be on the march (back from the dunes) and I'll have to miss it. None the less, I'll pray to our transfigured Lord to allow you to discern ever a little more clearly

---

[1] Georges Goyau, the French Catholic writer, who had been one of the first to support the forward policy of the *Ralliement* movement urged by Leo XIII. His writings included some notable studies of religion in Germany.

[2] Gaudeau, a French Jesuit theologian, favoured what was known as the ' integrist ' line. His *Panthéisme contemporain* was published in 1914.

his ineffable perfections, the source of all peace. Kind messages to all of you.

PIERRE

I'd like to be sure that your father is having a holiday. Tell him that I don't forget him.

22nd August 1915

A thousand thanks for your very long letter of the 17th. I too wish that we were talking freely together, so that as I read what you say I could put my own ideas to you ... since it's all we can do, we'll have to use the pen; it's too slow, but it has its good points, for it forces our thought into precise terms; it fixes it more solidly than speech when it confronts those whom we would make see and reach convictions and our own most personal way of seeing things.

First of all, in case you are still at all worried about it, let me tell you that I am writing to you from a place that is absolutely quiet. Some days ago, we left the ravaged countryside through which the Yser front now runs, and are peacefully billeted in a smiling farm, from which one's eyes, wearied by the monotonous plains, rest with delight on the low windmill-crowned ridges of the Cassel hills. Last week, I must admit, was pretty tough—not because the trenches we held were the scene of every attack—but because the Boche was so very close indeed to us, with only the width of a canal,[1] as I told you, between us. To reach the group of dug-outs and saps protected by the parapet (sand-bags) of the front-line, you had to go through 1800 metres of communication trenches dug in ground that was flooded by the least fall of rain, and too often invaded by the fetid stench of corpses, half buried or concealed. When you 'got home', shells were no real menace (we were too close to the 'other side' for them to risk sending over anything that

[1] The Yser-Boesinghe Canal.

might have fallen on their own men) but you had to play hide and seek with the various sorts of bombs and grenades that might at any moment land among us, their arrival heralded by the short sharp report of their firing,—not to mention the bullets that at times fell like hail on the parapet, burying themselves in the earth with a dull thud, tearing the sand-bags to shreds, cracking in the air like a whip-lash, mingling their various sorts of whistlings with the detonation of bombs that sound like an enormous groan when they explode.—I won't deny that, at some other times, when there was a sudden lull, there weren't minutes of profound sweetness and intensity, spent in contemplation of the silent desert in which two invisible armies lie in wait for one another among the yellowing pastures; I eagerly took advantage of these minutes, particularly when the sun, a great red mass, was setting over France,—before the nightly fusillade began again. On the whole, and in spite of the undoubted compensations accorded to curiosity, to poetry, to the intensity of life, I must admit that it was not a very agreeable situation to be in.—Three officers were wiped out at one go, by a mine, in a dug-out close to mine . . .

Having told you that to reassure you about my present lot, I come to your letter. I have read carefully what you have to say about the value of the present war. It's true: we are beginning again, on a national scale, the work of moral formation that has still made so little progress among individuals. As Breuil[1] wrote to me yesterday, ' We are all, Boche and Allies, floating downstream towards a cataract hidden from us by a bend, but whose roar we can hear. What will come next, we don't know. Civilization is in the melting-pot again; but what the mould will be we do not know . . .'

About your own personal concerns—listen once more while I repeat what is one of my firmest convictions, as your cousin and as a priest: ' Don't worry about whether your life is worth-while, about its anomalies, its disappointments, its somewhat

[1] The Abbé Breuil, the well-known prehistorian, a great friend of Père Teilhard's.

obscure and sombre future. You are doing what God wills. In the midst of your anxieties and dissatisfactions you are offering him the sacrifice of a humbled soul bowing, in spite of everything, to an austere Providence. You are deprived even of the joy of feeling that you are resigned, that you accept, that you love, and yet at the same time you want to be resigned, to show that you are faithful. Don't be afraid; all this toil is set to your credit and is a magnificent use of your time. It matters little that others may do more good than you, and at less cost: the great thing is not to do good but to fill the place, even if it is more lowly, willed for you by God.—It matters little that in your innermost self you feel, like the natural drag of a weight, a tendency to wrap yourself up in your sorrows and short-comings: there are plenty of other ' natural' ' gravitational' forces in us, what we call enjoyment, egoism, following the line of least resistance; but doesn't *truth* consist in freeing oneself from these in spite of the *compulsive* attitude this temptation imposes on us?—It matters little that, humanly speaking, you feel a ' wash-out', if God for his part finds you a success, as he would have you be. I know that it is just this last point that you question. You don't want to admit that in your case suffering sanctifies. Believe in all humility what you are told by our Lord's promises, by the example of the saints, by the assurances of those who speak to you in the name of God. Bit by bit, our Lord conquers you and makes you his own. No doubt, peace in one's heart, its dilation in the warmth of grateful affection, gives life a pleasanter and more normal harmony, lends itself to greater ease of action, than isolation and ruptures (it's just the same in the relation of health to sickness . . .). That is why we should seek, through our own personal efforts, to make sure we have the backing of good solid friendships, to save us from the weakness of body and soul . . . But if God intervenes to *wean* our heart, forcibly to divert to him alone the appetite for well-being and mutual love he aroused in us during the happy days of youth—then we must not complain. Don't hold it against our Lord if he wants to make of you more than what you call 'just a Christian woman'. Since your activity has to be far-reaching, it must emanate from a heart that has suffered: that is the law, and ultimately a kind law . . . I beg you, when you feel sad, paralysed, to *adore* and trust yourself to God. Adore, offering God your existence that seems to you to be spoilt by your circumstances: what finer homage could there be than this lovely renunciation of what *one might have been* . . . Entrust yourself, lose yourself blindly in your trust in our Lord, who seeks to make you worthy of himself, and will make you so, even if you are left in darkness until the end, providing you hold his hand all the time, clasping it more tightly the more you feel disappointed and saddened. Put aside every excessive concern with interior aesthetics, with your own internal state, every debilitating analysis of your precise degree of sincerity and moral integration. Right to the end we shall carry with us a burden of inconsistencies and unachieved aims: the great thing is to have found the centre of unification, God, and to have tried loyally throughout our lives to make him reign in our own person—the little fragment of being that we rule and that is so little our own. When, one day, which will not be long in coming (all life is brief), Jesus Christ makes himself manifest at the heart of our being, all the elements that we have worked so laboriously to orientate towards him will move of their own accord to group themselves in their real place. In one sense, success for our efforts counts little (God can correct everything in the twinkling of an eye): all that's worth while is the effort.

Goodbye. Enclosed is a bald draft for an essay on the problem of evil. If this letter finds you at Sarcenat give Guiguite a kiss . . . and let her see the essay.

I pray for you.

PIERRE

I'm glad to hear your news of Robert.

[Basseux-Rivière] 20th September 1915

So you're just on the point of starting a new scholastic year, the first in your *own* house; for my part, I'm on the eve of going back to the trenches in conditions that will perhaps make a long leisurely correspondence difficult for me—at least for some time. I want therefore to take advantage of the quiet afternoon I still have free today to send you some sort of ' counsel '. If it should ever happen that I should meet with what we call a stroke of bad luck, or if I should simply find myself so placed that I had to expose myself to the risk of one (don't imagine that I'm obeying any particular presentiment about this: I'm simply making an objective estimate of possible chances) I should feel stronger and more at peace in the thought that you were absolutely clear in regard to my views about you—views, I hope, that coincide with our Lord's—in whose name alone I have always tried to speak to you and bring you peace. First, then, and above all, I believe that you are in your *right place*, the place for which you were made, and to which you have been led by a series of events that have been painful and chaotic for you to feel and witness, and yet have been willed for you by God. I believe that the fact that you have found your place is *reconcilable*, perfectly reconcilable, with the constant state of revolt and distaste in which our Lord allows you to languish and at times to be engulfed in—in order to produce in you what precise shade of holiness? That I don't know—but it's certainly to make you more humble, more trusting, more detached, more sanctifying and effective in your work, the less you believe in yourself, the less you worry about your personal success.—At the same time I believe (though the contrary may be true, and should not, in that case, upset you) that you will not undergo this trial indefinitely: as I've told you more than once, it seems to me that you're in a *phase of transformation*, you're going through a crisis that will resolve itself one day in the calm and fulfilment of total abandonment to the will of God, when once that will has finally penetrated and won you. Every transformation, however, every maturing, takes *time*—time which it is physically, organically, impossible to reduce beyond certain limits—time during which you don't know where you're going or whether you'll ever get there—and yet you have to go through it, with your eyes closed, borne up only by trust.— I believe that while you're waiting for God's hour, the hour of calm and light, you must not allow yourself to sink into the slough of despond, where courage and joy drain away from you; on the contrary, you must root yourself in a confidence that becomes more tenacious and profound the more the shocks produced by external setbacks, and the *pseudo*-natural bent of your mind tend to eat away your energy and make you slide back into sadness.—This confidence in a God who is leading you triumphantly—fairer and more successful every day in his eyes—by dim and difficult paths, to his own divine centre—this confidence you will find, I believe, in an ever closer *union* with our Lord, sought for with faith and perseverance in the Eucharist, seen and loved in his will as it appears to you, humbly prayed to that his hand may be laid over your eyes and his arm draw you to him.—Tell me, why should you set such store by your own self, to the point of losing heart if you find that it is not so developed, not so favoured, not put to so much use as you would wish? What is our own individual success compared with God's good will? And then, what are these ambitions of ours? To be seen, to make some noise around us, to create some noticeable stir in our own little sphere of action? ... is that really what measures a life's value? Don't we know, rather, that the real worth of our existence will ultimately by judged by the *degree of faithfulness* and obedience we have shown in submission to the divine will, *no matter what*, apart from that, may have been the brilliant or lowly function we have served? Basically, I mean, you must be happy. You must be at peace. You must be untiringly gentle. Don't be ' astonished ' by anything, whether your physical exhaustion or your spiritual weakness. Let the ' smile ', the reflection of our Lord's, be born and seen always on your face, whose will it is to work through you and, that he may do so, to replace you ever more and more by himself. You dread the length of your trial . . . but it's nearly over already, and even while you are complaining, time is passing, as precious in its sorrows as in its joys. This is what I have to say to you again this evening for the nth time, looking forward, if God so please, to the nth + 1. This is what I am constantly praying for, fervently begging God to make us co-operate in his kingship and to help each of us to love him more.—Take heart, then, for the grand and essential work of education you have undertaken: even if it doesn't bear for you all the fruits you would wish, it still provides you with a wide basis for action and influence. And so, God bless you and grant you his peace. I'll send you a line again soon.

Ever yours,

PIERRE

[Hersin-Coupigny] 7th October 1915

I'm taking advantage of a lull to send you fuller news than can fit on a postcard. And this letter can serve also, if you like, as an answer to yours of September 25th.

To begin with the news, I can now tell you, without giving away any secrets, that until September 28th I was to the south of Arras, near a village called Wailly. It was there that for a fortnight we watched the slow approach of the great day of the attack which everything told us was coming, from the digging of assault trenches to the preparations for evacuating the wounded. Unfortunately, I'm not among those who are directly endangered by an offensive; even so, I was sharply aware during this time of what it means to see that one's life will become a rather problematical affair in the near future. When that happens, the mind can no longer dwell on any distant prospect, and you gradually find yourself living as though you were no longer of this world. At Ypres we were thrown into battle without having had the time to realize what was happening to us; this time

71

we could savour at leisure the slow approach of the great day, —and to all those who were capable of reflexion, this anticipation brought a ripening of the soul. I made a tour of the trenches on the eve of the attack to see people I knew and to give communion to some (all to whom I offered it accepted; I was limited by the smallness of my pyx). You can't imagine what emotions I then experienced, nor what one feels is conveyed in the clasp of a man who shakes one's hand, at a bend in a communication trench, after one has given him God—while the shells are going across, almost like a solid vault overhead, with a continual hum, on their way to demolish the trenches 200 metres further on, the trenches that we'll have to move into as soon as the bombardment stops. There's no doubt about it: the only man who knows [who experiences] right in the innermost depths of his being the weight and grandeur of war, is the man who goes over the top with bayonet and grenade. In that moment training, of course, and a sort of intoxication play a large part; but even so it is still true that the infantryman leaving his trench for the attack is a man apart, a man who has lived a minute of life of which other men have simply no conception at all.

I am ashamed, as you may imagine, to think that I stayed in the communication trenches while my friends went out to their death. So many of them never came back—first among them, my best friend in the regiment, and the finest soldier I've yet known, poor Commandant Lefebvre; to make sure that his Africans followed him, he was the first out of the trench, waving his *képi* and shouting, '*En avant, mes amis, c'est pour la France !* ' Twenty paces further on, he fell, making the sign of the cross ... I personally ran only the normal risks of being shelled in a communication trench, where you're sheltered from anything but a direct hit, though that's often enough. It's a stupid, passive sort of danger, that drops on you unawares just when you're least expecting it—like this evening, for example, when I was quietly coming back to my dug-out and missed a shell falling right on top of me by no more than a dozen yards.—In our case, the tough part of the attack—murderous, it was, too—

was very short. Two days later we were brought back to the rear, and we haven't been up to the trenches again. I hope my brothers, especially Olivier, came through safely in Champagne, but I've had no news of them later than the 25th.

What is going to emerge from this ghastly struggle? It's more and more the crisis, the desperately slow evolution of a rebirth of Europe. Yet could things move any more quickly? ... We must offer our existence to God, who neither wastes nor spoils, but rather makes use, better than we could ever anticipate, of the struggle in which we are enveloped. If I said that I didn't feel any weariness, I wouldn't be speaking the truth. As soon as the trenches lose the attraction of novelty, you easily become heartily sick of them,—particularly, perhaps, when, like me, the work you've given yourself to involves witnessing all the miseries, one after another, without sharing in the battle or victory. Pray to God that he may give me the strength to hold out as long as he should wish me to. When the regiment, for the third time, fills up with new faces, it's hard work to start making friends again, to form relationships, in the hope of being able to give someone a word of advice or absolution when the next attack comes. (Doesn't that picture just fit the monotony of your school re-opening, too?) God grant that we may remain to the end his workers.

When I started this letter, I said that it was in answer to yours of the 25th. Like you, I hope that activity will shake off your weariness and that once again, in good heart, you'll plough a good furrow from which new growth will always spring for heaven, while your feelings of distaste and revolt will now be, even for you, a thing of the past. You ask me to pray to our Lord that he may help you to accept his will, from day to day to grasp opportunities of bowing to it a little more lovingly. That's as it should be. Have confidence, I tell you once more, and leave it to time. At the moment, it's impossible for you to see how you'll stand tomorrow in the dispositions of your heart and the love of God; believe me, you have only to let yourself be led, mindful only of setting your foot each day on the spot that Providence marks out for you. And then you'll find peace.

I was interested to read your lecture to the Fénelon Association and your remarks on the problem of evil. Reading the first, I couldn't help thinking, once again, that if you were able to get such good sense over to a rather wider audience, it was because you're chained to the distasteful office of Principal of the Institute. As for the second, here is my answer: 1) There is no contradiction between the natural genesis of evil and its historic genesis; they are two different things that can perfectly well be reconciled in one and the same reality, in one and the same world.—Just as, for God to make a sanctified soul (physically augmented, in life, by grace) he first has to make a natural soul which he *then* super naturalizes, so (with due allowance for the scale) to make the 'miraculous' cosmos from which suffering was to be banished, he had (?) to take a universe in which suffering was the natural condition of life and progress;—and it is this natural world that reappeared as a consequence of original sin. 2) You say that one inevitably comes back to this question: 'If God could make a more perfect world, why did he not do so?' My answer is: you're using 'more perfect' ambiguously. Every conceivable universe has its own special shade of beauty, which is incommunicable, and by which it is *more perfect* than all others. Another universe, with less evil, would be called by us 'better' because we reason like weaklings who are terrified of effort. But would it be a fit setting for the growth of the saintly qualities that are born in the shadow of the cross?

That must be all for today. I have said enough to show you that I don't forget you or the Institute. I'll send you a card soon, if there's any news. I pray for you all.

PIERRE

[*Corons du Maroc, Hersin-Coupigny*] 15th October 1915

I must send you a line, at any rate, with the answers I owe to Mme Parion and Mlle Tardieu.[1] I'm writing from a mining

---

[1] One of the teachers at the Institut Notre-Dame-des-Champs.

village in the firing line. A large number of little workers'
cottages, airy and well laid out (in which you see triumphant
evidence of concern for and improvements in social conditions
during recent years) are still intact (the walls, I mean), and in
these we sleep comfortably on mattresses, trusting to the kind
hand of Providence to keep shells off our roof. Our trenches
are pretty active, and rather bad. They are partly composed of
German trenches captured by the British at the end of last
month. A huge mine crater between the lines forms a broken
stretch of ground disputed by both sides, giving free scope to
the ingenuity and courage of the troops.—If you let yourself
think about it, this landscape of gutted houses, of devastated
mine-workings and featureless expanses furrowed by communication trenches, is a mournful sight. In fact, you don't think
about it;—normally, it's a very jolly party that sits around the
dixie bubbling with soup made of vegetables from the abandoned
gardens.

About what will happen to me next I have no idea.—Shall
we stay in this sector? Will there be an offensive? Shall we
go back to quiet trench life with the possibility of leave? There's
no telling. The most contradictory rumours and wildest yarns
circulate all the time. For the last three days I've been deprived
of saying mass, and I don't know when I'll be able to say it
again. I try to make up for it by mentally (too infrequently and
neglectfully, alas) performing the two fundamental acts of
religion, offering and union, of which the mass is the most intimate expression of all.

May our Lord unite us so thoroughly with himself that he
may be seen in all that we do, above all through his kindness
and great love [1]: that is what I ask for you, and for myself,
and for all I love. The September offensive seems to have
spared the family. Not so with my Jesuit colleagues. We have
had many losses in the Society, and are gradually sacrificing the

[1] cf. St. Paul, Titus, iii. 4. ' The kindness of God, our Saviour, dawned
on us, his great love for man.'

cream of our finest minds. I often mentioned to you last year my friend Rousselot (Professor of Theology at the Institut Catholique).[1] I didn't tell you that four months ago he was reported missing, in the Argonne; we're very anxious about what's happened to him.—*All* is vanity, you see, except *holding on loyally*.

Talking of the Institut Catholique, why don't you go and have a talk with M. Verdier [2]—you liked his retreat. You really *must* have some support. You see, you're too much on your own, and I'm too far away, apart from not being, perhaps, just what's needed.—At least you know, don't you, that I shall always do all I can to help you come closer to our Lord?

Ever yours,

PIERRE

[*Corons du Maroc*] *2nd November 1915*

It's too long since I wrote to you. I'll do so as soon as we're resting again, and tell you what I think of the *Sens de la Mort*[3]— an appropriate book, indeed, for the date I'm writing on.—We came out of the front line yesterday, and at the moment we're living in more or less ruined workmen's houses. The only at all memorable incident of this last spell in the trenches was that a 210 mm. shell blew up the dug-out opposite mine (luckily its occupants were out); all I got was the shock and a certain amount of earth.—Filthy weather.—Before long, no doubt, we'll have a few days in the rear, and then it'll be easier, as I said, to write to you at greater length. You know that I don't forget

[1] Pierre Rousselot, s.j., whose most important works are his *L'Intellectualisme de St Thomas* (1908) and the section dealing with the Christian religion in the symposium *Christus*, published in answer to Salomon Reinach's *Orpheus*.

[2] The Sulpician, later Cardinal-Archbishop of Paris.

[3] By Paul Bourget, of the Académie Française.

you (or the Institute), particularly before our Lord. Remember me to your family, to Mme Parion . . .

PIERRE

[*Hersin-Coupigny*] *7th November 1915*

Owing to some muddle about the take-over, we had the pleasure of finding our spell in the trenches prolonged. As a way of ' getting through ' another afternoon—of those I still have to spend here in the second line—I can't think of a better occupation than catching up with my correspondence with you. I'm writing in a cellar (not quite as solid as it might be, I must say) in the basement of a house that has been pretty well knocked about, like most in the neighbourhood. In this, with a few candles to give us light, fifteen of us are living, not to mention a dog and her four puppies. We have a stove, chairs, mattresses and tables. If it wasn't for the monotony of this mole-like existence (I'd much rather rat it up and down the communication trenches) we wouldn't have much to complain of, for we're warm and dry. All the same, the notice to move off is always welcome when it means withdrawing to some little post in the rear. I hope we shan't have too long to wait for that bit of luck.—As I told you on my last card, of November 2nd, the military side, so far as our sector is concerned, is at the moment very lacking in excitement. On all sides you can see preparations for winter. Communication trenches have been dug and minor headquarters set up. There won't be much change in the general appearance of the line until the spring. Only events that affect one personally can still add some interest to our lives, such as, on the bad side, the fall of a heavy shell or a light 88 uncomfortably close, perhaps, or at some distance, and, on the good side, the imminence of leave or meeting a comrade.—As to my own leave, I expect I'll get it about the end of the month; and I assure you again, although I know you don't doubt it, that I'll do all I can to spend at least an hour with you.

As to my comrades (by whom I mean my fellow-Jesuits, real friends, and, most of them at least, men I've known for a long time) there are quite a number of them in these parts, and thanks to them I can, at long intervals, spend one of those hours in which one can enjoy the bliss of forgetting the long days passed in an atmosphere that stifles the mind.

Le Sens de la Mort has brought me three or four such hours. No doubt, as you say, the pragmatism that Bourget borrowed from the ' new philosophy ' is a little limited,—since ' to succeed ' is a *necessary* but not a *sufficient* condition of the *truth* of a position. Moreover, one would like to be sure that, in the author's mind, this actual idea of ' truth ' is really intact; by that I mean that, in a religious context, it implies the *objective* existence of beings and of degrees of higher beings that stand on their own feet, and not simply a hypothetical higher dynamic quality more or less imaginatively attributed to a transcendant world whose reality is only a magnification of our own selves. (I'm afraid that here I'm being a little over-subtle, and uncertain of what I'm trying to say; so don't try to extract too precise a meaning from what I've just written.) Apart from that, however, it's an excellent thing and fundamentally important, to show the positivists that they can't dismiss the supernatural without destroying their own dogma of being slaves of experience; and nothing is more urgent, if we are to impose Jesus Christ on an intelligence that has long observed and understood Life, than to show it a religion that is alone competent to bring triumph over death (over its terror and reality) to the urge—that can never be denied or baffled—towards ' ever greater fulness of being ' which governs the existence of each and every one of us. Bourget's book makes us think, as Christians and as intelligent beings, about our destinies. It approaches the solution of the problem of Evil on the most effective lines: by showing that Evil and diminishment are transformed, in the name of Jesus Christ, into the good and the heightened. On all these grounds I liked it very much, and also because the force of a sincere emotion has swept away all the psychological frippery and worthless sensuality that still cluttered up the *Démon du Midi*. The war has matured Bourget and made him greater. It's interesting to compare the *Sens de la Mort* with that long-winded and unhealthy novel (I forget the title, *Jean X...*)[1] you made me read eighteen months ago. You'll be able to tease Em. de Margerie by showing him how deceptive it is to trust the emotional impressions aroused by reading novels in which the author makes the atheist die, as it suits him, either as a stoic [...] or as an outcast (Ortègue). I hasten to add that I think Bourget's novel is infinitely more objective and generally true in its treatment of the psychology of the unbeliever than du Gard's.

Well, what else is there to tell you? I've lost your last letter, by putting it in too safe a place, but I remember two other things you mentioned in it. First, you are doing your best to master small individual difficulties (and even to make over to me the merit for doing so ... that means a great deal to me, I assure you; in that way, as we were saying in April, we are working together) without attempting yet to come to grips with the great task of total acceptance;—and then that for you the great stumbling block is not so much that you can't see as that you can't manage to overcome a reluctance of the will.—I think that in all this you have judged the situation and behaved with great humility and wisdom;—yes, you are quite right to confine yourself at first to small efforts, hidden and commonplace. You could give our Lord no better indication of humble and suppliant good will than to confine yourself to your own ' poor best '; gradually, believe me, you will gain ground on the capital point of abandonment without reserve to the divine will; even the humiliation you feel at the thought of not making sufficient progress in the ' essential ' should be for you the occasion for acts of most sincere and intimate adoration. The smaller you feel you are, the better will you adore, for you will be speaking from the inmost depths of your heart; and the better you adore, the more will God enter into your imperfections and make use

[1] Roger Martin du Gard's *Jean Barois* deals with the same problem as Bourget's *Le Sens de la Mort*.

of you, poor though you may be, to allow much good to radiate from you. You are distressed at seeing the growth of virtue around you, while you yourself make no progress. Humble yourself, pray, implore . . . but don't *worry*. The great thing is not that the most saintly soul, the most loved and privileged soul, should be *me*. All the better, if there is great love for our Lord around me (you have the consolation of being able to add ' and, a little, because of me, who have kept these souls in an actively religious atmosphere '): my sole ideal is to be the servant, the handmaiden to whom the Master gives the place he wills for her in his heart, and who seeks only this: to be faithful. Deep down in your soul, set above all things, immovably, as the basis of all your activity, as the criterion of the value and truth of the thoughts that invade your mind, the Peace of God. Everything that contracts you and disturbs you is false—in the name of the laws of Life, in the name of the promises of God. You think there's no point in going to see M. Verdier because the trouble lies not in understanding your duty but in your will. But are you overlooking the great strength to be found in the support of someone in whom you can confide? Laying bare one's conscience is a painful business, but the very act of doing so is salutary and soon brings solace; in any case that difficulty *in itself* should not deter you. All this, of course, I say without in the least wanting to force your decision.

Now I must stop. You'll find my handwriting rather illegible and my thought perhaps a bit foggy. I feel I haven't been able to express to you all I wanted to say. It's the fault of this cellar, with its stuffy atmosphere and the various discordant noises it's full of. I'll make up for it the next time I write. Until then, I shan't fail to pray frequently for you and your two families.

I had a nice letter from Marcel, the day before yesterday. Make the most of his leave. It's so infrequent.

Ever yours,

PIERRE

Would you tell Mme Parion that I got her letter and will answer it.

[*Corons du Maroc*] *2nd December 1915*

I'm writing to you from my front-line dug-out to which—by a transition that I didn't find unpleasant in its salutary abruptness,—I found myself sent back the day after I returned here. My heart is still overflowing with the kindness I found at the Institute and the joy of having seen you again, and I can't wait any longer to tell you so in a letter which will at the same time assure you that I had a good journey. Indeed, the Lord is good to give us these happy moments in which our energy is rested and strengthened. If only, don't you think, he will make us really understand that he is even better than all that,—and that the surest means we have of progressing in a fruitful friendship is to *converge* on him, each from his own side, helping one another by prayer and effort to do better.—After those excellent talks we had, we have a fresh basis for understanding one another. Everything I feel about you can still be summed up in: *Pax tecum*. There's only this, that our Lord himself must deign to say these words to you in the depths of your soul. Be sure to tell Mme Parion, please, that I was very conscious of her kindness during my short stay in your lovely house. I'll send her a line immediately.

What can I tell about the Artois? . . . I arrived in time for the end of the frost, though all there is to show for it is an excess of mud in the communication trenches. On the afternoon of the day I reported back to H.[1] there was a bombardment of the local midden which cost the Sisters, where I generally say mass, six hens. I was given the best of them for my stew: that's something to reconcile me to the 210's, I must say. As I told you, I think, winter routine in the trenches is as tolerable as is possible, particularly in length of tour. In consequence, when

[1] Hersin-Coupigny.

81

this letter arrives, I shall be on the point of returning to the rear, and not far from a fortnight's rest. So you can be easy in your mind. But better still, think to yourself that our Lord will keep me from all harm, if he so wishes; and if he does not so wish, it will still be all right, even for you, because if not for everyone, at least (it's St Paul who says this) for those who love God, *everything* works together for the greatest good of the soul.[1] His ' optimism' is qualified, but very consoling. Every kind message to all of you, in both your families. You know my deep affection for you in our Lord.

PIERRE

[*Hersin-Coupigny*] 11th December 1915

Just a word, this time, to reassure you that all goes well with me. We came out of the trenches three days ago, and we still have ten more days' rest here. I think I told you that I'm very kindly looked after in my free time by the Sisters of Charity of the little mining town we're in. As a result of a bombardment that obliged their quarters to be evacuated by an ambulance section that was monopolizing it, the Sisters can now receive us (me and some other priests) more freely, and if the Boches don't worry us too much with their shells we shall soon be building up an interesting little group in these parts. This club, if I may call it so, will be a great help in overcoming the boredom of winter quarters. Our week in the trenches, at the beginning of which I sent you a letter, and which has just ended, went off, so far as I was concerned, without any mishap but not without some unpleasant passages and adventures. Quite apart from the shelling—pretty intense at times—we had to put up with persistent rain that soon reduced the communication lines and trenches to a lamentable state. You have no idea what an effort the ordinary ration fatigue calls for from the men in such

[1] Romans viii, 28: ' Everything helps to secure the good of those who love God.'

conditions: to make your way down 1800 metres of communication trench, carrying a can, sinking up to the knees in mud, more often than not with shells bursting right beside the shattered parapet, becomes a real hardship. The men accept it as nothing out of the ordinary: if only they knew how to endure their toil with a full Christian awareness!—I was still in my rain-soaked dug-out, down at the foot of the Crassier-Double that has been mentioned in recent communiqués, when your welcome letter of November 30th arrived. It gave me great joy and touched me deeply. Yes, I believe the year that has just gone by has again improved and strengthened our friendship. May God deign to make it ever more holy and of greater service to his cause. I forgot to tell you that the two masses I said at the Institute were for the house and its Principal. You know that I never forget either of them when I'm able to say mass.

God keep you. And may our Lord grant you peace, his peace, which comes to souls of good will—of which you, you may be sure, are one.

PIERRE

I've written to Marcel.

[Azincourt] 24th December 1915

I can see that this letter is going to cross with one of yours again—which shows that we often have the same thoughts in mind at the same time:—but I'd rather take a chance again and let you have a rather fuller proof that I am remembering you and the Institute on Christmas Eve. First of all, let me tell you that we too are going to have our Christmas celebrations. At the spontaneous request of the officers and men I shall be saying midnight mass in the village church very beautifully decorated by the daughter and son from the château, with whose help, too, I have been able to teach the men some carols;—apple tarts, cleverly baked by two of my *poilus*, are waiting in the room next door to appear at the *réveillon* . . . what more do we need to forget for a few moments the war and the trenches we'd be floundering in at this moment but for the sudden change that sent us off to the rural depths of the Pas de Calais. As I see it, this Christmas that is not without some religious feeling, is an opportunity to be eagerly grasped of appearing openly as a priest before the new draft in the regiment, the officers particularly, with most of whom (the new ones, I mean) I haven't yet made the full contact that will no doubt be found this evening at the C.O.'s table. Pray that I may acquire and exercise a sanctifying influence on these men, more than one of whom I shall probably see die.

I need hardly emphasize that your memory will be present in my best prayers. May our Lord, seen as the only factor, the only conquest necessary and sufficient for success in life, grow greater within your heart. You could hardly believe how vividly when I have the chance to collect myself a little and think and pray (as happened to me during the last fortnight at Hersin) I become aware of the growing light of this truth, so simple and yet so infinitely rich and fruitful, that God is all. In directing ourselves ever more completely and loyally towards him, in striving towards him with all our strength, we use up all the available energies of our body, with no wastage:—we come closer, unerringly and with no danger of losing them, to those we love;—we make ourselves fitter to do good around us, to radiate peace and goodness . . . In one single act, in one single attitude, we fulfil the whole complexity of our aspirations and duties. Isn't that the truth, and isn't it good to dedicate oneself to the blessed oneness of God, in which all things and all persons are achieved, with absolute certainty and permanence.

One of these days I'll lend you a book[1] (not by a Jesuit!) in which similar ideas are treated in a way most useful for a headmistress, no less than for a soldier-priest. You must tell me what you think of it.—As for news, I have hardly any to tell you. All you need to know, I expect, is that I'm not exposed

[1] See letter of 8th January 1916.

to any shell-fire, even very distant. The men are rather lost and homesick in these parts, where wine is dear and there's no tobacco. I like it, however, in this remote countryside which is that of my childhood. Aren't the château and its kindly masters just like those we knew at home? . . . You'll understand what I mean if I tell you that sometimes when I've been a little while with some lady who reminds me of Maman, and a girl of just the same sort as Françoise or Guiguite, I find it a little bitter to have to shrink back among my men, so vulgar and raucous. But that's just our own unpleasant nature, isn't it? If our Lord had not stepped down to our level, he would have stayed in heaven, without ever coming, loyally and lovingly, to consort with our coarse nature. I must tell myself, and I think I'll come to feel it, that no Christmas night will ever have meant more to me than this one I am about to spend on the straw this evening, by the side of men whom I shall be the more certain to love in real charity the less I feel I have in common with them.

God keep you. So far as you have leisure and strength, go on visiting the poor. I'll be thinking of your Christmas tree.

I've had Mme Parion's letter telling me there's a parcel on the way. I'll answer her when I write to say it's arrived.

Ever yours, and, in case I don't have time to write before then, a happy New Year. I've received the *Revue hebdomadaire*.

PIERRE

[Oost-Dunkerque] 8th January 1916

I sent you yesterday Dom Chautard's book [1] which I mentioned in my letter of 24th December. I want you to read it, slowly

---

[1] Dom J.-B. Chautard was abbot of the Trappist Abbey of Sept-Fons, near Dompierre-sur-Besbre (Allier). He was known chiefly for his *L'Ame de tout apostolat* and by the part he played in 1902 when the religious congregations were under discussion. His friend Georges Clemenceau had him called to defend the cause of the religious life before a committee of the Senate.

and right to the end: I think it will do you good, the worthwhile sort of good that is measured in an improvement and rectification of the deep current of one's life.—But I must add this piece of advice: while recognizing that your life sins (as is true of all of us) through the defects the author points out, take care not to be distressed or think that you haven't so far done any good at all. It's no use being disheartened; what you have to do is to see how you can act more effectively. I know you well enough to be able to assure you, in the name of our Lord, that up to the present you have been a good servant to him, and that it is in peace and expansion of spirit that you must advance along the austere path he has opened up for you. It's always, however, possible to do better. Besides, there are ways of ' doing better ' that God discloses to us only gradually because at first we would not have understood them.—I think that the time has come for you resolutely to set the activity of our Lord at the centre of your influence,—to count for the full success of your work primarily on your own degree of union with the presence and will of the master. You realize, I hope, that this possession of yourself by God can come about without your having to adopt the externals of a nun. I think that you can remain extremely ' lay ' (in the good sense of the word) and at the same time, in your own intimate life, extremely close to our Lord. He himself will gradually mould your attitude to his own liking. What you have to do is to adopt him definitely as the God of your life, who alone can give full life to your activities.

There are, of course, some things in Dom Chautard's book that I don't like so much or that should be taken with some qualification. It's all very well to run a young people's club only with supernatural resources; I'm quite ready to do without brass bands . . . At the same time that shouldn't make us forget the natural aspects of education (physical training, domestic science, cultural development) which, normally, make souls fitter to know God and serve him. Within such education there must be a hierarchy (the one complementing the other) but no

abrupt divisions, no cutting off short. Christianity should form
and ' inform ' (as the scholastics say) the whole man.

I completely agree with Dom Chautard about the importance
of ritual and ceremonies: it is essential to Christianity both to
be a social body and also to have the precious gift of the sacraments, whose action *ex opere operato* is so divine a reassurance
when we feel conscious of our shortcomings and weariness. To
my mind, however, the chapter dealing with this is a bit woolly
and laboured. It's often difficult to see whether he has in mind
the formal, or social, character of ritual, or simply its pageantry
(a very secondary and superficial factor). The ' liturgical life '
he suggests to us gives the impression of a rather complicated
and Benedictine way of presenting elementary truths, of which
every one who has some sort of enlightened interior life is
already completely convinced.

I haven't yet thanked you properly for your letter of December
22nd. Yes, may our Lord become more and more the light of
your life, the light that grows in intensity and is cherished ever
more dearly as the years run on, as the ' outlets ' we dreamed of
in our youth close up, as we suffer more and more disillusionment
about ourselves and others.—You are absolutely right in working
to make love of the poor supreme in the Institute: it's the most
Christian attitude, the most social, the most educative, that you
could make your pupils adopt. To make them turn with real
sympathy to the destitute is in some way to give them, in one
single habit of mind, the quintessence of all humane and Catholic
training. You can never go too far along those lines.

Goodbye. I'm using my pack to write on—and my writing
suffers. Tomorrow we go into the front line. I'll send you
some details about the sector. In the book I sent you'll find two
picture-postcards. They're of places I often go through.

Ever yours,

PIERRE

This is in answer to your letter of January 5th, which arrived, of course, an hour after I'd posted a line to you. Thank you for your New Year wishes: once again, may the peace of God and the pervasive love of our Lord be increasingly within you! It may well be that you feel very far from the ideal unification of your whole being with God you so long for. Just be patient and let yourself be led. The great thing is, in your desires, and prayers, and efforts, to direct yourself, to raise yourself, towards the centre of all life and all happiness. Good will, humbly enduring through the inextricable determinisms and the incurable mutability of the soul that we have to control— that is all that is asked of us. When God finds this good will in some human monad,—then, sooner or later, even if it be but at death, he completes his creature's work and takes it for his own.

I am writing from our aid-post in the line. If you could see me, you would hardly believe that I was playing such an honourable role, for apart from the light being poor (owing to the numerous broken panes having been replaced by boards and sacks) the room I occupy is the last word in comfort: a huge fireplace of real white marble, carved in deep relief, a massive table in a beautiful hard wood—a ' modern-style ' glass-fronted bookcase which still holds half a Larousse and a fine collection of art books—an electric light artistically covered with an old-gold shade . . . We're installed in the still intact part of a fine house, completely riddled and gutted on the side facing the Boche, rather better preserved on the other. What a change from our rain-soaked shacks in the Artois! Our elegant interior, of course, is not safe from shell-fire. Still, we have to trust to luck, and so far all goes well.—You'll realize that the post I've just described isn't in the actual trenches (they're a quarter of an hour away). This is due to the lie of the land and also to my exalted position as corporal, which means that I now live next door to an M.O. instead of having to bunk in a sand-bagged dug-out in the front line.

That, no doubt, would be less comfortable than this; on the other hand I have come to be bored in my drawing-room, where there is too complete an absence of the vicissitudes you always meet with during a spell in the trenches. Whenever I can, therefore, I get away from it. We're not allowed to go about much during the day (in order not to attract the attention of the Boche to the various primitive communication trenches and assorted gangways used for traffic in this marshy sector). I make up for it in the evening, at dusk or on light nights. I have to learn to find my way, I can tell you, in the labyrinth of causeways and canals the sector consists of! That's one good reason for solitary—and how romantic—'noctambulations'. Yesterday evening, in particular, I was favoured by a wonderful moon. Not a sound, except the dull thud of my muddy hob-nailed boots on the duckboards in the trenches. Nothing but light and shadows: the silvered surfaces of the marshes edged by the black line of the causeways; here and there all along the front, the sparkling cascade of rocket lights;—the beam of the Ostend lighthouse turning in the distance for the benefit of some submarines. I savoured as a rare experience this veil of poetry flung over the formidable array of two civilizations, at grips, right before my eyes, with one another. And, instead of going back to my house, I would have preferred to stay with some of my friends in the sand-bagged shelters put up in the midst of this shimmering solitude, where you break off in the middle of a joke to listen to the Boches working, talking, coughing, without being in the least put out by it, any more than they are.

We are coming out of the lines this evening for the change-over, and moving to a camp in the sands. In an area so quiet as this, a rest is less needed and less enjoyed. I'll take advantage of it, I expect, to meet again three young Jesuit soldiers who are in this neighbourhood; They aren't the sort of friends or intimates with whom one can relax and unburden oneself, but fine souls whom it does one good to see, no doubt, but who mostly look for advice and comfort from an older man . . . This is less pleasant and less restful, but more useful and more pleasing to God. We must indeed let others find support in us even when we feel that we ourselves are very uncertain and much preoccupied with finding something to lean on ourselves! Well, we shall have to come second.—I hope that the *Voyage du Centurion* will reach me in time for this interlude. The article in the *Revue Hebdomadaire* on Psichari made me want to read him.

God keep you. I pray for you, and for your two households. Affectionate regards to Mme Parion.

PIERRE

P.S. **My ideas** about the chance of a ' chaplainship ' are coming on a little. I am beginning to want it. But will it be possible? At the moment I can see only one way in. And I don't know whether it's open.

[Nieuport-Ville] 22nd January 1916

I am writing to you from my villa, ruined but with its furnishings unchanged, while waiting for the relief that will send me back to a camp in the middle of the sands.—Very calm, as is usual in this sector, have been the days spent here,—hardly distinguished by some slight bad temper from the Boches, put rather sharply in their place after some manifestly ill-timed conciliatory advances.—It is fortunate, indeed, that in the life I am now leading everything limits the horizon of what one can foresee and encourages an existence that just flows on from one day to the next. Without this contraction of one's preoccupations (brought about simultaneously by physical lassitude and a lack of interest in an unsettled future) war would become altogether too long-drawn-out and irksome.—For me, as it happens, the days go by quickly and painlessly, vaguely illuminated by the dim conviction that they are spent [lost] in the essentially impersonal work that has been swallowing up so many lives during the last eighteen months, in order to lead men God knows where.—To be truthful, I must confess that there are some breaks in this fine serenity. For lack of any well-founded hope of obtaining a position as chaplain, I am beginning to toy with the idea of profiting by the present lull to do some intellectual work. Sometimes I feel that my heart is full of things that should be said about ' mighty Nature ', about the meaning and the reality of her appeal and of her magic, about the complete realization, surpassing all hopes, which Christianity grants to the pantheistic aspirations (properly understood) that will always arise with increasing intensity in man's heart, about the different aspects of matter, etc. It's an ambitious plan . . . but isn't it the only way of speaking intelligibly to men, to their hearts, following the road to the heart? What will emerge from this leap in thought, the fruit, no doubt, of a work of slow accumulation and of reactie against a prolonged stifling of the life of the individual mind? It would be rash to prophesy. Meanwhile I am making notes and I am doing all I can to open up my mind to contact with God. A little more responsiveness to his influence, a little more union with him! What more solid enrichment could there be than that?[1]

The day before yesterday, I heard from Boussac,[2] just off, for the nth time, for an unknown destination. If I mention this, it is because, as with news from Breuil, hearing from that source has the gift of bringing me back to an awareness of my own small interests and personal plans. Yes, indeed, God had placed sympathetic and friendly minds in my path, in whose company it would have been a joy to do the work of a Christian and a scientist . . . Will he allow us to meet again one day, or does he ask for the sacrifice even of that, a better thing often than the fulfilment? . . . I believe that I would not be cast down by the second possibility. Since the beginning of the war, so many others have learnt to ' lose their lives ', simply for their country. What should we not be able to do, to give up, if we

---

[1] The whole of this paragraph heralds the dominant themes of *La Vie cosmique*.

[2] The geologist, son-in-law of Pierre Termier. He held the Chair of Geology at the Institut Catholique de Paris, later held by Père Teilhard.

believe in Jesus Christ? Forgive me if I sound rather a bore today, abusing the kindness of a listener to talk interminably about selfish, hollow things. I felt this evening a need to drag my problems out into the open and see just where I stand; and so I have taken advantage of your indulgent friendship. You see how much I rely on you.

I don't know whether I answered your letter in which you told me that you had begun your visits to M. V. I'm glad to hear this. Carry on faithfully with the experiment until you can see clearly one way or the other. You and all your doings will certainly gain a blessing for this humble and perhaps costly effort.

I expect I'll hear from you before long,—perhaps just as I'm sending off this letter. I can assure you in advance that yours will be welcome.

Every day I can cross the Yser and say mass in a chapel fitted up by the sailors (as I think I've already told you) in the ruined town.[1] There I pray for you and yours.

PIERRE

[Nieuport-Ville] 2nd February 1916

To answer your letter of January 24th, I am glad to choose this feast of the Presentation—the Candlemas of our worthy ancestors—which this year I am spending in the grey atmosphere of the banks of the Yser and the bleak self-contemplation it inspires. The Rosary in the fog. The men are suffering more than ever and accumulating the substance of an inexpressible sacrifice. Why must it be that their agony should lack the element of adoration and oblation through which the wearisome task of co-operating with life is transfigured and made intelligible? It will have been a joy to you this morning, I am sure, to take, as though in your hands, your good will, your hopes, your ambitions, your fears too, and all the things that repel and

[1] Nieuport.

disgust you, and present this whole bundle—so living, so full of feeling and tremors—to the keen glance, to the good pleasure, to the purifying influence of our Lord.—I would like this oblation of your whole self to have been united to that which I was privileged to make of the one victim of the world, at the same time, in the little cellar-chapel at Nieuport. We often say to God, ' I give myself to you, I wish to unite myself to you.' We say this sincerely, but do we not forget that it is he alone who can give himself and raise a being to some small degree of union with himself? The attitude that incorporates us fully with the truth is indeed that of the Presentation, in which we humbly expose ourselves to the radiation of the infinite Being, ardently longing that he may penetrate us and transform us into himself.

Thank you for the encouragement you give me to allow my personal thoughts a little play, and along the lines I spoke of. Some reasonable reconciliation must be made, I am sure, between God and the world, between the detaching aspirations of Christianity and the ineradicable passion that makes our whole being vibrate when we experience something of the soul of the mighty whole of which we are undeniably a part. But over the vast horizons that these ambitious aims open up to the mind and heart, my thought still wanders—like a flight of wild duck over the Allier—without finding the precise, central, point on which to rest. You are quite right in seeing in St Paul the great bulwark, the surest theorist, of a sort of Christian pantheism (one could almost say the same of St John). For St Paul all energies hold together, are welded deep down into a single whole, and what the humanity of our Lord does is to take them up again and re-weld them in a transcendent and personal unity. St Paul speaks in terms of the world at least as much as in terms of the individual. That's one of the reasons why reading him grips me more than all the rest.

Just now, there's no need to send me anything except the *Revue Hebdomadaire* (and, when it comes out, the *Voyage du Centurion*). I haven't yet finished Newman's *Apologia*. Did you notice, in the latter, what is said about the writer's tendency to immaterialize the world, to see in everything only spirit and the action of spirits? I still don't think, myself, that the domain of the Angels is the mysterious region which, under the vague description of ' energies ', links together, at different levels, the physical atom and the social monad. Still, there is a possibly fruitful idea in that, that could well be straightened out or recast.

So far as my external life goes, there's nothing of importance to tell you. We've been back in the line for some days (though I fear that for me this doesn't mean the trenches), and things are very quiet, though the Boches are very sharp on any head shown too long over the parapets.—Paris is the danger spot now! So you've received your baptism of fire. I'll be interested to know whether there was an alert in the Notre-Dame-des-Champs area.

God keep you. Kindest greetings to Mme Parion and your sisters. You know that all goes well with my brothers. Joseph, like Robert, has just had his leave postponed. The day before yesterday I had a letter from Anne-Marie,[1] and yesterday I hastened to answer her.

Ever yours,

PIERRE

[*Nieuport-Ville*] *27th March 1916*

By this same post I am sending you back your MS, registered. You'll see that I've read it very carefully, and you mustn't be horrified at the number of notes I've made. I've read it for you as I would have done for myself, rephrasing or emphasizing some passages,—as though I were correcting my own work. I wouldn't, of course, seek to impose any of these alterations on you, nor do I claim that they are always an improvement on your original inspiration.

First of all I must say this: it's a very fine lecture, very Catholic and very lofty in tone. You must certainly have made

[1] Anne-Marie de Cathelineau, a cousin of the Teilhards.

all who heard you prouder of their faith and fuller of love for our Lord. And you couldn't hope for a greater success or a richer reward than that.—All the last part of your work (especially from *L'Étape* onwards) is excellent, and makes me wish that you weren't hampered by the need to quote from and follow the thought of another (even though it be Bourget), but could pass on, in some work that was completely your own, some of the fullness of your personal experiences—for they gain in warmth and urgency, and are thus the more contagious and ' catching ' the more they are coloured by inward suffering. Why don't you, too, give us *your* book—the book of your life— like Psichari?

But to go back to your lecture: after making it quite clear that I liked it very much and was even very moved by it, here are a few improvements in detail that I suggest (they are given in more detail in the notes with which I've loaded your MS).

a) Keep an eye on improving the style, not only by avoiding jarring phonetic effects and repetitions of words—but by enriching your vocabulary, by getting more depth into your wording: there are verbs that are now quite colourless (to be, to do, to have), for which as often as not one can find more expressive and vigorous alternatives. But you know that better than I do.

b) Avoid any obscurity in phraseology, ambiguity in the use of demonstrative adjectives and pronouns (this, that, its, etc.).

c) Try to mark out clearly the various steps in your thought by means of transitions that don't simply connect, but, if I may put it so, synthesize—summing up in a single line both what you've just said and what you're passing on to,—showing just how far you've reached and what the next step is going to be. This is a much more difficult art to acquire and presupposes, of course, great precision and maturity in the formation of one's ideas. But it's essential if the thread of your exposition is not to be lost in a maze of quotations.

d) The first part of your paper, especially the description of the state of mind of the intellectuals (pessimism—naturalism) after 1870 could well perhaps have been shortened, and in any case clarified and condensed. I've indicated a few corrections for you. This is the only part I think needs any considerable revision.—You might note that in the development of Bourget's art the stage of knowledge pure and simple corresponds to this state of mind.—After that, conscience arose in opposition, as you very well point out.

In short, your work still contains a number of careless passages due to haste in composition and to the fact that it was *spoken*. If it is to appear in print (as I hope it will) it needs some slight improvements in form and style, some cutting of the quotations too, I expect, which should not take you long.

So far as the apologetic value of the *success* of Christianity is concerned, note (I've written a few lines about this in the margin of your work) note that it is real, even if insufficient, if one *admits* (as very few people, particularly in this age of Bergson, refuse to believe) that Life cannot be mistaken, cannot develop successfully other than in the direction of the true (from which it follows that the true must exist), [must be sought] *in the number, in the direction taken by*, the things that succeed. The *true*, moreover, must have the same *stability*, the same objectivity as the life it supports and the tendencies it arouses and maintains: if God were no more than a figment of the imagination, an *illusion* with no reality or truth other than that of making it easier for us to act, we should have to say that the *conditions of viability* of our existence are less real than the existence itself, which would be absurd. It would be like saying that the lungs could breathe immaterial air . . .

So much for that. Thank you for the confidence you showed in me by letting me see your work. And thank you, too, and Mme Parion, for the parcel. The camphor was used straight away.[1]

Some other time I'll tell you how my ideas about the 'Cosmic life'[2] are coming on. They're taking shape and I'm beginning

[1] To get rid of lice.

[2] *La Vie Cosmique* is dated 24th March 1916; cf. Claude Cuénot, *Pierre Teilhard de Chardin.*

to get it down on paper. What you say about the role of music and poetry is *very true*. Those arts do not lead us exclusively to pantheistic and pagan bursts of feeling. All they do is to arouse the soul *in a general way* to the search for the most beautiful and the greatest: *they make it sensible* to the whole, they *cosmicize* it, if I may use the word, sometimes by causing it to lose itself in the lower nirvana, sometimes by causing it to unite itself ardently with the great effort towards the higher spheres. Have I got it right, this time?

I'm quite all right; and things are still quiet. I constantly pray a great deal for you. May the abiding peace of our Lord dwell within you.

I was very pleased with M. Verdier's comments on feminism. —Leave things to Providence. Your vocation is taking shape and your place in life is gradually being prepared.

PIERRE

About the apologetic value of success as a living force—I once read a little book of Joergensen's [1] (translated by d'Armailhacq, published by Plon (?), out of print, but you'd find it no doubt in libraries) whose title escapes me at the moment, in which the argument is put with clarity and a quasi-biological backing, which are impressive.

[*Nieuport-Ville*] *9th April 1916*

This is in answer to your letter of April 4th. But before I thank you for it and say anything about it, I must first of all tell you what a painful shock I had to read in yesterday's paper of the death of M. Auffray,[2] your friends' father. Please pass on my condolences to M. de Margerie. But my thoughts are most of

[1] The Danish Protestant writer, best known for his books on St Francis of Assisi, published in 1909 and 1910.

[2] He was connected with the Margerie family, friends of M. Teillard-Chambon.

all for you, who have lost, I imagine, a support and a friend. I don't know why (or perhaps I too readily feel why!) we imagine that the framework of our lives should be as durable as ourselves. We can't admit that those we have always known, or whom we have at some time looked on as our support or as part of our own permanent personal environment, should disappear before ourselves ... As though the countless ruptures that we witness daily should occur without violating the little domain of our own affections.—I hope that this new sorrow and disappointment—coming on top of so many others, will not make you lose heart. We have but one permanent home, heaven: that's still the old truth that we always have to re-learn, —and it's only through the impact of sad experiences that we assimilate it. I don't know whether I told you how, while I was helping Boule[1] in September 1914 to put away in safety the most valuable of the Museum's treasures, handling the fragility of human hopes with such a direct physical contact, I felt buoyed up with a sort of triumphant joy: because God, his will, not to be attained by anything that grows less, and yet attainable in spite of every disaster and ruin, became manifest to me as the only absolute and desirable reality ... And even now, in my bad moments, however awful the future that menaces our country, I still retain this triumphant joy, based on a conviction of the transcendence of God. Yes, even if, contrary to all expectations, the war should end badly not only for us but for the real progress of the world (though God knows how much I believe in the ultimate success of the world and the progress, in spite of everything, of Life,—I have faith in life); even then, I would feel like repeating over all these seeming victories of evil, the ancient cry of the Greek festivals, *Io, triumpe*. And yet I love beautiful things, science, progress, almost ingenuously. I am a man as much and more than anyone else. But there it is: We believers have the strength and the glory of having a faith in God more profound than our faith in the world: and that

[1] Marcellin Boule, director of the Natural History Museum and professor of human palaeontology.

faith in God re-emerges and persists even if our faith in the world should be crushed by the impact of events. I've rather wandered from what I wanted to say to you and perhaps you'll find me hard and brutal. But bear in mind that I'll be saying at least one mass for M. Auffray and his family and that I pray our Lord to make you feel that he can and will replace by his own self all the human supports he takes from you.

To come back to your letter: I know just as well as you do the sort of distaste you feel for a piece of work you've just finished: everybody, I imagine, feels something of the sort. And yet, if one is to produce something really worthwhile, one must be able to recast the general design, give sharpness to one's ideas (they often become really clear in one's mind only after the first draft has been made), and even resign oneself sometimes to the trying labour of a complete reshaping. I hope that you'll turn the lecture to good account (I assure you again, it gave me real pleasure) and I'm by no means without hope (whatever you may say) that some completely personal work will gradually outline itself and take shape in your mind,—to bring comfort to the masses of young girls to whom ordinary horizons offer no hope, no interest to live for. If I can form a picture of the type of woman you are trying to describe, I shall pass it on to you, you may be sure.

And now, once again, take heart for your efforts for your former pupils. What you tell me about that gives me real joy, because I believe I can see that God is little by little leading you where he wants you to be.—I am glad to think that you're going to Sarcenat; if nothing occurs to upset things (and we're now at the rather critical part of the year) I expect to go on leave at the beginning of May. I'll do my best to see you. By that time I shall perhaps have finished the few pages in which at the moment I'm writing down my ' testament of an intellectual ' [1] and I'll probably entrust them to you.

Just recently, by which I mean yesterday, I had a sad blow:

[1] By which, as Marguerite Teillard-Chambon says in her introduction on the war, is meant *La Vie cosmique.*

a young and attractive little Jesuit, a corporal in the artillery whom I often saw and who delighted me with his zest and his wide openness to all beautiful things, had both his legs broken in his observation post by a shell. I believe they've been able to save his life, but he's had to have his legs amputated. I'd seen him only the evening before, and a few days earlier he'd done me the honours of his observation post. I'm going to try to visit him, for his hospital is near our rear headquarters. I'm not at all worried, of course, about his morale (the first thing he said to one of his cousins, who told me the news, was, ' You know, old man, I've lost my pegs') but it's very sad to see such a splendidly active person so (apparently for ever) handicapped.

God keep you. I pray for you and yours.

PIERRE

[*Esnes*] *18th June 1916*

As I'm writing to Mme Parion to acknowledge a Nîmes sausage and her letter, I can't not send you a line in the same envelope. I'm writing from the bottom of a solid shelter half buried in the earth of a desolate plateau near the d'Avocourt wood. Outside, a beautiful sun has dried up the incredible mud in which we were bogged down at first. We're not too badly off, and anyway it won't last for long. So much to reassure you about my external circumstances.—Interiorly, I haven't yet completely emerged from the sort of torpor into which I've sunk as the result of an existence made up, since I last saw you, of perpetual moves, towards or within an area that is both desired and dreaded. Once again I've felt that I'm no longer the individual monad full of plans for personal activity but the monad lost in the great clash of nations and brutal forces: this has made me rather dizzy and depersonalized me. Add to this my being deprived of the sacraments,—though I have some compensation for this since I've been carrying the Blessed Sacrament on me. I thought I should have the joy of seeing that I found a source of real energy in my cosmic ideas. Evidently, however, war is an extreme and abnormal case of renouncing the individual's rights and hopes.—One thing that has marked my time here has been the absence of any particularly interesting events either for the regiment or for myself: just the slow tedium of being exposed to a moderate amount of danger in which everything (apart from a certain number of more important incidents on either flank) passed by unnoticed—that's been the formula for these last ten days. This, as you can appreciate, isn't much of a 'tonic'. I've had only two or three moments of 'excitement'. Don't imagine, though, that I'm depressed; if I were, I don't think it would affect me much; for in *a sort of* way I feel that I've lost interest in myself... I'm writing this to you as though we were talking to one another and to try to straighten things out in my mind by forcing myself to reflect a little on my own self.—Under these conditions I feel I can better understand the difficulties you meet with in your own circumscribed existence.

God keep you. May our Lord, who rests on my heart, bless you and grant you his joy and peace. The knowledge that you have courage and are in good spirits is a great source of strength to me.

Ever yours,

PIERRE

[*Esnes*] *19th June 1916*

I wrote to you yesterday, at rather greater length than before, at the same time as to Mme Parion. But that same night I was given your long letter of the 15th and I can't stop myself from answering it immediately. First of all, thank you for all the heartening and Christian things you say. Yes, you are indeed more of a support to me than you could imagine, when you speak to me of the virtue of the blood of Christ and urge me to converge with you on the heart of our Lord. At times, it seems, duties are shared. In these days, you pray and think for me while I lead rather the life of a machine.

If I've only sent you brief postcards it's first of all, as you've guessed, for lack of facilities for writing. Moreover, until my arrival here, I've been living (and am still) rather as though on my toes for the next move, an attitude that hardly favours reflective introversion or unburdening of my mind. To tell you the truth, I've been rather weak about this;—it would have done me good to write to you from a deeper level and so force myself to define my inner attitude and regain contact with what is going on deep within me. However, better late than never. I already feel that I've benefited from writing to you yesterday and writing today.—I told you before, and I can only say again, that I still have considerable difficulty in analysing myself and also in shaking off a sort of numbness which comes from too much exteriorization. I'm quite sure that (if things turn out well) this phase will be followed by a more comforting and fruitful period of reaction. At the moment, all I can do is to hold on patiently and put up some sort of fight.

As I was telling you yesterday, what has so far marked my time in the Verdun area (now nearly finished) has been a sort of moderate degree of danger without the consolation of apostolic work or the occasion to show any particular devotion to duty. Nothing to really arouse or spur on the will or make it vibrate in tones of unsuspected richness.

Neighbouring battalions have shared the toil and glory; our own has remained in an out of the way corner. Since our Lord so willed it, then it's humbler and better that way. However, as you can imagine, it lets down morale or makes it an easy prey to every annoyance. I don't, you see, hide anything from you. Pray for me, and believe, too, that by God's grace I haven't got the *cafard*. It's just that to me Verdun has been completely prosaic,—how salutary, perhaps. When we're in the rear again I'll send you more concrete details about the places we're in and the life we lead. At the moment I won't say more than that the fine weather still continues and our dug-out is nearly dry.

Here is a thought that came to me some time ago about the will of God: has it occurred to you that it is in some way materialized, or even made incarnate, in our inmost depths, by *time* (or, as Bergson would say, duration), time that carries us along and gives rhythm to our lives, time that passes too slowly or too quickly, time that separates us mercilessly from a longed-for date, or makes the hours of reunion go by too fast; time which stands in our way to prevent us from achieving in the twinkling of an eye the improvements we dream of in ourselves or in those around us; time which makes us grow old ... It's the creative activity of God that is the source of this fundamental and universal determinism: we should acknowledge it and love it.

Did I tell you that Boussac and I have gradually opened up a correspondence on subjects you'll guess (the relations and connection between the life of faith and the life of man)? He's a great deal more individualistic and much less cosmic than I am. He is inclined to take an entirely gloomy view of war and progress. Fundamentally, however, we have the same ideas and the same aspirations.

It's Breuil that I'd now like to meet again.

Goodbye. Yes, don't let yourself be disheartened by the ' petty cares ' that hamper you, and often, no doubt, overwhelm and baffle you. The power that small things have to influence our lives is no illusion, and as you say, it doesn't prevent us from doing useful work. Good luck for the *Correspondant*. So far as personal work is concerned try to be patient and foster some ideas that you really care for, and they'll end, you'll see, by emerging fully mature. May our Lord bless you.

Ever yours,

PIERRE

[*Beurey-Meuse*] *25th June 1916*

For the last two days we have been billeted in a delightful village in spite of having been partly burnt (in 1914), near

Bar-le-Duc. This evening I'm going for a walk along a little river, its waters smoothly flowing but with a powerful current that runs, silent and strong, between woods and great fields of hay ready for cutting. We have sunsets of garish gold over meadows of even more garish green. The country smells as it did when I was a child. It's a real relaxation after Verdun. I lack only one thing, and that the most important: someone to whom I can unburden myself and so relax any number of tensions. For this, I'm reduced, if I may so put it, to our Lord and correspondents such as you.

I promised you some details about my life at Verdun. In fact, there's very little I can tell you for our time there was very ordinary. Our battalion occupied a favoured position between Hill 304 and the d'Avocourt wood, on which no attack was made. On one occasion only we were shelled by heavy guns, but fortunately without damage. Practically the whole of my time was spent in a dark shelter hollowed out of the d'Avocourt plateau. I hardly left it except for a spell in the front line or at Esnes in the rear. From up there, there was a magnificent and entrancing view stretching from the Argonne to Vaux, but inexpressibly mournful. The ridges that are fought over are completely torn up and as though pock-marked by some disease: between the green and richly wooded banks of the winding Meuse you'd think that the hillsides had been ravaged by fire. Further to the rear the picturesque ousts the terrible. There's a fascinating strangeness in the great undulating expanses, half buried in woods, in which the supply tracks criss-cross and countless mysterious telephone lines run. Everywhere you see the path of war. The war has completely taken over this whole countryside. The villages near the firing line are the objectives of heavy shelling so you only approach them with some nervousness. I've mentioned Esnes to you, which is the headquarters for the sector's ambulances: there, the shells fall almost continually, reducing the ruins to rubble and often, too, wiping out a human being. Would you believe it, from a neighbouring height I witnessed a regular target practice with 77 and 105 mm.

guns on our ambulances? One spot along the evacuation route was under observation by the Boche and each vehicle as it appeared was fired on and followed with shell-fire, coming and going. After two hours of this game they finally scored a bull though fortunately most of the wounded were saved. Apart from the regular bombardments, the danger in our part lay in the numerous lighter shells that were being fired pretty well all the time at random at the few ill-made communication trenches that connected the front line with the rear. In the end we took practically no notice of the whistle of shells, big or small, unless they came altogether too close. In fact, I was never in any particularly serious danger; but, perhaps through some physical or moral weakness, this spell at Verdun (which I in no way regret) has left me terribly exhausted. It's a case of learning to say with St Paul, ' When I am weakest, then I am strongest of all.'[1] It's not a bad thing, is it, to feel out of one's depth: one clings more genuinely to our Lord's hand. Between now and Friday I'm going to try to bring myself as close as possible (with you, of course) to the heart of our Lord. My need is great to steep my soul in him again, so that I may have more faith, more devotion, more kindness. Reassure me that in speaking to you like this, in all frankness, of the poorness of my courage, I don't upset you.—My mind is still pretty well empty of ideas and inclinations—and I don't know whether our rest will last long enough for the current of familiar thoughts to start flowing again. We have no idea what's going to happen to us and all we can do for the moment is to take advantage of the rest. I myself take advantage of the church, where for the last three mornings I've begun to say mass again. You have not been forgotten, nor anything that concerns you.

God keep you. I'll write again from here.

PIERRE

---

[1] II Cor. xii. 10.

This is in answer to your nice letter of the 22nd, which reached me on the same day that I sent you my last. I greatly appreciated the affection and encouragement in what you said. I repeat that you can do a great deal to help me; there are always times when no one has strength for himself.—I believe that you're perfectly right in thinking that the sap of my thought and activity is sentient rather than intellectual. Even though the distinction between the two powers, the 'affective' and 'apprehensive' is much less sharp than at first appears, and that to feel intensely involves almost necessarily a very intimate vision of what is experienced (my poor friend Rousselot[1] thought that all knowledge is 'sympathetic' and therefore reducible to love), there are temperaments in which intuition is born from an excess of tension or vital ardour much more than from methodical effort: and probably it's to this type that I incline. I am much more enthusiast than scholar (forgive that pompous word, too weighty for my qualifications). You're quite right in your judgment of me.—This is a great weakness and at the same time a precious source of strength; and I've come to learn this only too well recently. This appetite, this passion for living, which you envy me (and which I certainly owe to some extent to the fact of having always been successful on the whole, and having found help and sympathy ready to hand)—this appetite and eagerness to act is something, then, of which we are not completely masters: it's a fountain that springs within us quite independently of ourselves, and we can use it, direct it, but not feed it nor keep it going. If this prime energy weakens deep within us no reasoning and no industry can restore it. '*Si sal evanuerit, in quo salietur?*'[2] That is a *primum datum* corresponding in the practical life to the apprehension of first principles in the intellectual life.—May our Lord, then, preserve deep in our souls this impulse towards progress and fuller being;—and may he at

[1] cf. letter of 15th October 1915.

[2] 'If salt loses its taste, what is there left to give taste to it?' Matthew v. 13.

the same time direct this deep-rooted urge towards himself alone.—He, as the source of life, is the only master and dispenser of this twofold fundamental energy . . . I repeat, I have had deep experience of this dependence, this inability of ours to give ourselves the appetite (so essential) for living. That is where I am vulnerable. And wasn't this, in some small degree, the deathly weariness of our Lord's agony in the garden?

For some time now I have been feeling impelled by questions that have been put to me and circumstances in which I was necessarily involved, to get to the bottom of this question of weariness, of disgust, of the state of a soul naturally embittered, and submerged by life. This too, of course, may be used for God and become in a high degree sanctifiable. But there must be a psychological theory of it, essential to sound ascesis,—and a ' philosophical ' theory too, justifying such states of soul. My ideas on this, I hasten to add, are still imprecise. But I've always noticed that the important thing in a problem is not finding a solution but expressing it clearly . . . From the practical point of view I'm glad that tomorrow happens to be the feast of the Sacred Heart. The master above all of the interior life. I feel that it will be with a complete renunciation of any confidence in myself that I shall ask him to bring life to my soul (and to the souls of those who mean most to me). And secondly, should he prefer us to plod along cheerlessly, that he may at least keep alive in us the desire to love to do his will, for its own sake.—I have gone a considerable way in regaining my spiritual foothold. If the future were less foggy I could perhaps get back to methodical work: unfortunately, however, we're still in too undecided a position for me to be able to make any sort of serious start.— Today, the feast of St Peter, my patron saint. I keep remembering what our Lord said to him (John xxi) at the end of the gospel: ' When thou hast grown old, another shall gird thee, and carry thee where thou goest, not of thy own will . . .' It's strange how much, in spite of all my arguments and all I say to the contrary, I feel an instinctive, ineradicable preference for the determinism of the world, for ' the hand of God upon us ' . . .

There again you have one of those primary, fundamental, predispositions that act as the nerve centre of our lives and over whose birth and continuity we have no power.

Goodbye. Tomorrow I shall be praying to our Lord for you and your affairs, more earnestly than I can tell you. At those times when the war's vast burden of wickedness weighs us down, menacing and implacable, even the warmest human expressions of sympathy may seem very fragile and empty; yet, if they rest upon our Lord, they are in fact extremely potent.

We are all following with intense interest the slow development of the great offensive. This is now more than ever the moment to hold fast to the conviction that all that matters is that the greater glory of God should emerge from this chaos,— and to the belief, too, that this greater glory deflects events towards itself and knows how to extract from them the marrow and sap which are lasting.

I've received the socks and the tin that came with them. Thank you, and Mme Parion too. Be of good heart for the end of the year. We're still in the same peaceful billets.

PIERRE

[Bois Saint-Pierre] 10th July 1916

This is in answer to your good long letter of the 4th which reached me just after I'd sent you my own few lines, enclosed in my letter to Mme Parion. Since then, I've had from you four numbers of the *Revue Hebdomadaire* and the *Daily Mail.* Many thanks for this intellectual fodder, much appreciated by me and many of those with me. Reading Richet's article on alcoholism (I haven't yet read P. Bureau's on the fall in the birth-rate) I was greatly struck by the fact that it's necessary for so many people to be kept in or brought back to healthy and good conditions and ways *by force*. In the case of religion, of course, which calls for interior assent, and in which the things of which one can be certain do not belong to the experimental order, the use of constraint is a matter of infinite delicacy; even so, it's easier to understand, by comparison with the abuse of pleasure-giving poisons, the legitimacy of preventive measures (the Index, education—designed to give a particular ' bent '), which revolt us at first, but which go with the privileges of truth and light. In any case I am more and more convinced that humanity is not yet ripe (if it ever will be!) to be led by reason, and that for a long time still the masses will need to be kept on leading strings.

I'm writing to you in wonderful sunshine, and still from a wood.—This one is in the shell zone, and a dozen times by day and night they come crashing down among the trees, with a roar like thunder, without, however, the least excitement. A dozen sausage balloons are floating in the air above us. Apart from that the front seems extraordinarily quiet: which augurs an uneventful tour in the front line for us; for—so it seems—we are at last having a second spell in the trenches in the same area as before. There's no need for you to be particularly anxious about me. Just pray more earnestly to our Lord that during these days he may make me adhere more scrupulously to his will and achieve what may be to his service. It's a good thing, when you come to think of it, to be the pebble tossed by the divine ocean. Then, as you tell me you've ' seen ' more clearly, everything of ourselves that is lost in the service he calls for is a solid gain, a part of our being put permanently in safe-keeping. —Aren't those flashes of light the most precious and gratifying that from time to time enable us to see and really assimilate some one of the fundamental truths that are on everybody's lips and are yet so slow to reach the heart? Have you ever tried, when they come to you, to get them down on paper? It is then that little by little the cast our Lord seeks to give to our soul gradually takes shape. In the small effort of writing, the light we have glimpsed becomes sharper, concentrates, in a form that we might not perhaps be able to give it later; it prepares the way to extensions of itself:—in blacker moments we hold on to the words in which thoughts born of joy and clarity are expressed.—

I have always found it an excellent thing to note down in this way the stages, even the least important, of my interior life.[1]

Would you believe it?—The day before yesterday I had the extraordinary good luck and the great joy of meeting Boussac again; his battalion arrived from the Aisne to take over the very positions we're leaving. Although he's the sort of man with whom I get on more easily in correspondence than in conversation, a talk with him was a real comfort to me,—mixed, as you will appreciate, with a sharp pang of regret for all the fascinating work the war has cut us off from. Yes, as you quite rightly remind me, a most attractive future awaits me, after the war. But, you know, my own personal development and success have, almost naturally, come to seem of secondary importance to me: hardly anything moves me now except the values and causes to be defended (and I don't doubt that that's how you see things too) . . . It's true that these values and these causes are much more enthralling than a purely personal success.—I think, as you do, and I said so to Boussac to counter his gloomy forebodings, that what will enable us to avoid a revolution and class warfare (at least in the immediate future) will be the joy with which the *poilus* will fall back into the pattern of familiar work and the new ardour with which most of them will throw themselves into it again.—I found Boussac, then, still a bit depressed by the war. When I recently tried to show him that by doing his share of the fighting he was, one way and another, co-operating with the progress of the nature he so loves, he answered that ' he would never confuse, nor even could he ever compare, the brutal doings of military men and the insincere clap-trap of diplomats with the noble and silent transformation of Nature.' And yet isn't it essential to establish the validity of this comparison, to bring about this fusion? I often experience Boussac's feeling of revulsion but I believe it's based on an illusion . . . Yes, the moral and social development of humanity is indeed

[1] In the following month he wrote the *Maîtrise du monde et le signe de Dieu*, whose theme is adumbrated here.

the authentic and 'natural' consequence of organic evolution. This development has an ugly look to us because we see it at too close a range and because free will has its own particular and alluring forms of corruption, but it is in fact the normal term of a process which no doubt is 'noble and silent' simply because we see it from so great a distance,—just as shrapnel bursting around an aircraft, seen from a long way off, makes a very pretty picture, purely ornamental in appearance. All moral perversions are found in embryo in the most 'natural' of activities, the most passive (in appearance) in the hands of the first cause; and therein they are tamed but not by-passed nor surmounted, nor overcome.

I believe that in his lectures Bergson embarked upon this study of the nature, place and biological persistence of moral evolution; otherwise, I'd have a dig at it myself.

I'm glad about your successes, and also about the approach of the holidays; it's always a pleasure to know that you're at Sarcenat. You'll see what a nice person Caro[1] is.

Goodbye. Every sort of kind message to all your family and to Mme Parion. Tell her that the Nîmes sausage, eaten here in the woods, was greatly appreciated by all of us.

Ever yours,

PIERRE

[Esnes] *14th July 1916*

This morning I received your card of the 9th and I'm answering it from the bottom of my dug-out on this glorious day of the festival of the Republic. Since the day before yesterday the battalion has been in the front line, holding the same positions as last time. The sector seems considerably quieter than it was three weeks ago: and apart from a not very vigorous attack two days ago on the battalion we've relieved, the place is almost

[1] Gabriel Teilhard de Chardin's wife, Caroline Jeannerod.

as free from danger as the Nieuport area. Only the mud is still in full control; and so yesterday you might have seen me going about plunged above my knees in glutinous mud, at the bottom of one of those crumbling and shell-torn ditches we dignify by the name of communication trench. Fine weather indeed!

I'm personally one of the lucky ones, since I have the relatively comfortably shelter of the aid-post to rest in and get dry, instead of being reduced, like my comrades, to sleeping on a muddy embankment. Even so, morale is high.—At the same time it's a little humiliating to have been in these parts without experiencing anything at all exciting or heroic. However, for a Christian, humility is the queen of the virtues, isn't it? Never, perhaps, do I feel so conscious of the bliss of belonging to God as when I see myself tied by the divine will, as I am now, to a fate less glorious than I might have dreamed, and which I am ready to accept rather than get distressed about it. To be on the safe side, in case of a sudden attack, I have taken to carrying the Blessed Sacrament on me again; and it is thus, with our Lord so close to my pen and this letter, that I am praying to him with more confidence than ever to add to it a fruitful blessing for you and your work. This morning, as I thought about the Master so close to me and yet still so incompletely united with me, I was entirely filled once again with the infinite mystery of the contact and fusion of beings. Some sort of coming together, or at any rate some sort of bond within matter lies at the root of union. But the stages in the intimacy [the progress] of co-penetration are indefinite: each within the other, the two beings can be tossed indefinitely, like a pebble in the ocean,—and when it's a question of union with God, it's in carrying along with us the whole world that we advance further into the bosom of God: and that bosom itself is in all things; and all things, purified and concentrated, meet and are found again in God's innermost self.

God keep you: and be of good heart for the end of your year. Don't worry about lacking strength or apparent fervour...

But, as you yourself very well say, ask our Lord with confidence to give you strength and to make good what you lack.

Ever yours. And remember me kindly to everyone.

PIERRE

[*Sermaize*] *22nd July 1916*

I've just had the pleasure of receiving your note of the 17th, from Sceaux. We're still in the *brouhaha* of arriving at our rest billets, which makes it difficult to write properly: but I don't want to put off writing to you, so that you can know without delay that I'm safely back from the hill 304 area. As my brief letters from up there will have told you, this second time I had, spiritually, a less difficult spell than the first. And I attribute this both to my better physical condition and to the twofold fact of having been able to do more and to give more of myself. It hardly needs saying: the more you refrain from thinking too much about yourself, the more you put others first, and the better and nicer you are,—the happier you are, and the more influence you have over others. We should know how to smile always.

Our last days in the line were favoured by magnificent weather: I wished you could have shared the last sight I had of the Avocourt wood: the sun was setting, huge and red, behind a forest more leafless than in December; and from the trees there rose, with shattering explosions that rocked the ground, the smoke from land mines. This was the regular time for bombing duels. Fortunately, there were times when it was much quieter. Anyway, we're now back resting in a delightful village not far from Revigny. We've most probably finished with Verdun, at any rate with the bank we occupied; it's always pleasant for the mind and at the same time an added relaxation to live with a rather undecided future to look forward to, offering the prospect of something new or different. The village I'm living in has no parish priest, but there's a church in

113

which, starting tomorrow, I shall say mass. This morning I said mass again for the first time in the neighbouring district (served by the former parish priest of Les Eparges, an extremely nice young priest). You may be sure that I remembered you: and you were, as always, well up in the long list of intentions accumulated in the last three weeks which I offered to the bountiful and almighty action of our Lord. I hope that Cécile has passed her exam. Why must the tyranny of haymaking make Papa put off your visit to Sarcenat? (I learnt this from a letter of Guiguite's, full of regrets.) I would have liked you, at least, to have gone up there. Evidently, however, that might have been a bit difficult ... to counter the boredom of the trenches I've been reading Thureau-Dangin's *Newman Catholique*, which Guiguite sent me. I feel more than ever in sympathy with the great Cardinal, so undaunted, so firm of faith, so full, as he says himself, ' of life and thought ',—and at the same time, so thwarted. And once again, I was conscious within myself of the inspiration that calls me to the great work of reconciling the supreme and absolute love of God with the lower (but still legitimate and necessary) love of life embraced under its natural forms.—A host of Newman's ideas: That it is more important to fight against fundamental errors of thought than to make a few conversions or confine oneself to sectarian disputes; that the intellectual function of the Church consists primarily in eliminating, in choosing, in selecting from within, the positive dogmatic development expressed primarily in the body of the faithful.— Those who try to win the day for a truth, *before its time*, run the risk of ending as heretics. . . . these and other similar ideas, so far-reaching, so open, and hence realistic, have entered into my mind as into a dwelling long familiar to them. And what has made it all the more heartening to me to find this community of inclination and appreciation, is that the man who felt them so deeply had bitterly experienced, without being scandalized, the bitter temptation of being born before the due hour or season for his thought.

I've been reading some poetry, in an anthology picked up

by chance in the trenches. Musset seemed to me, beneath his harmony, to have some most disturbing weaknesses of thought. In the end it was Ronsard and Vigny (particularly the latter) that I found most soothing and refreshing. I think, too, that I'd get great satisfaction from reading Maeterlinck (hush!) but I don't know his work well enough. I had a nice letter from Robert a few days ago. I'll answer him straight away.

Goodbye. Have a good holiday, and I hope that Nature will make you feel more at peace. Let yourself relax in the sort of contemplation that takes you outside yourself and in thought that flows, as the whim takes it, along its own familiar path ...

Ever yours,

PIERRE

[Sermaize] 4th August 1916

I expect you found a letter from me when you arrived at Le Chambon. It was written long enough ago for me to give you some more news—if not outside news (which you won't need after being at Sarcenat), at any rate interior (which is the real) news.—I must tell you first of all how glad I am to learn that I misunderstood my family's plans and that you were able to go to Sarcenat; I imagine that you could find nothing more relaxing after Paris than the peaceful company of Guiguite and Caro. Mind you tell me what you thought of the latter.

I'm still resting near Sermaize, but since yesterday rumours of a move have suddenly started circulating,—but where is anyone's guess. I'm quite unmoved by these reports. If anything new does crop up, you'll soon hear of it from me.—For me, of course, a move back to the lines no longer has any of the attraction of novelty ... But once the time for action comes round again it's very seldom that my earlier keenness doesn't revive. Moreover, they may perhaps intend us for some interesting operation: it would be about time, if the war is really (?) approaching its end.

Since I last wrote, my life has been very much the same, hardly interrupted in its sort of peaceful monotony by the appearance of Boussac (a most welcome event) and a first anti-paratyphoid injection (an unpleasant event). I've also formed most cordial relations, which look like becoming closer still, with a priest from the colonies, who has recently joined a regiment in my brigade (as chaplain): he's a straightforward, forthright, open character, not a bit ' ecclesiastical ', and I immediately found him easy to get on with; and he's already had occasion, at Vaux, to show his mettle.

Meanwhile, I've been trying, in the friendly solitude of the forest, or in the quiet and rather musty coolness of our little village church, to get my thought to develop. I've been feeling a certain need to progress and to enjoy it (no doubt, also) intellectually, and I've answered the ' call ' as faithfully as I could. To tell you the truth, no really new vein of thought, no really satisfying centre for my ideas, has emerged from this self-scrutiny, from this plumbing of my own depths. Even so, I've prospected certain problems, of which one or another will serve to lead me towards some useful lines of thought. First of all, it seemed to me, in support of my theories of Christian co-operation with progress, that there was a real law or natural duty of pursuing research to the very end. Don't you agree that it's a matter of loyalty and ' conscience ' to strive to extract from the world all that this world can hold of truth and energy? (*There must be nothing* in the direction of more-being that remains *unattempted.*) Heaven wishes us to help ourselves [to help it].— It seems to me impossible to concede that revelation should have come to release us from the duty of *pursuit*; and in the grave defect (or rather temptation) of ' extrincisism ' from which churchmen suffer (in wanting to make theological and *a priori* judgments about all reality) I see as much laziness as complacency. It's not only from cosmic enthusiasm but also *as a strict natural moral duty* that we must strive to see more clearly, and thus act more effectively. Under pain of sin, we must try every road ... [*plumb all things, even since the coming of our Lord*].

Next, I found that I would be hard put to it to defend rationally, or at any rate scientifically (in the wide sense of the word) the precept of charity.[1] In general, since charity fits in with a shallow or conventional sentimentality, or, if one is a Christian, because it is pre-eminently the first of our Lord's precepts, the law of fraternity and love is accepted without question. But why, foremost of all, should there not stand the force that organizes, disciplines, selects? (Forgive me for speaking as Teutonically as a Nietzsche . . .) but is it because, placing suffering above all evil, we see the moral ideal in a universal pacification [alleviation]? I like to believe that philanthropy has a more noble basis than that. Is it that mutual love, the law of love, is the very *meaning*, the final fruit, expected of the universe, mutual love being a value [a harmony], a perfection in itself? Maybe . . . that's as far as I've got. What about you?—It's a good thing that facts are more important than theory and that we know for certain, from our Lord's own words, that we must love our neighbour as ourselves. Explanations don't matter: one can always be contrived. All the same, I'd almost class the precept of charity as the revelation of a mystery.

These days, you know, I've been champing the bit internally, to get into the Red Cross. It's undeniably an extremely divine and priestly role to be employed in pouring oil and wine into the wounds inflicted in the struggle for life; but I can't help realizing that my own nature is much more that of the drill that pierces, than that of the oil that eases the advance of progress.

God keep you. May our Lord give you a restful holiday. I commended you to him once again, this Friday.

Ever yours,

PIERRE

Every kind message to all at Le Chambon, especially my uncle and aunt.

[1] For a later and more exact statement of this question, see *The Divine Milieu* pp. 142-4.

[*Nant-le-Grand*] *23rd August 1916*

I'm writing to you from an old country house that stands at the entrance to a little village lost in the most mountainous part of the Bar-le-Duc country. We alighted there yesterday from our dusty vehicles, and if it were not for the too real and too numerous gaps that yawn around me I could imagine that the fortnight since we left Sermaize was no more than a bad dream. I want to start my rest period by sending you a few words to bring you up to date about my position, without prejudice to later letters in which I'll revert to various ideas suggested by your letter of the 11th.

This time, then, we were sent to the right bank, between Thiaumont and Fleury, and we spent ten days in that hazardous area. I'm not allowed, of course, to describe in any detail the operations I witnessed, but I can at any rate tell you that the time I spent there was at once arduous and quite extraordinary, and during it I lived just like a machine, almost completely exteriorized in what was happening.—The setting was that of the worst battlegrounds of Verdun. In front of ravines still more or less clothed in bare woods with trees that are now no more than posts, stretches the area that still has some green growth. Beyond that, there's practically no vegetation; it's all churned-up rubble, and more often than not clay torn and ploughed up to a depth of two or three metres: a real lunar landscape. It's the part where the trenches end and one hides in shell-holes, roughly inter-communicating, and from which all too often, if one wants to make room for oneself, one has to turn out some corpse, Boche or French. Fortunately we had good weather, cool, with hardly any rain: and so we were spared one great trial. On the other hand, shelling, attacks, artillery barrages, happened several times each day. I spent two days in a shell-hole, bracketed for hours at a time by shells falling as close as less than a metre from me. This sort of life, you can imagine, is something of a strain on the nerves. However, our Lord kept my morale firm.—One small compensation, of course, for the horror of such things is the sight of astonishing displays of mechanical and moral energy. For 48 hours I was occupying a hole perched rather like an eagle's nest on the side of a hill from which I could see, very close to me, the line from Thiau-mont to Fleury, 200 metres away. At the moment when the barrage opened up every slope and ravine burst into smoke: it looked like a huge volcano, its sides pierced by countless sulphur springs. Then suddenly, a hundred metres from me, I saw the waves of infantry emerging, at a walking pace, as they made their way back to Fleury, curiously unhurried, tossing hand-grenades into the shell-holes . . . We have had a good many losses, very painful ones. Many of my best friends in the battalion never returned from up there. In the chaos of churned-up clay in which we moved, bullets are treacherous: you never really know whether you're under observation or not.—Going up and returning I went through Verdun, a most interesting visit. The towers of the cathedral are intact, but one side of the apse is completely ruined.

I have said that my morale remained good. Except at times of intense shelling, when life becomes more animal, absorbed in and completely concentrated on the whistlings and explosions, I preserved my appetite for thought. What I regret is not having been sufficiently competent, perhaps, to hearten or comfort this or that one of my friends. But until you suddenly learn that they've had a bullet through the head, it seems so unlikely that men whom you see hale and hearty in the line, should meet with so swift an end, that you feel embarrassed at speaking bluntly about its nearness . . . I don't know what sort of monument the country will later put up on Froideterre hill to commemorate the great battle. There's only one that would be appropriate: a great figure of Christ. Only the image of the crucified can sum up, express and relieve all the horror, and beauty, all the hope and deep mystery in such an avalanche of conflict and sorrows. As I looked at this scene of bitter toil, I felt completely overcome by the thought that I had the honour of standing at one of the two or three spots on which, at this very moment, the whole life of the universe surges and ebbs—places of pain but it is there that a great future (this I *believe* more and more) is taking shape.

I'm not writing about it at great length today because I'm showered under by letters that I have to answer from all sorts of people. I'll write soon. You know that I pray for you. Yesterday, after a fortnight of not being able to say mass, with so many friends to remember, with so many dangers safely avoided to thank for, and with the consciousness of the crying needs and bitter sorrows of the world, I said what was perhaps the most fervent mass of my life.

Ever yours,

PIERRE

I've just had your letter of the 20th. Thank you.

[*Nant-le-Grand*] *29th August 1916*

Just a word to keep you in patience until I can send a rather fuller letter. I'm still quiet and resting,—but, just as though, to prevent me from enjoying the solitude of the room which the local *curé* has put at my disposal, all sorts of extraneous occupations devour my time these days. Not to mention a second anti-paratyphoid injection I had yesterday, and which always makes one a bit muzzy for forty-eight hours, I'm having the ghastly business of making the arrangements for a service for the regiment's dead, which is to take place the day after tomorrow. The trying part of the affair is that the idea came from a certain excellent fellow who wants, however, to give the ceremony a distressing glamour: with high-ranking officers present, and visiting artistes—a piano brought from Bar-le-Duc (liturgy! oh dear!). My share will be a short address into which I hope to slip some sound ideas. You can appreciate that I regret the fruitful tranquillity and peaceful reflexion that seemed to await me here. You have had occasion to know such renunciation so well yourself . . . I hope that after Thursday my free time won't be so disturbed.

I've received and read with interest your last *Revue Hebdomadaire*. Boutroux's [1] article on freedom of conscience once again made me deeply aware of the necessity to reconcile, on the basis of a sincere love of natural progress, the claims and absolutes of believers and unbelievers—each being able, later on, to add to his human work the principles and corollaries that his more or less enlightened good faith reveals to him. But what do you think of the crass religious ignorance of so fine a mind as Boutroux's when he says that ' religion ', as commonly understood, ' denies creatures any existence of their own and any intrinsic value' (p. 434)? One can recognize, under this grossly erroneous expression, the fundamental mistrust of a faith which, in his view, deflowers the world by denying its evolution any absolute value. (This is just what I had in mind when I wrote the *Vie cosmique*.)

I liked the article on feminism, and I recognized in it the qualities that make you want to preserve it among your papers. I hope that the author, in developing his views, will be able later to show that some sort of emancipation of women, eminently desirable in itself, can be achieved without their becoming at all masculine, and particularly without depriving them of the light-giving and ' idealizating' (forgive that ghastly word) power they exercise by the mere act of being present, by just being quietly there. The ancient French view (rather narrow, of course, and jealous) that saw in woman a luminous and inspiring influence, and set her apart from the tumults and banalities of everyday activity, is, in my eyes, the most perspicacious of all: we must preserve it by giving it fresh vitality.

I expect this will find you at Bagnoles. I hope that you'll be able to have a thorough rest there, in preparation for your new task, or rather for going on with your never changing

[1] Émile Boutroux (1845-1921), the philosopher whose *Contingence des lois de la nature* (1874) and *Science et religion dans la philosophie contemporaine* were of particular interest to Père Teilhard de Chardin.

task!—It's quite true: one's often tired of oneself and wishes that one could start some new work from scratch. It's just one more servitude in which the creative hand of God is made manifest in us,—and which we must accept in a spirit of adoration,—without forgetting that the most sacred and most living depths of our soul (if not the whole course of our life and the complex of our habits) can be renewed and rejuvenated in an instant by grace!—You are quite right to resist the bitter-sweet impulse of feeling self-pity for your past. I well know that tendency . . . Set against it the vigorous conviction that happiness and life lie ahead, in God.

Goodbye. Another time, if I have some ideas on the subject, we'll talk about the *Action Française*. I've noted what you say about your longing for a more autonomous life, less burdened by command and authority. But I'm not yet clear about what advice I should give you. I join my prayers to yours that our Lord may enlighten you. It seems to me that, given your present responsibilities, such a change would call for some *occasion*, something hinted at by circumstances, which would present you with a new situation without abandoning the old.

Ever yours. After all, I see, I've written you four pages.

PIERRE

I'll send you back the *Revue Hebdomadaire*. Mme Parion has written to me in great distress. I've answered her. Send me Marcel's address.

Just had your letter-card of the 25th.

[*Nant-le-Grand*] *8th September 1916*

This is a happy date on which to answer your nice long letter of the 4th, which came yesterday. I included in my mass this morning a fervent intention that through the mediation of our Lady, light and peace may descend upon you during your silent 'retreat' in the Normandy countryside. I need hardly add that, following up the ideas which you and I have been turning over recently, I also asked our Lord, through her whom he chose to set above the world and church as a never-fading nimbus, that woman may become among us that which she should be, for the perfecting and salvation of the human soul. It pleases me greatly to offer mass for some of these far-reaching world-intentions; I feel that it's a much worthier object, and much more devotionally strengthening than the over-frequent commending of intentions that are often too trifling or at any rate too personal.

I'll begin by giving you some distressing news about one of my dearest friends. Three days ago a letter from Mme Boussac (Jeanne Termier) told me of her husband's death. On the 12th of August, while I was on the right bank, he had gone up to the left bank again and was coming back from the night fatigues when a shell splinter struck him in the back, at the entrance to Montzéville, of evil memory. He was brought down from the front in an ambulance (to Jubécourt) and died there a week later, without my having the least idea of what had happened. You know that I'd seen him as recently as some time about August 5th . . . This loss is more than a sad event for me, it's shattering. One of the pillars of my ' future ' disappears with Boussac. At first I thought that my reaction would be an embittered rejection of all that I had 'adored'. Instead of working to improve things in the world and extend its conquests (in the spirit you know) would it not be better to abandon to its own sort of suicide this ridiculous world that destroys its finest products, —and then, devoting one's mind entirely to supernatural things, sing a dirge over the ruins of all that here below seems beautiful and precious? . . . But then I pulled myself together. I reflected that God constantly, even when it's a matter of what are manifestly most saintly undertakings, allows the premature disappearance of the instruments best fitted to achieve his glory. I told myself that man's labour, whatever form it may take, must be essentially tenacious, patient, gentle,—and that it's by uncomplainingly putting right the disorders and obstacles that a new order is doubtless taking shape and painfully clearing a place for itself in the world,—an order by virtue of which the brutal shocks and blind disasters that still bruise and so often crush humanity as it blossoms within the chaotic complex of determinism will be reduced to a minimum. And I told myself that I would continue, should God spare me, to work at the earth's task.—However, there it is. With Boussac's death I feel that one of the strongest ties that bound me to geology has slackened. It's some months ago now since I began to ask myself whether it was really too late in life to start on some new line, richer in problems and hopes, than the history of life on earth. In its broad outline, that history has given all that one expected of it. I think now that there are other directions of search, more aggressive, more synthetizing, in which we can pursue our study of the real. Today, we have got our general bearings in the world sufficiently clear. The time has now come to get to grips with matter, organic life, collective life, and to master it, subject it to experiment, make it give up its secrets and its power. No doubt this work has already been begun; and in many of its branches, physics, biology and experimental psychology, I realize that one needs too much technical luggage for me to have the time to take it up at my age of 35. But there may perhaps be something else to try; I can't quite see what it is, but I can dimly apprehend it. Now that the bases I had relied on for my geological career are disappearing, I shall eagerly, if it lies open to me, take the most direct road that leads to the heart of terrestrial reality,—or at least I shall signpost it and point it out to others.

You'll be giving me very great pleasure by sending me Tourville's *Pensées*[1]: it's exactly the sort of book I need. When I was at Ore Place[2] I read a short life of him: and, though I can't quite recall what I liked about it, I do remember that I was

[1] The abbé Henri de Tourville, a contemporary sociologist, was one of the first disciples of Le Play, the founder of the school of social science based on observational methods.

[2] The Jesuit house at Hastings, Sussex.

very pleased with it—particularly, I think, because of a sort of revelation it brought me of the interest to be found in social phenomena. As to Fonsegrive's [1] article, you'd better wait before sending it to me, until we start a new rest period, as our present one is just about to end.

From what you tell me in your letter, I gather that you have received not only the first letter I sent you from here but the second one also. I've little to add to the details I gave you about my life here. However, there have been a few extras. First of all, the memorial service for the regiment's dead at Verdun, took place with, to all outward appearances, great success. Mme Scott (alias Nelly Martyn, of the Opéra Comique, wife of the designer)—since Nieuport, she's also an honorary corporal-bugler in the 4th Zouaves, a regiment in our division—sang with most laudable modesty—and I said a few words which succeeded in pleasing the brass-hats present. The next day I went to a performance—a sight to be seen once at any rate—given by the ' actors with the forces ' to the colonial troops in our brigade. As I wrote to Sarcenat, one would have to have lost the capacity to be astonished by anything not to be moved by such a scene: Parisian actors playing under the village chestnut trees to an audience of Senegalese, Martiniquans, Somalis, Annamites, Tunisians and French . . . I brought back from it the very definite conviction that, among other results of the war, will be that of mixing and welding together the peoples of the earth in a way that nothing else, perhaps, could have done. With some Africans, no doubt, the fusion is distasteful, but even so it may well bear fruit. In any case, with the Russians, Australians, etc., it will have most valuable consequences.—Meanwhile, this village on the Meuse that shelters so many savages presents a most picturesque scene. There's the negro quarter, with Somalis, and the yellow quarter, with Annamites, grouped together, and these various exotic peoples retain their own cooking, their

[1] A French philosopher whose numerous works sought to demonstrate that Catholicism is not incompatible with science or democracy. He died in 1917.

customs, and even their ceremonies. I mustn't forget to add that one group of Annamites is Catholic. You see them praying at the Lady altar in angelic attitudes, or murmuring prayers in a group with the fervour of eastern neophytes.

On Monday, I had the great joy of seeing Joseph arrive. He had faced a sixty-kilometre bicycle ride to come and see me. I hadn't met him since January 1915 when he was leading an unhappy office life at Moulins. He looked extremely elegant, as you can imagine, in his Cadet's uniform. His sector, north of St-Mihiel, is still comparatively quiet; but I doubt whether it will remain so much longer.

With all this, and various other excursions, I'm leaving Nant-le-Grand without having written anything worth talking about. That will have to wait for the autumn and winter campaign. I've at least drawn up a plan of moral studies (interpretation and justification, from the point of view of natural evolution—replenished by the light of faith—of morality, chastity and charity); but I haven't yet got down to writing a draft. There'll be a first chapter which I'll do probably separately, on ' the duty of research '. I think that man has a fundamental obligation to extract from himself and from the earth all that it can give; and this obligation is all the more imperative that we are absolutely ignorant of what limits—they may still be very distant—God has imposed on our natural understanding and power. To grow and to fulfil oneself to the utmost—that is the law immanent in being. I do not believe that in allowing us glimpses of a more divine life God has excused us from pursuing, even on its natural plane, the work of creation. It would, I think, be ' tempting God ' to let the world go its own way without trying to master it and understand it more fully. We must do all we can to lessen death and suffering. We must develop the significance of revealed dogma through a more searching criticism of truth. I should even go so far as to say that religious faith can be justified only in a mankind that constantly exercises such a leverage on the unknown that every divinity other than our adored Lord would appear if, *per impossibile*, it still remained hidden from us ... It would be so grave an objection to the truth of the Church to be able to reproach it with making men lazy!

You'll give me very great pleasure indeed if you'll let me know what you envisage as a fresh [less restricted] orientation to your line of action. In view of our warm friendship, this confidence does not surprise me; I only want to advise you well. Our Lord will reward your faith, if not my merits.

As things go now, I may get leave at the end of the month, or at the beginning of October. But since future operations are so uncertain, don't count too much on my coming then.

Goodbye. Don't let these eight pages prevent you from listening in silence to our Lord, one word from whom is worth more than all the prolixity of human speech.

Ever yours,

PIERRE

[*Nant-le-Grand*] *18th September 1916*

I received your long letter of the 12th yesterday and read it with infinite pleasure and care. And even though I don't think that I'm yet sufficiently clear in my mind to be able to give you a useful answer, I am anxious to send you at least an acknowledgment, and of course to thank you very much indeed for Tourville's *Pensées*, that arrived safely the day before. I've already begun to look through the little book. I do believe that if you'd sent me a duplicate of your copy, I would have guessed where your pencil-marks came—quite apart from the fact that mine would often have noted the same sentences.—Yes, it's most heartening to find a really holy man who doesn't hesitate to urge you to ' be yourself ' resolutely. It's a rather dangerous line to take, no doubt. But shouldn't one be able, for love of God, to risk (if that's possible) even one's holiness or even one's complete orthodoxy?

Moreover, if people try to be ' pioneers ' not out of personal pride and ambition but from love of the Church and of truth, and with absolute trust in God and acceptance of his will before all else, can God allow them to cut themselves off from him? . . . We must pray for one another, then, that our Lord may keep us both humble and fearless, supremely united above all to his divinity, the source of every really fruitful activity . . . One could be heartbroken sometimes, don't you find, to feel deep within one so many powers, so many sources of illumination, that remain buried, stifled in the impenetrable throng of people who surround us without knowing or understanding us . . . What peace it is then to know that there is a living centre of all things, through whom our desires and our points of view can unerringly make their way and reverberate in the very depths of souls, of each individual soul,—anonymously but divinely.

It's a great source of regret to me that I'm an ignoramus and a Philistine in educational matters, so much so that I'm unable to throw any truly authoritative light on the really vital question that confronts you.

Basically, I feel that I entirely agree with you on the advisability of allowing much more play to the spontaneous development of character, at the expense of authority (visible and threatening). I think, as you say, that in seeing that modern methods can be advanced upon and improved, you thereby at once do in fact advance upon the static ideas of nine-tenths of educationalists. However, there's this question: how far is it possible in practice to apply what seem to you to be the ' theories of the future '? to what category of pupils? in what type of teaching?—there will always be a high proportion of unformed or defective minds that need to be *forced* into the *mould of truth* . . . Can the experiment be started except by trying it out in *individual* cases? And, if so, is not your organization, the Institute, sufficiently flexible and you yourself in a sufficiently commanding position, to prevent any particular child being exposed to the evils of standardization and conventional regimentation?—The objections you enumerate to a ' revolution ' in methods are very grave; the experiment would be too serious to be tried out hastily on an organism so constituted as your present establishment. The best advice that I think I can give you provisionally (until I can get some other ideas or, please God, we can have a good talk about it) is to foster your ideas, check them with people who are both experienced and bold, try them out in your circle, gradually and individually, defend them by word of mouth and by your pen, if possible . . . and pray that, if God should see fit, the providential indication for a change may come to you.—If you knew how much I share your repugnance for rigorism, ' because almost all forms of life are beautiful and defensible ' . . . For a similar reason I hardly dare anathematize any proposition—which is rather a weakness, of course, from the point of view of action . . . But it's a weakness that some people must have so as to make up for those who are too blunt and hard in their censure.

Goodbye. This isn't, I repeat, a real answer to your letter. I'll think again about what you say; and there are some points you touch on to which I haven't referred here, although I ought to talk to you about them some time.

I'm still resting. Everything goes well.

PIERRE

[Nant-le-Grand] 9th October 1916

I have to thank you for your letter of the 6th, so full of really good things,—and to assure you that, with me, things are still quiet. I imagine that the extension of our rest is due to the bad weather; and I'm even wondering if, instead of the excitement we expect and hope for, we won't, when the time comes to make a move, have to put up with a prosaic holding tour in the trenches.—Yes, I'll let you know, so far as possible, the whole truth about what my position really is. Only, you know, it sometimes happens that it's only at the last moment that the real military situation becomes apparent; and, much as I agree that you should be aware of any danger I am in, when such danger exists, I would equally reproach myself for giving you any false alarm.

Until the days of mud and blood return, I have fallen back into a peaceful routine, in my room in the presbytery at Nant-le-Grand. Talking with you has revived and given a new start to many ideas and impressions in my mind. As the best way of depicting the beauty of our Lord at the heart of things—as I see him in my mind's eye—I thought of something that pleased me greatly. It would consist of three stories in the style of Benson (*The Light Invisible*), three sorts of vision (The Picture, The Monstrance, The Pyx) in which Christ would appear glorified by everything that is blessed in reality and infinitely attainable and active in each creature ... It would take too long now to go fully into my idea, or more accurately, the intuitions and impressions I want to arouse.—During our next rest, I hope to get this little piece, which, as I told you, appeals to me greatly, finished, and then you can read it.[1] Don't you think, too, that it would be a good idea, as a way of filling out my (our) ideas, to give a picture of the saints we were speaking of, those through whom, most particularly, there shone a sanctified, deep-seated passion for all that made up the life of their own times? (St Francis of Assisi, St Angela of Foligno, St Catherine of Siena, etc.)—not, of course, complete biographies, but biographies from a particular point of view: ' Holiness nourished by an intense communion with the earth.' My ideas are still vague, but you'll be able to help me to get them into shape and document them. What one would have to write would be a sort of history of the ' Christian cosmic feeling ' ... I think it could be quite easily done, and fascinating. You read much more than I do, so make a note for me of anything you find, won't you?

Well, what plans! We have the happiness of thinking that

[1] The reference is to *Christ in the World of Matter*, three stories in the style of Benson (published in *Hymn of the Universe*, Harper, 1965), dated from Nant-le-Grand, 14th October 1916.

our Lord rewards good intentions and makes them bear fruit, even though we may never achieve them.—One thing in your letter seemed to me particularly true and heartening: it was the idea that our paths coincide too exactly for their meeting to be fortuitous rather than providentially willed by God. ' Obviously,' as you say, ' there's our Lord's good pleasure in that.'

You reproach me for not giving you the text of my army citation. Here it is (without comments, which, *a priori*, you would say were uncalled-for): ' A model of courage, self-sacrifice and coolness' (I assure you I blush to write this . . .) ' From the 15th to the 19th August he directed the parties of stretcher-bearers over ground torn up by artillery and swept by machine-gun fire. On the 18th August he went to within twenty metres of the enemy lines to find the body of an officer who had been killed, and brought it back to our trenches.'

So much for today.—Don't be downhearted, will you, about your monotonous work, or your own personal work and your lecture work. Every sort of message to Mme Parion and to your family.

PIERRE

[*Nant-le-Grand*] *13th October 1916*

I wouldn't be surprised if I heard from you shortly, but seeing that the post may not be too regular these days, I'd rather not wait before sending you some news.

We're continually on the point of going up the line again for a tough spell. If you read in the papers that things are hotting-up where I was in August [1] you'll be able to tell yourself that I have a very good chance of being there as spectator or actor. I'll send you some postcards, but it may not always be easy to do so. So don't be surprised if possibly you don't hear from me.

It may, after all, be a simpler business than I anticipate. But

[1] Fleury-Thiaumont, near Verdun.

in any case I'm going to try to commit myself to this new affair as though I were abandoning myself to a vast and kindly current of divine will that will carry me along and use me where and how it pleases. The only essential thing, surely, is to cling to the divine action, ever present, and the more to be adored the more our destiny outruns our anticipation and control ... I like to think, these days, that you too, for your part, will be equally amenable and full of trust in God, not only in what concerns me (which would really be too little) but in all things.

If it turns out to be a false alarm that has made me write to you, and we remain here, I'll send you a card the day-after-tomorrow.

Ever yours. Kind messages to all of you.

PIERRE

[*Nant-le-Grand*] *15th October 1916*

We're still here! Owing, it seems, to the bad weather. It can go on like this until spring, if one is waiting for a fortnight's sun in this fog-ridden country ... Yesterday I received your letter, or rather letters, with the ' Meditation '. I liked the latter greatly and, as you appreciate, it's on the same lines as my own ideas. However, you feel, as much as I do, how complicated these questions are and how they need to be treated in conformity with the spirit and living tradition of the Church ...

So far, I've been concerned primarily with reconciling human effort and detachment. You, for your part, are faced by a similar and related problem, but even more delicate; the conjunction of enjoyment (in the noblest and widest sense) and Christian perfection.—Everything you say is perfectly right and *must* be said and emphatically repeated. *Amo quia odiosum* expresses a mistaken idea, very common, at least among those who observe us from outside: it is the fruit of an excessive Christian reaction against selfishness.—The truth is that if we are to love our neighbour ' other than do the heathen ', we must learn to supernaturalize our sympathies: and this supernaturalizing will always be suspect or incomplete if it is not haloed by a love that extends to the wretched, to the least interesting and least attractive people. It is in this particular sphere that charity reigns supreme, detached from every outward human appearance. (Even then, moreover, it is still a truly human feeling: the poor wretch who is helped and cared for in a Christian way, is truly loved for himself, clearly seen in his right place, as a member of Jesus Christ.)

The example of our Lord, which makes your thesis irrefutable, also completes it: while our Lord had *his particular friends*, at the same time he showed a certain *predilection* for the sick and for sinners . . . I believe that each of these two types of predilection has its special function. The first *fulfils* the soul by associating it with other souls destined for it;—the second marks an effort of the soul (the soul completed and strengthened by holy friendships) to extend the divine radiance.—It's always the same conclusion that emerges: the kingdom of God makes use of *everything*, success *and* suffering, attractions *and* repugnances. Its supreme triumph is in the latter, but it rests equally on the former.—The ' deviations ' of which you speak and the ' attractions from below ' are eliminated from the loving charity you describe to the extent that that charity equips us for a wider, more universal love, and gives us greater zest for the love that is less sustained by natural attraction.

All that I've just written is still rather confused. My ideas are far from being distinct and would need close checking by people who were at once very saintly and very human.—In any case, go on crystallizing what you have in mind by putting it down on paper. If your present thoughts, or mine, still lack the Christian perfection we would desire, God will be able to lead them gradually to it, once our good will is complete.—After all, what do attractive ideas matter? It's the substantial reality of God that should supply the interest and joy of life.

I'll send you back your little essay with Maurras' book. It

might be useful to you.—If I get any ideas on this subject I'll let you know.

Yesterday I finished a draft of what I mentioned to you, ' Christ in the World of Matter. Three stories in the style of Benson.' [1]

Ever yours,

PIERRE

Be of good heart in the work you've undertaken. You may be sure the time you spend on it is very precious in the sight of God.

[*Nant-le-Grand*] *20th October 1916*

Yesterday I received your welcome little note of last Monday. Since then you'll have learnt that mine was a false alarm and that I'm still living in my very damp and wooded valley. Thank you for remembering me before our Lord and for thinking of telling me that the first month of your school year is wrapped in peace and a certain pleasantness. No news could give me greater pleasure.—This calm and this clarity, mark you, are *truth*. Before long, perhaps, they may become somewhat dimmed or overcast: when that happens, don't think that you've been under an illusion or that you have to change the views you formed when your mind was at peace. It's trouble and anxiety (at least in the case of souls of good will) that are *abnormal*, are *less true*. That's what St Ignatius says in his *Spiritual Exercises*: and it's a truth that is of great value in helping us to understand and judge ourselves.

I think you'll have had my answer to what you told me about your views on ' supernatural charity '. It seems to me that I pretty well gave you the substance of my thought, and, on reflexion, I find hardly anything to add. There's one thing we have to do, and another we must not neglect. One must use with loving care and welcome with gratitude the friendships our

[1] cf. letter of 9th October 1916.

Lord puts in our path, either by forming with them a *new principle* of Christian action and renunciation, or by making them serve to sanctify certain souls more effectively through the sharing of views, tastes, activities, that ' destine ' us providentially (as you so well say) for these rather than for those. And then at the same time we have to prove to others and to ourselves that the core of our power to love is not rooted in selfishness but comes from God and leads to God: that's why it's important to love the less lovable, too—first in a spiritual ' offensive ' against passive enjoyment,—and also because we must show our Lord quite clearly that we love him above all the pleasant things in the world. Experience shows that this affection shown to unattractive or even repulsive creatures (themselves, too, placed in our path as a ' vocation ') can be very possible, very human, and very sincere. It is the salt that savours all our other affections, and through it, much more perhaps than through all our efforts in thought and action, we make the world a better and happier place. Remember Françoise [1] and her old man!... All this, I'm quite sure, was implied in your *Meditation*. If I repeat it to you, it's because I too need to confront the complexity of this problem of human affection, how to use it and make it divine.

At the beginning of the week I sent Guiguite (as a souvenir of our common admiration for Benson) the stories I told you about and asked her to send them on to you afterwards. You'll see that the second story mentions your little room at the Institute, or at any rate is told by the light of its lamp. And you'll understand, of course, as I told Guiguite, that what I've written is simply an imaginative fantasy,—in which, however, I've put a great deal of myself.

I had a letter yesterday from my friend de Bélinay, a captain in the 8th infantry Chasseurs, who has just made his final vows at Paray. I'm copying for you this passage which struck me greatly:

' Yes, I must confess that I'm almost frightened by the

[1] Françoise Teilhard de Chardin, a Little Sister of the Poor, who died in Shanghai on 7 June 1911.

sense of fulfilment in every direction, provided by this
profession (religious), by this intoxication of leading a
company of picked troops under fire and taking a village
(Berny-en-Santerre). All my life I've had the painful
feeling of being just a half-baked kid, and that the age of
maximum vitality was going by without bringing me the
manliness the lack of which is so noticeable, so undeniable,
I mean, so easy to put your finger on. And now the
war brings me the lot. Whatever happens, I'll bless our
Lord eternally for having let me see what I have seen, and
for having given me this feeling of strength and confidence,
and the trust shown me by the men which is so moving. . . .
In the *Correspondant* for October 10th you'll find an
article of mine (Hearty), amusing in its mixture and
contrast of priest and tough customer.'
Isn't that excellent?—a splendid union of the natural and the
supernatural, and a living demonstration of their fruitfulness
when one combines them (even though it be only to suffer for
it because Providence does not provide the great desires
we foster with the opportunity to reach out and find fulfilment).

As I said at the beginning of this letter, there's nothing new
here. Since this morning the weather has turned fine and cold.
Putting it at the best, we have still a week or so before moving.[1]
We could do with more activity and movement. This prolonged
calm tends to send the mind back to its peace-time concerns,
and these are barred both by our present resources and by the
shadow to come. And then one loses one's bearings. Besides,
in the solitude of the countryside and of my heart, I seem to feel
more vividly aware of the savour of God.

---

[1] The next day, 21st October, the regiment was moved in lorries to
Verdun.

[Verdun] 30th October 1916

I think you'll have received my card of the day before yesterday, in which I told you that we were being relieved. The take-over is still incomplete, for I'm writing to you from the depths of the Verdun casemates. I think, however, it won't be long before we'll be off for a more refreshing spell in the rear. I'll then send you some fuller details of these last days of fighting, during which I've seen many extraordinary things and, of course, have been in some quite risky situations (not excessively so, however).—For the moment, I'll say no more than that I'm very well. Up in the line, my morale wasn't as high and unshaken as I should have liked ... It's indeed the supreme difficulty to be ready to disappear in death, even though it be in the finest of causes and on the most magnificent of stages! When you feel that you are really at the foot of the wall (or the edge of the ditch, if you prefer) that is the time you feel apprehension—and you feel that only our Lord can give us true forgetfulness of self, sincere, deep, and real.—The apprehension, I believe, is worse than the reality,—for all whom I have seen die, died so simply!—I've received your various letters (Sunday, Wednesday, Thursday) with great joy. If you only knew what pleasure it gives me to know that you feel happy *in your action on others!* Once again, if a few clouds should pass across these rays of light, it matters little. At last, *you have seen clearly.* When things are quieter again for writing to you, I'll try to take up with you some of the ideas you put to me about the nature of real and total charity, which retains and purifies nature,—which doesn't kill the joy of loving but cuts out its selfish side ... Thank you for sending the book on Lotte[1]; it's arrived, but I haven't begun to read it yet. Your idea of a study of the Péguy literature is interesting. Don't let it prevent you from being your own self and developing and presenting *your own*

---

[1] Joseph Lotte, a University teacher at Coutances, a friend of Péguy, whom he had known at the Collège Sainte-Barbe. He founded the *Bulletin des Professeurs Catholiques de l'Université*, which first appeared in January 1911.

ideas.—Yes, I find the 'new women' most interesting. Love them, and defend them.

Goodbye. I'm glad you liked my stories.

PIERRE

Thanks for having taken my place at mass! Do so again. I don't know whether I'll be able to say mass on All Saints and on All Souls. We must all pray for one another on these days so intimately bound up with the Communion of Saints.

[*Ménil-sur-Saulx, Meuse*]   *2nd November 1916*

Here I am pretty well settled in, in a little village of the Barrois, not far from Nant, where I was a fortnight ago. Although I haven't yet found the peace that favours correspondence, I want to send you a few lines to let you know first that I am now right in the rear—and to give you a few details also about the last battle; once that's done, I can pass a sponge over these rather disturbed memories and take up again in the solitude of the woods hereabouts the course of silence and reflexion that, in the absence of any company, serves as a rest-cure,—and, I hope, helps me not to waste my time too badly.—You'll have learnt from my postcards that I took part in the last Verdun offensive. My regiment took the village of Douaumont; the colonial troops of my brigade captured the strong-point. You see that we had our share of the glory, and that almost without loss, at least during the attack itself. My battalion was in reserve, so that I didn't see the attack itself, which in any case it was quite impossible to see in the smoke and fog, and the mud in which mud-coloured figures were moving. It was only the next morning, at dawn, that I moved into position on the ground we'd taken. And I must say that that was not the best moment. I spent a most unpleasant day with my C.O. in a shell-hole just by Thiaumont farm, under a long-drawn-out continual bombardment that seemed to want to kill us off piecemeal. Such hours are the other side of the glory of attack.

What can I tell you about my impressions? I find it's difficult to focus them and analyse them. Basically, I note that I experienced a sort of depression and inertia, partly due to the not very active part played by my unit. Fortunately this lack of activity, this lack of ' go ', were gradually put right by the stimulus of having plenty to do. All the same I didn't feel that my spirit was really heroic.

From a more speculative, almost ' dilettante ' angle, I profoundly enjoyed, in short bursts, the picturesque side of the country and the situation. If you forget that you have a body to drag over the mud like a snail, the Douaumont area is a fascinating sight. Imagine a vast expanse of grim, naked hillsides, wild as a desert, more churned up than a ploughed field. All this we recaptured. I saw again the places where, in August, I huddled in holes that I can still distinguish,—and in which my friends fell. Now one can make one's way over them without fear: the crest above, and two kilometres beyond it too, are now held by us. Hardly any traces of the Boche can be seen,— except round certain shelters, some appalling sights that one looks at without turning a hair: everything has been buried by the shells. To get back to the rear for rations you have (until some communication trenches have been contrived) to make your way for three-quarters of a kilometre across this chaos of enormous shell-holes and treacherous patches of mud, following a few makeshift tracks. I was just getting down to a picturesque description: and I light on what was the greatest misery of the battle, the ocean of mud in which one had to find one's way and watch one's step at the risk every moment of getting lost and falling down. A few concrete pill-boxes were still standing, at long intervals, marking the painful route. You can't imagine how odd it was to see these shelters lost in the chaos of the battlefield, particularly at night. Just as in the inns along a main road or the mountaineers' huts among the glaciers, a whole motley population of wounded, stragglers, somnambulists of all sorts, piled in, in the hope of getting a few moments' sleep,—until some unavoidable duty or the angry voice of an officer made a little room,—soon to be occupied again by some new shadowy figure, dripping wet and apprehensive, emerging from the black night. It's an odd life, and very tough, you lead up there at Froideterre, where, quite apart from the shells (you completely forget these except when they stalk you when you're immobilized, with nothing to do) the earth itself presents such a force of inertia to a man's attempts to move, even on his own and with no burden other than his coating of mud, that it often happens (how often, too!) that he simply falls down, exhausted, with tears in his eyes . . . that's what Verdun is like all the time. —All these horrors, I should add, are to me no more than the memory of a dream. I think that you live so immersed in the immediate effort of the moment that little of them penetrates to your consciousness or memory. And on top of that the lack of proportion between existence on the battlefield and life in peacetime (or at any rate in rest billets) is such that the former, looked back on from the latter, is never anything but a fantasy and dream.

And yet, the dead—they'll never wake from that dream. My battalion had relatively few casualties. Others, on our flank, were more unlucky. The little White Father who went to see you at the Institute last February, was killed. Pray for him. Now once more I'm the only priest in the regiment.

Thank you again for thinking of me and for your letters,— and for your prayers and those of the Institute. Some time later I'll send you another letter, not so full of ' exteriorities '.

On opening your parcel, I found that it contained not Lotte but three copies of the *Revue Hebdomadaire*. They're most welcome.

I have no difficulty in saying mass here every day.

PIERRE

[Ménil-sur-Saulx] 6th November 1916

This is in answer to your short note of the 3rd, which arrived yesterday. Yes, I wrote to you from Verdun at the same time as to Mme Parion; perhaps your letter has now reached you, with only a little delay. In any case I wrote to you again, and at greater length, on the 1st or 2nd of November. I hope that this second one will have had better luck and arrive more promptly than the first.—Do you know, I'm a little annoyed with myself for having sent you my stories before going up to Douaumont. The last one will have moved you needlessly. Still, it can't be helped—I wrote it under the emotion of the moment; and so it was true.

Now I am back again in the peaceful autumn, in the middle of the woods, without the shadow that hung over my last days at Nant. At that time life seemed so problematical, beyond the next few weeks or even days, that every earthly reality seemed shrouded in obscurity. I don't think it's a bad thing to go through such an experience from time to time. A sort of habit gradually grows up of bringing death into life; and one effect of this union is to produce a great strength and a great widening of the mind. All the same, in the freshness of emotion I feel as I enjoy the fine wild autumn, the high-banked rivers wandering, flanked by green meadows, through the rust-red woods, it's a great thing to have the joy of being re-born and living again. I revel in the damp smell of dead leaves . . .—and I am living a tranquil life, with hardly a thought of our future, which again has the attractions of an unknown destination and a distant date.—All this is restoring me to an atmosphere congenial to recollection and thought; only the duty of doing some parish work, in particular saying a few words at the evening service, intervenes to distract me from the task of pursuing my habitual line of thought.—Fundamentally, I am experiencing with new intensity the intense joy and longing of clinging to God through everything. More clearly than ever, the great three-fold effort of the world (the effort to dominate the real, the effort towards social organization, the effort of endurance in suffering) seems to me to be the life-sap to be sanctified,—that which, supernaturalized, must feed the growth of the kingdom of God. In human effort, we have the very marrow of the universe. And it's there that we have to strike.—Don't you think that instead of working directly on souls, it would often be better to concentrate on transforming their *environment*, that is on gaining acceptance for, on bringing to the man in the street, certain points of view, certain ideological currents, that would win over and lead towards God all who shared them, without there being any necessity to bring any external or other pressure on them? If you preach effort above all things, if you urge the sanctification of effort, must you not inevitably stimulate the desire for Christ and bring about his reign, while at the same time you make use of the noblest and most precious human language? Of course, there's effort *and* effort . . . but there can be no real difference of opinion about the meaning of *good* effort, which is victory over selfishness and emancipation from faulty matter? Just think what solidity, what consistence, what interest, every life holds for a man who has understood that the infinite reality of God is apprehended [is apprehensible] at the term of every work of conquest, of every act of social charity, of every suffering endured . . . You'll be amused to hear that Maurras came to my assistance the other day, in a conversation on religion. It was right in the very depths of the citadel at Verdun, in the officers' mess. I was having a comfortable glass of beer with a lieutenant who is a friend of mine, and observing with curiosity the Spanish mission who were loading one another with congratulations around their cups of tea. Our conversation gradually turned to moral life; and then I saw that my companion was a fervent disciple of the ' religion of the spirit '. His attitude is this: he believes in our Lord, he reads the gospels constantly, he offers up to God all his actions as so many prayers . . . but he wants no dogma, no ritual, no ' organized religion '. He's above all that . . . I tried, without much success, to show him how contradictory his attitude was, since, with no dogmatic tradition, it was quite arbitrarily that of the countless pictures of Christ he chose this one (the Catholic) rather than that one (Renan's, Harnack's). (In actual fact, he lives, through sentiment, from an impetus acquired earlier in a very Catholic family.) I pointed out to him that the dilemma is becoming more and more imperative: either integral Catholicism or agnostic liberalism. I don't think I convinced him,—even the most intelligent men (and he is intelligent—very much so) are so little concerned to introduce a little light and order into their basic attitude and their thought.

However, while I was talking about ritual and practice and external institutions, whose necessity is less evident than that of dogmas,—I couldn't help feeling the attraction of this apparently more spiritualized form of religion, of a religion that seems to be contained entirely in the heart and will (I should add that I have always had a weakness for this view). It was then that I remarked that I was behaving just like Isocrates (cf. *Quand les Français ne s'aimaient pas*, p. 334), who killed the spirit of Athens by trying to separate it from its political basis. And I reminded myself, fitting it to my case, of this truth, drawn in fact from the *Action Française*, that the emancipating spirit of the Church is indissolubly bound up with its existence in an organized body, whatever may be the vulgar corruptions and inconveniences inherent in this incorporation, Vatican intrigues or repository trash . . . And even if my friend wasn't convinced, I at least felt more certain in my own mind.

There are various other things I'd like to tell you about, in particular a piece I'm thinking of writing, which would form a chapter at any rate of a collection I'd like to call *The Book of Peace*. But that will be for another time, if it sorts itself out.

Meanwhile, forgive me for writing at such length about myself. It's from friendship that I do so; for the rest, if you only knew how small I feel, and powerless, and unworthy . . .

I pray a great deal that our Lord may be with you and bless

your effort at the Institute, especially your 'kindergarten'.

Devotedly yours,

PIERRE

P.S. Tell Robert that I've received his last letter and will answer it. My love to Marcel.

[*Ménil-sur-Saulx*] *13th November 1916*

This is in answer to your long letter of November 5th, which I don't need to tell you gave me great pleasure. For the last week there's been nothing noteworthy in my existence, from any point of view . . . this letter will tell you at any rate that I'm not forgetting you.

As to what you say in yours, the first thing I have to say is that in my case, the apprehension of death doesn't take quite the form you imagine. No, what frightens me is not the destruction, seen and felt, of the more or less precious edifice I've been able to build up within myself; nor is the breaking off of points of contact multiplied by the search for and cult of the true and the real what seems most distressing to me. It would really be altogether too simple-minded to set one's hopes and find one's joy in things that ' round off ' or enrich a personality so fragile and doomed as ours . . . what fascinates me in life is being able to collaborate in a task, a reality, more durable than myself: it's in that spirit and with that in mind that I try to perfect myself and acquire a little more mastery over things. If death attacks me, it leaves untouched these causes, and ideas and realities, more solid and precious than myself; moreover, faith in Providence makes me believe that this death comes at its appointed hour, with its mysterious and special fruitfulness (not only for the soul's supernatural destiny, but also for the later progress of the Earth). Why then, should I be afraid and grieved, if the essential core of my life is left untouched,—if the same design is still carried on, with no break or ruinous discontinuity?

. . .—What I am apprehensive of in death is (why shouldn't I admit it), besides the suffering, fear of the unknown, of a change of world (or at any rate a change in the outward aspect of the world). As you say, which comes to the same thing, the realities of faith are not felt with the same solidity as the reality of experience . . . And so inevitably, providentially, there must be terror and bewilderment when one has to pass from one to the other.

That, however, is just the moment to achieve the triumph of adoration, and of trust, and of the joy of forming part of a whole greater than oneself. I think that if anything can assuage the bitterness of death, it is still, and always will be, the practice (properly understood) of the passive attitude I have often urged on you. I don't mean that through death we shall return to the great current in which all things are absorbed, as the pantheist view of happiness envisages; yet at the same time we are caught up again, invaded, dominated, by the divine power—contained within the forces that disturb the most intimate depths of our organic being,—those which are present above all in the irresistible urge that will lead our disembodied soul along the further paths that await it (as inevitably as the sun causes vapour to rise from the water on which its rays fall) . . . Death surrenders us totally to God; it makes us enter into him; we must, in return, surrender ourselves to death with absolute love and self-abandonment,—since, when death comes, all we can do is to surrender ourselves completely to the domination and guidance of God.—Even as I write this, my thought is feeling its way; that's why it finds difficulty in expressing itself and appears trite or muddled. All the same, I feel that there'd be something to say about the joy (the healthy joy) of death, about its harmony in life, about the intimate connexion (and at the same time the barrier) between the world of the dead and the world of the living, about the unity of both in one and the same cosmos. Death has been treated too much as a subject for melancholy reflexion, or as an occasion for self-discipline, or as a rather hazy theological entity . . . What we have to do is to see it in its true context, see it as an active reality, as one more phase, in a world and a 'becoming' that are those of our own experience.

I very much enjoyed and approved of what you say about the renewed (and fuller) sympathy you feel for your environment seen in the light of the divine good will. This is indeed a supernatural and holy charity, which makes you truly maternal and clear-sighted . . . Cherish this precious disposition with care. Have you noticed, that when you do this, you to some extent transport yourself into God, into his heart, for you sink your affection in his (just as in doing his will you identify your activity with his operation)? There is no more perfect, more intimate, communion . . . Not only do you love *as* our Lord loves, but you love *through his love itself*. No fusion of beings could go further . . . Continue along this road, and pray to God that he may help you to be always more his own by working bravely to be yourself. Tell me about your kindergarten and the 'contagious' progress of the new ideas in your establishment. You know how much that interests me.

Yes, I'll send you the next piece of writing I manage to complete. At the moment I can't yet see any sufficiently matured idea. But that can come later. I'm at the stage of having a number of different, incoherent, thoughts, with nothing to dominate, centralize, penetrate, and animate it all . . .

Ever yours, and be of good heart, both for Péguy and, above all, 'the rest'.

PIERRE

[*Ménil-sur-Saulx*] *23rd November 1916*

I haven't heard from you since the letter in which you told me of your great sorrow: and I perfectly realize of course that you have other things to do besides writing to me. But I do want to send you a brief word again, to show how much I am at one with you in your distress, and how much I want you to be strong, to find consolation, to be Christian, in your grief. These days, particularly at my mass, I have been praying for you continually, for all of you, for the soul so dear to you.[1] You will see that our Lord will be able to convert the sacrifice he imposes on you, into heartening and unifying grace. Deaths such as my uncle's, in some way shake the past of a whole family. Nothing after it is quite the same as it was before, for the old setting of our memories and of our earthly abode is spoilt or shattered: it is that that makes us weep and feeds our melancholy. But are we wise to allow ourselves to slide down this slope? Isn't there, rather, a providential economy of all life that burns our boats behind us, and drives us on, in continual detachment (which has its own meaning and its own sweetness when we know that it leads to an eternal home in which there is room for all of us)? This continual advance, no doubt, brings its suffering, meritorious and inevitable. I, too, have been feeling it these days,— partly because of family bereavements that gradually leave so little of our youth remaining with us, partly because new deaths of friends, fallen recently in action, made me realize how precarious is my own immediate future. And I've come to think that the only, the supreme, prayer we can offer up during these hours when the road before us is shrouded in darkness, is that of our Master on the cross: ' *In manus tuas commendo spiritum meum.*' To the hands that broke and gave life to the bread, that blessed and caressed, that were pierced;—to the hands that are as our hands, of which we can never say what they will do with the objects they hold, whether shatter them or care for them, but whose whims, we may be sure, are full of kindness and will never do more than hold us close in a jealous grasp,—to the kindly and mighty hands that reach down to the very marrow of the soul,—that mould and create—to the hands through which so great a love is transmitted,—it is to these that it is good to surrender our soul, above all when we suffer or are

[1] Cirice Teillard-Chambon, Marguerite's father, who died on 16th November, 1916.

afraid. And in so doing there is a great happiness and great merit. So—let us do so together.

I must leave you now, because an untimely training exercise claims me for the rest of the day. But I am not forgetting you.

PIERRE

[*Ménil-sur-Saulx*] *5th December 1916*

This is in answer to your letter of the 29th, that brought me, the day after we parted, the details I wanted to know. I am particularly glad that you were able to talk to your teachers and tell them what you felt about charity. When your heart is full of something else to get across to them, let it again, freely and faithfully, unburden itself. No light is given to us for ourselves alone; and when we share it it finds fresh fuel in us.

But, to go back to our meeting, you may be certain (as I said when leaving) that I left you better and stronger, and happy to have found you as I hoped you would be and as you wish to be. You've now reached the most difficult time, perhaps, the time when the emptiness of absence, as you say, is replacing the feeling of presence, and no longer has, to fill it a little, so many or such lively sympathies as at the beginning. I should like you to think that I wish my remembrance of you to grow with the increasing feeling of isolation you are perhaps experiencing. Above all, I hope that the silence that descends, perhaps bringing sorrow with it, upon your soul as it becomes increasingly conscious of its 'aloneness', may encourage a more irresistible intimacy with our Lord. 'He and I,' says Newman somewhere in his *Apologia*, speaking of the profound feeling he experienced on a particular occasion of the only two essentials meeting face to face,—those in which all the rest is summed up and between which it falls into place. I pray that you may feel this fundamental and peace-bringing simplification of the world asserting itself more and more rapidly in your mind. I pray a great deal that that may happen—during this Advent that culminates in the

feast of peace. You won't be surprised that, in these days, I find
a particularly deep meaning in this expectation of him whom I
may well meet at the first turn of the road ... My only surety
then, I think, will be the thought that if I have made more than
one false step it will have been in a clumsy effort to love life and
truth too much. And I feel, too, that in all my efforts it is truly
the divine will that I have ardently striven to fulfil,—even though,
perhaps, it has not always been in so Christian a way as I should
have done ... Since we've mentioned the Liturgy, let me tell
you also that I will remember you most particularly on the 8th.
For me the Immaculate Conception is the feast of ' passive
action ', the action that functions simply by the transmission
through us of divine energy. Purity, in spite of outward appearances, is essentially an active virtue, because it concentrates God
in us and on those who are subject to our influence. In our
Lord, all modes of lower, restless, activity disappear within this
single, luminous, function of drawing God to oneself, of receiving
him and letting him penetrate one's being. To be active in such
a way and such a degree, our Lady must have been brought into
existence in the very heart of grace,—for no later justification,
no matter how immediate, could replace this constitutive, inborn, perfection of the purity that watched over the birth of
her soul. It is thus that I see the Immaculate Conception. May
our Lord give you and me too, a little of her translucence, which
is so favourable to God's action.

About my own situation, at the moment there's nothing of
much interest to tell you. The lull continues, although there
are some rumours of our going back to the trenches. I'll keep
you up to date about everything, as you ask. As yet, of course,
I don't know anything about how my paper was received by
Études.[1] I still don't have anything definite on the stocks. I can
see plenty of useful things to say about the ' evolution of death '
(how the outward appearance of a same sort of end can [must]
disguise, at different stages of life, extremely different realities,
different ' transitions '),—or on ' the flesh and the spirit ' (an

[1] Presumably *Christ in the World of Matter*.

interpretation of the human complexities and dualism found in our ' larval ' condition, if I may use the word),—or on ' the soul of the world' (the world being conceived, from its lowest stages, as being committed to producing from itself souls that draw from it, and gradually exhaust, its real being, and then bit by bit rebuild the real world by the side of the old) ... But I'm not quite clear in my mind about the central idea, or about the structure and shape of what I want to write. I would like it to be in a way both a great encouragement to live, and a great solace for having to let oneself sink ' into the arms of death '; —and this because of considerations that have their roots in intuitions (augmented of course and completed) of the experiential order, in harmony with natural order and coherence.[1]

I've sent you back the copy of *Études*. I forgot to tell you that reading Fonsegrive made me want to read *Jean Christophe* (although it would probably grieve me to find the statement of a thought too akin to my own expressed by another ... Oh! the incurable egotism, and perhaps something else as well), and that Péguy's verses ' Happy those who died ...' struck me more than any other poetry has ever done. I forgot to re-read it sufficiently to learn it by heart. If you think of it, copy it out for me in one of your letters.

God keep you. Have a good rest and take care of yourself; and don't be disturbed if you feel at all slack. I had Mme Parion's letter yesterday. Thank her for it. I'll be answering her.

Ever yours,

PIERRE

[Ménil-sur-Saulx] 8th December 1916

I can't send my answer to Mme Parion without adding a word of remembrance for you—particularly on today's feast. I am

[1] This passage contains the germ of all Père Teilhard wrote in 1917, 1918 and 1919.

praying most earnestly to our Lady that she may show herself specially maternal and consoling to you,—and that she may make you learn that the only real treasure is that of a soul united to God through grace and submission to his will. I should very much like to be sure that your heart is not too heavy or embittered at this moment. Don't forget, will you, that it was particularly for those who feel life burdensome that our Lord came, and that it is for them that he has the warmest welcome. I often ask him in my prayers to console you;—what you are suffering now, you may be sure, is profitable and fruitful,—and your life will emerge from it stronger and finer, for you will have learnt to love God more really . . . —We're already getting well into December. I very much fear that the spell in the trenches we're threatened with won't be over before Christmas; don't hesitate to go straight to Sarcenat, and stay there as long as you can. —About my ' paper ': I had a nice little note of acknowledgment from Léonce.[1] ' . . . It seems to me a sort of high scientifico-cosmic philosophy (if you'll forgive the phrase)—well yes, they may perhaps find it a bit evolutionist. We'll see . . .' ' They ' are the censors who have to read the article before it is published. (They're certainly personally quite sympathetic to me, but that may not be enough . . .) And I thought I'd been so careful! I'll tell you the outcome of the adventure my poor ideas are involved in.

Affectionately yours

PIERRE

[*Verdun*] 11th December 1916

This is to let you know that we're going up to the trenches tomorrow (the same ones still, more or less) for a tour that will in all probability finish by Christmas. I'm telling you this, because I know you want to be kept informed.—I'll send you

---

[1] Fr. Léonce de Grandmaison, s.j. editor of *Études*, whose best-known work, *Jésus-Christ*, was published in 1928, a year after his death.

postcards, so far as I can; and I'd be happy to have a few lines from you. If the mail doesn't allow this, I shall think that our Lord stands between the two of us, and he will give us strength, I am sure, through one another. I'm ' going up ' without much enthusiasm, but without much anxiety either. As the war loses its novelty and ceases to be ' fun ', going up the line seems continually more grim. But then, on the other hand, one has an increasing awareness of following our Lord and of being in his hands. I have made up my mind to spend the time, hour by hour, lost as far as possible in the will of God. I want any hardship I may suffer, too, to serve as an added consolation and source of strength to you in the more hidden, but not less distressing, trials you are undergoing.—The greatest pleasure you can give me, when you get this letter, will be not to worry fruitlessly but to find rest in the heart of our Lord from every engrossing and enfeebling anxiety. That's how you can help me most—Don't be afraid. This spell will soon be over. And then leave will bring a new day.

Give Mme Parion every sort of kind message from me, and pray for me as I do for you, most fraternally.

PIERRE

P.S. I'm writing to Léonce to ask him, should my ' paper ' not be approved, to send it on to you. You keep it for me.

[Ligny-en-Barrois] 22nd December 1916

At last I'm back in rest billets—and in particularly pleasant conditions. From my room in the presbytery (with a real bed!) I look out over the valley of the Ornain, its canal and the main line from Nancy, along which runs the civilian and military traffic,—on the other side the plateau of the Barrois continues towards St-Mihiel. Immediately behind the house, finally, the great forest of Ligny ends, where I shall be able again to indulge in the walks and dreams I enjoyed at Nant and Fouchères. As it is highly probable that we shall be here for a good many weeks, I am delighted at having landed up in so congenial a resting place. But I'll have plenty of time to tell you about all this. I must let you have a picture of what's been happening during this last week. So here goes.

As you can have had no difficulty in guessing, and as the papers will have told you, if you remembered that I belong to the 38th division (de Salins), we took part in the attack of the 15th. It was our brigade that recaptured Louvemont and the adjoining area. The operation had the same features as that at Douaumont: Very few losses during the attack, rather more during the shelling, and great difficulty in bringing up stores and getting the wounded out. On the 24th October we were moving along a big ridge, but this time we had to make our way over ground cut up by ravines, sometimes deep, and formerly wooded, in whose complete wildness there was much that was picturesque and grand. On the whole I wasn't in any serious danger. During the assault there was a pretty nasty barrage to get through, in a ravine; a great many heavy shells were falling, shaking the ground and sending the pine-trunks flying, while we were slowly advancing, with frequent hold-ups, along a rather poor communication trench. In these circumstances it was pretty heartening to see the flood of prisoners that was beginning to arrive. For the rest of the time, the shelling I experienced was never sufficiently dense or accurate to cause much anxiety. On the other hand I never saw the war in so picturesque a light. The Boches' deep dug-outs in front of us had remained intact, so much so that when we went into them it was most entertaining to explore the stores piled up in them: kitbags, arms, letters, cigars, wine, beer, tins of food, etc. . . . Here and there, too, you could see trench-mortars in position and guns—we were properly in Boche land. On the night of the attack I slept in one of these dug-outs I've just been telling you about, along with three wounded Germans, who seemed harmless enough. In the morning I had to take charge of a dozen prisoners who had the job of carrying out the wounded. I managed to have some sort of conversation with them. They gave me the impression of being most unwarlike, mostly young-sters, sometimes sorry for themselves. Only the officers, as a class, give themselves airs. There's no doubt that, without their artillery, these types would never hold on. We held out before Verdun with no entrenchment but shell-holes, while they get themselves picked up by hundreds in dug-outs that afford pro-tection from any shelling!—I told you that in places the ground was very difficult. Particularly at the beginning, when we didn't yet know the best way through, we experienced again the misery of being bogged down, and of having to carry the wounded through treacherous clay. When on top of this the frost came there was an epidemic of frost-bitten feet. I came out with just a touch of a cold and a slight pain in one foot. It didn't amount to anything.—Trying to analyse myself, I found once again that when one enters the battle-zone one experiences a sort of trans-position in the way one looks at things and judges them, which makes one accept it as natural (I don't say pleasant) to see men die and to be exposed to death. One becomes a ' war-monad ', a depersonalized element in a supra-individual operation. One is no longer the same person one was before. This transposition, of course, doesn't take place all at once. Bit by bit, through a series of minor horrors experienced and mastered, one's new state is born and consolidates. When one is back again in the rest area, and one's earlier state of mind is restored, one seems to have been living in a half-dream! and that's partly why (quite apart from reflexion being swallowed up in action) it's difficult properly to express war memories that aren't purely anecdotal.

Your remembering me, and your prayers, which I knew I had, have been a powerful solace to me. Thank you for having thought of ' offering up ' for me the humiliation our Lord sent you the other Saturday. You are quite right in believing that these distasteful vexations disguise a great power that God places in your hands, for the good of many around you. Never forget that.

I've received all your letters and postcards. Next time I'll write at greater length about yours of the 8th. The 'treasure-ships', too, came safely to port this morning (Lotte, de Tourville, two parcels of socks, tea, sausage, tins of food . . .) with your letter of the 18th. Thank Mme Parion. I'll write to her shortly.

No chance, alas, of our meeting at Sarcenat. I don't think I'll get leave before January 10th,—and then you know I'll spend most of it at Lyons. (Don't tell Guiguite yet, either that it'll be so soon,—or that I'll be going to Lyons).

Stay up there as long as you can. I'll be one with you in heart on your sad pilgrimage. Ever yours, and a happy Christmas.

PIERRE

No news yet of the article for *Études*.

[*Ligny-en-Barrois*] *23rd December 1916*

I hope that this short note will find you up and about again, and able to travel to Auvergne without getting too tired. I'm anxious in any case to send you my Christmas greeting in time to arrive before you leave. You may be sure that on this feast I shall pray earnestly to the Lord of Peace that he may give you an abundance of his peace, and make you understand how great is the sanctifying power of the burden of life when it is carried in a Christian spirit.

I have to tell you that my article was not passed for *Études*. I'm not really surprised. In addition to treating of matters that objectively are controversial, the general tone would have upset the quiet and cautious readers of the review (this was the censors' primary objection). I'll show you the letter Léonce wrote me, very kind and very fair. ' Your article,' he says, ' is intensely *exciting* and interesting to read. It's a canvas of thought covered with delightful images. But rather strong meat for our readers, who are peaceful folk . . .'

In view of all this I hardly see how my ideas can ever see the light except in conversation or in manuscript form, passed surreptitiously from hand to hand. Our Lord will do as he sees best. I have made up my mind to carry on straight ahead along my own road, out of loyalty to my own self,—in order to be true, as Tourville says. If the worst comes to the worst, if I die without ever having been heard, I feel confident that I shall have served my purpose. For ideas to prevail, many of their defenders have to die in obscurity. Their anonymous influence makes itself felt. Moreover, I have absolute faith that our Lord will use the sacrifices I shall have to make to obedience, to assure the spontaneous success of any good there may be in my aspirations. He will carry them into many souls who will think they hold them by their own right; and these will win the day for them more effectively than I can ... You may be sure, in any case, that I am in no way upset. Take care of yourself. Always yours.

PIERRE

[*Ligny-en-Barrois*] *28th December 1916*

In view of the time it takes (particularly round about New Year) for a letter to get to Sarcenat, I think it better to write to you at Paris, so that you'll find this when you get back. My wishes for 1917 will thus arrive a little late; but you know so well, don't you, that I will have expressed them in my thoughts and my prayers, at their right time, so that this delay matters little. You know what I would wish for you: that in joy and sorrow, in work and passivity, in success and failure, in meetings and bereavements, our Lord may grow within you, and take the first place in your activities and affections. And next—if he so will it, and if it accords with his plans,—that visible and tangible success may reward your Institute, and peace be felt in your heart and in your family! I like to think that the year now beginning will mark, as did its predecessor, a new progress in our friendship, and bring us closer together and more united to pursue our fraternal journey towards God.—I hope that we'll be able to meet often.—I very much felt, as you did, the incompleteness of those meetings of ours, always overshadowed by the imminence of parting . . . After all, isn't that partly what makes them so precious? Don't be afraid, mind, of being unable to express in a letter all that you feel. One way and another, by literal expression or by intuition, I know that we understand one another completely. And that's the great thing. When the time for a peaceful unhurried meeting comes again, I shall bless God. But I don't believe it's indispensable for the progressive development of our friendship.

You'll have received my last short letter in which I told you about the fate of my article at *Études*. Today, at the same time as your letter of the 25th, I received one from Léonce, very kind and very illuminating, which I'll show you also. Without disguising the difficulties of publishing anything that deals with the questions that interest me, he warmly encourages me to ' integrate within Christian philosophy (even negatively such, that is, compatible with the Christian life) the results, suggestions, and interpretations, even hypothetical, that guide modern scientists.' To do this ' would be to render an immense service, one that a life would be well spent in.' So you see that, fundamentally, I am understood and encouraged. This impels me to classify more exactly my views on the reconciliation I glimpse between the passion of the earth and the passion of God on the meeting-ground of human effort, even natural.

You are quite right in what you say in your letter of the 8th, that nothing is so fine as the strength that achieves. One of the things I have acquired this year is the conviction of the necessary effort, the effort without which *some part of being will never be achieved*. Only a fortnight ago, at Verdun, when I was seeing and experiencing the astonishing effort made by thousands of active units to mount an attack whose success was still in *the balance*, I had a profound impression of the *contingency* of any success in this world, and of its subordination to our own *tenacity*, to our own diligence. In fact, the sound principle is that of action that tackles everything resolutely and energetically, without wasting too much time in fruitless discussion. ' *Don't chat, but try!* ' That's always true.

At the same time I am still faithful to my cult of the other component of the real, by which I mean the dominating energies that force our resistance, even at its most vigorous, to bend before them and acknowledge their mastery. I very much like Blondel's lines on sorrow that you sent me, because through every word shone the creative, formative action of God whose influence alone has the power to take us out of ourselves ' in order to put in us something that is not of us '.—' The joy of another's action in ourselves ', that's exactly what makes the passivities of existence seem so sweet to me, so worthy of adoration (since it is through them that God asserts his primacy over us)—so much so that if I didn't react against this feeling I'd forget that every creature's success is bound up with its active good will, and that no immanent inevitability drives us towards success.—The more I think of it, the more I see that death, through the great invasion and intrusion of everything new that it represents in our individual development, brings freedom and solace,—even in spite of its essentially painful element (because essentially transforming and uprooting) . . . It would be so stifling to feel oneself ineluctably confined to this superficial and experiential facet of our cosmos.

I pray for your safe journey to Murat. And I am happy to think that you'll soon be near Guiguite. I'm sure that your last week, all flu and boredom, will have found great favour in the eyes of our Lord, since you surrendered yourself to his will. Ever devotedly yours,

PIERRE

[*Ligny-en-Barrois*] *1st January 1917*

It's a joy to me to spend this misty afternoon of the first day of the year in sending you my greetings for the coming year . . . Last year, on the same date, I remember, we were in the lines in front of Nieuport, for our first day. During the night I had taken possession of the comfortable sitting-room in the ruined villa, where I had little idea that, for three long months, I would have so much leisure for agreeable meditation. I had spent the morning in a tour of our new sector, still very badly organized, and I had begun deeply to enjoy its damp and pervading melancholy . . . You can't imagine what charm I find, looking back on it, in that time by the Dunes and the Yser, which brought me so lively a reawakening of the urge to think and write, dormant after a year of war. To find a comparable harmony (and reciprocal influence) of place and self, I think I'd have to go back in my past as far as the happy days when I felt the intoxication of the desert. Who can say what invincible power it is that sometimes makes us tremble before the earth, or the sea, or the huge past, as though we were close to a beatifying presence that still hides itself from us . . . and who will ever bring about the happy conjunction of this vague summons, so deeply felt in the heart of every man at all worthy of the name, and the call of a personal God! Would you believe, reading Lotte, which you sent me, I was surprised to find Péguy so close to me (it would be less conceited to put it the other way round). His concern to defend and praise the ' carnal cradle ' of Christ fits in with my own most personal prepossessions. And, just for a moment, I have a slight grudge against him for having taken the subject of Eve. *Eve*, the ' natural ' mother, whose face, so full of mystery, blends into the distant past, shrouded in symbol and legend. What an admirable personification of the ties so essential and so vital which indissolubly bind our human bundle to nature's laborious and patient advance. If only for having found this central core to his thought, this pillar on which his thought rests, Péguy is a great man. I wish a similar inspiration would come to me.

At the moment, my ideas are rather at sixes and sevens,— progressing a little in every direction, but without converging yet quite as I'd like them to. My leisure, perhaps, is not yet sufficiently undisturbed, broken up as it is by trivial little tasks, disturbed, too, by the expectation of leave any moment. What interests me most just now is what I might call the *impasse* in which evolution finds itself caught. In the first place, one can't foresee what will follow the awakening of thought in the world. Secondly, without a sort of emancipation from matter (which would be a complete break with the process of transformism, which is a skilful, but pliant and submissive, use of matter) it's even more difficult to see what thought can do to free itself from the cosmic passivities and mortality, within which it seems doomed never to flourish except precariously and by hazard. And further: *by the very fact of its appearance*, thought is an element of disorganization, of decomposition, for the living stem. The monads refuse any longer (rightly or wrongly) to submit to the laborious task of extending life blindly with docility.—Either they look only for enjoyment, and follow the line of least resistance; or else they try to break the links that attach them to others: they have of their nature a constitutional urge to exist proudly and selfishly . . . The appearance of reason necessarily marks an organic crisis. The former cosmic framework no longer suffices to contain [to satisfy] the new activities born with the human soul. Thus the equilibrium of the universe urgently demands that all men should be given a transcendent interest and outlook and thus with the cohesion imposed by the new ties be prevented from frittering themselves away.—Isn't this the obvious place for the liberating function of the body of Christ and the moral teaching of Christ (charity, humility, renunciation) by which are neutralized the risks of deviation inherent in the thought of our independence? Thus *morality* and sanctity take on an organic and essential significance in the economy of universal becoming . . .—through Christ, the bundle of all created matter that was in danger of falling back and disintegrating is re-formed in a higher, terminal, unity, balancing the lower, radical, unity drawn from incorporation in one and the same matter. I think there'd be something I could write along those lines. But I'd like to find a form [a setting] that's not too heavy or diffuse—(not to mention that from the theological point of view one would have to avoid the classic snag of giving the impression that nature can demand super-nature . . . But one can steer past that easily enough . . .)

Thank you for your letter of the 27th. I am thinking to myself with pleasure that at this moment you're at Sarcenat. Now that your sad pilgrimage is over, you must feel relaxed and at peace at having brought my uncle back to the land of his fathers, like a good patriarch . . . I'm expecting my leave some time during this week—unless I get put off until the next batch. Steps are being taken for me to become an ' honorary ' stretcher-bearer in the regiment, which means being free to serve as chaplain to the three battalions without being tied to any regular duty. It's the type of chaplainship that I suggested as the most attractive to me, and the most useful. It looks as though these steps will bear fruit in the near future. I pray for you.

PIERRE

Léonce writes that my rejected article will be sent round to you at the Institute.

[*Ligny-en-Barrois*] *4th January 1917*

I think that on arriving in Paris you will have found my last two letters, after a not too tiring journey. This is just a line to tell you that my position is still very much the same. Tomorrow, however, we're being moved to a place 8 kilometres away, just far enough to make me lose the advantages of my present billet. Providence, I hope, will see to it that I find a quiet corner and a table, if not a bed. I want this all the more that it seems to me that my ideas are beginning to become more precise and fall into place, as I shall tell you in my next, more detailed, letter. Still no leave-parties away! But it can't be much longer. Perhaps they're waiting until we're in our new quarters. I am posting Lotte back to you.

I'll send you a real letter soon. I'll pray very much for you tomorrow, the first Friday of the year. May the Sacred Heart make you progress even further in him, and make you find the real joy, ever renewed, of living. Ever yours,

PIERRE

[Boviolles?] 6th January 1917

I'm writing from my new billet, an admirable little ' thought cell ' [' pensoir '] that Providence offered me yesterday at the last moment, when I was already seeing myself with no refuge to hope for other than a corner of the sacristy. I'm in a snug little room, with a huge bed, a sky-light through which filters a half-light that encourages the ripening of one's ideas, sufficiently difficult of access (two flights of stairs to climb before you reach my attic) to keep off the bores and the undesirables ... It's ideal. A little way off, my mess occupies one of those little one-storied houses you find in the Meuse country, of which there are many in the village, where the chimney covers half the ceiling (it opens out into the kitchen like a huge funnel, letting in the daylight and the rain). Nothing could be more countrified and picturesque. Apart from the distance from Ligny, which is an interesting supply centre, I've lost little by exchanging Givrauval for Boviolles.

Yesterday, I received your letter of the 31st, and one from Guiguite too. I was glad to hear that your journey went so well, and that Sarcenat did you good. It's thus that, one by one, under the irresistible pressure of time, we surmount all the steepest obstacles of life ... After all the troubles and vicissitudes of the last two months, you're back again in comparative tranquillity, with sorrow no doubt in your soul, and with a somewhat different light (as you put it) cast upon things, but still at peace, and in the right mood to continue the blessed work of God and the earth. One day, just as simply, the whole formative period we find so painful will be behind us, and before us will be God, in whom to lose ourselves. I remember that Françoise was

162

borne up and strengthened by her intense joy in the anticipated possession of God. There's no doubt at all that that thought provides an inexhaustible source of joy and of obliviousness to the daily trivialities that we don't know what to do with. Thank you for what you say about my rejected article. On such occasions as this, particularly, you have no idea how precious to me are your sympathy and support. You're perfectly right, and M. Labauche, too, in saying that everything we give out from ourselves except to another soul is no more than dregs. In a way, the whole tangible universe itself is a vast residue, a skeleton of countless lives that have germinated in it and have left it, leaving behind them only a trifling, infinitesimal part of their riches. True progress never makes itself felt, is never realized in any of the material creations we try to substitute for ourselves in the hope that they will survive our life on earth: it is in souls that the advance is made, the real sparks in which the inner fires of the world are concentrated and embodied, and it disappears with them.—I was telling you in my last letter that I can now envisage an interesting angle around which to group the greater part of all that has passed through my mind these last weeks. Provisionally, I'd call it ' The pain of isolation '.[1] It seems to me that terrestrial beings, as they become more autonomous, psychologically richer, shut themselves up in a way against one another, and at the same time gradually become *strangers* to the cosmic environment and currents, *impenetrable* to one another, *and incapable of exteriorizing themselves*. In this there is both an organic inevitability (the consequence of individualization, which causes the vital current to become increasingly dispersed and scattered), and a fault both inborn and of the will in the monads, who are intoxicated by their independence and tend to dominate or repel others.

In any case, there is in this a most mysterious and profound source of pain. The soul dimly regrets the dignity and the

[1] ' *La peine de l'isolement* ' is the ' *Lutte contre la multitude* ' which Père Teilhard wrote in February-March, 1917. cf. Cuénot, *Pierre Teilhard de Chardin*.

insurmountable barriers that prevent it from bursting out and re-immersing itself in the whole. Sometimes it shivers at feeling alone with itself, never completely understood.—Sometimes it suffers the anguish of feeling lost in the midst of a multitude of strangers.—Sometimes it is seized with giddiness, when it realizes that emancipation has made it sole master of its destiny: it would be so pleasant and comfortable to abandon oneself to a vast current shared by all!—The monad suffers again at seeing the universe threatened by failure because its most noble elements, surrendering to anarchy, shirk the common tasks (this is the ' cosmic crisis ' brought about by the awakening of thought, that I spoke of in one of my recent letters): What can one do that will effectively sanctify and co-ordinate this effervescent multitude? How heavily the burden of the world weighs upon the spirit that is tied so strictly to it and yet is powerless to animate the whole! . . . Who will come to relieve us of the pain of solitude? The answer is obviously our Lord, who opens up to us in himself a beatifying centre of convergence and confluence. In him we find real fusion in a real unity, we find effective interaction and the inter-comprehension we need . . . both organically and morally, through the unifying activity of his body and the efficacious sanctity of his teaching. And so the monad finds solace and the crisis of the world is averted.—I believe there are valuable and profound things to be said on that theme. Death would have its place in such reflexions. For isn't it death, in fact, that liberates, that breaks down the barriers that keep the soul in isolation and allows it to lose itself in God?— And so death becomes almost something to wish for.

Such are my ideas at the moment. Apart from that, there' not much news. Still no leave for anyone. Today, the Epiphany I am asking our Lord to make himself a little more manifest to the world and to us, and through us; you, I know, will certainly have offered the same prayer, which it is so pleasant and so 'full' to utter. Most affectionally yours. Kind regards to Mme Parion.

PIERRE

I've received with great pleasure your letter of the 4th, and read it with great interest.

True enough, my taste for the earth is strange, and, at first sight, most anti-Christian. But it's precisely because I feel so intensely this basic thing in the pagan soul that I feel in a stronger position to speak advisedly (on equal terms) with those who worship the universe,—more certain, too, of the inter-relations and quasi-reconciliations possible between two passions I really believe to be to some degree united in me, and which in any case I certainly experience—a passion for the world, and a passion for God.—What I appreciate in the earth is obviously not its lower part, now outstripped and decrepit (although an instinctive charm still leaves in our hearts a certain weakness—isn't that so—for the age-old abode of the past, for ' the first earth and the first clay ').[1] What attracts me isn't even the myriads of non-human existences that surround our monad, but have no future, that are becoming further and further removed from us and so cease to be interesting.

For me the real earth is that chosen part of the universe, still almost universally dispersed and in course of gradual segregation, but which is little by little taking on body and form in Christ. In my mind I clothe this earth with all that makes up the beauty and solidity of the real and tangible universe—rich, concrete, vitality,—a precious future with which all our efforts and our industry co-operate, an intimate bond of union in matter and in the transformation that makes us evolve as one being,—a destiny that is not artificially imposed but organically based in our capabilities and built up by effort plus the help of God.— You're right in saying that our creation suffers from a discord that apparently dooms to failure all these efforts to find a term to evolution along the actual line of ' becoming ' that now opens before us. It seems that the mind cannot free itself except by some clean break, some escape, *of a completely different order* from

[1] Péguy.

the slow organization of matter that led up to the elaboration of the brain. In this sense there is indeed a discontinuity between heaven and earth. (That's where death comes in.) But the continuity persists in the impulse, the vital effort, the *spirit* in which the work of beatification is embraced and forwarded. To this task of sanctification we have to bring all the spirit that has instinctively animated and still irresistibly raises all terrestrial life. We have to transfer to heaven [go to heaven with] all our zest for the earth. Dynamic unity exists along this fundamental axis of aspiration and drive: if we place ourselves there we can make directly for God *without leaving the line* of all truly natural effort, the line that runs through the aspiration immanent in the whole of our cosmos. I don't think that transformation of organs holds out any hope to us, in fact, of any appreciable development of psychisms in the future. What advance could there be upon thought? As I was saying, the liberation of matter is an extra-transformist phenomenon [concept], which belongs more to idealist philosophy than to a scientific examination of things.—True progress, heir of the vital impulse, seems indeed to be confined to *moral* organization by which the conscious soul surrenders itself docilely to the duty, inherent in its constitution, of extending, freely (and to some degree blindly, it must be admitted) the evolutionary work from which it recognizes its own emergence and which must be good.—What natural organic connexion is there between this obedience, this humble fidelity, and the fulfilment of the monad that in the end finds itself ready to pass into God through Christ? That secret is beyond us, even though we can, maybe, discover some things that are consonant with it, some probabilities. The moralization and sanctification of the Universe are the real progress, the real extension of the work which produced the brain and thought. It is this that should be emphasized,—by insisting that neither moralization nor sanctification are a break, but a purification, careful as they must be to reject no fragment of the legitimate human effort and never to forget the fundamental unity of all the particles of our creation.

Reading Newman's *He and I* for the first time, I had the same impression as you, and I applied the same corrective: 'I' is not an entity isolated from all relations: it is, in a way, the whole universe centred on me, *whose destiny* (in a very true sense) *is played out in me* (in God's eyes isn't every soul worth the whole world, isn't it the whole world?...). Thus, in this essential confrontation of God and me, I feel *every* creature *behind* me ... And so the fundamental primacy of individual salvation leaves the soul all its fulness, as far-reaching as the Universe.

There's a great deal I could say about your letter. That will come gradually. Going back to what I wrote to you recently about 'man alone', I can see an interesting paragraph to write on *The unifying role of Matter*, through which we are able to enter into one another, and have the illusion (not completely illusory) of being able to arrive at the beatific union. This would indeed be one of the most irresistible attractions of matter, would it not (together with that of being the source of countless precious things)?

I realize that what I've written today is complicated, because not yet sufficiently matured. Forgive me. In these talks, you're the companion of my search.

Still no leave for anyone!?

Apart from that, all goes well. Had a letter yesterday from Marcel. I've answered him. Remember me to Mme Parion, and thanks for her card.

Devotedly yours,

PIERRE

[?] *13th January 1917*

This is in answer to your good letter of the 9th, received yesterday; it's always most welcome, any news from you, for if there be any intimacy on this earth that refutes, by experience, my views on the isolation of souls, then for me it is certainly yours. Talking of that, have no fear that the apparently disillusioned turn my thoughts have now taken is going to make me lose heart or become indifferent to the present life. I'm not feeling a heavier burden of distress or even suffering only from a more irresponsible melancholy. It's only that I do believe I've glimpsed one of the fundamental notes of our sensibility, one of the deep and continuous vibrations that we can now hardly distinguish any more, because they reverberate too universally and too persistently in us, but which are none the less the basis in our soul of our petty superficial passions.—I want, you see, to discern more clearly this complex of regrets and desires which in effect makes up our life and our most individually personal energy. This time, I felt that what I'd grasped brought sorrow rather than fulfilment or enthusiasm. You may be sure that I'm examining it with fascinated curiosity that has in it nothing morbid or debilitating. It's perhaps one of the mainsprings of the soul that is to be found there.—Must we not disclose it, if we are to be more consciously human, more effective in our action on others, more certain too of what we lack and what our Lord will give us?

I didn't know, I'm ashamed to say, that Schopenhauer had already spoken of the penalty of individuation. In a way, this concurrence flatters me and gives me more confidence. However baneful a man's influence may be, the importance it assumes in men's minds proves that it contains a precious element of truth, in which men have seen a correct reflexion of themselves . . . Just as in science and reasoning the most difficult thing is undoubtedly to distinguish and formulate clearly the fundamental problems, so in practical life and action we are half way to finding the solution to happiness when we are able to define accurately what causes us suffering and what we wish for.—Already, moreover, the axis of our ideas has shifted a little, and now (without abandoning the problems I discussed with you recently) bears upon the ' evolutive ' value and significance of Christian morality. I see that you fear I may tire myself out or ' distort ' my thought up in my attic. Nothing, of course, would do me so much good, from every point of view, as the opportunity for some really good discussions. But what can I do, all alone, except think?—In fact, I find nothing more restful or more nourishing to the 'zest for living'.—Anyway, I can assure you that if the lovely snow that covers our wild uplands hardly allows me to get out for a walk, rumours of a move (not to the trenches—so don't worry) which probably explains the lack of leave—lead me to anticipate for myself all the activity you wish.

Today, moreover, I've just been informed that my new job as honorary stretcher-bearer has just been decided and confirmed (for the moment, write to me at the same address as before). I am leaving the battalion to join the ' *Compagnie hors rangs* ' (C.H.R.).[1] So goodbye to my room under the eaves and my bed! I'll have to see what luck I have in the neighbouring village. To tell you the truth, as an old hand rooted for the last two years in the first battalion, I'm in something of a panic at this change. I feel personally rather at a loss, too, at no longer having any concrete or military duty. It's always an effort to make a change and get out of a rut . . . and, in this case, I must add that I don't very much like feeling that I'll belong to the category of 'denominational personnel'. Still, I mustn't hesitate. Pray that I may have both tact and courage, and that I may acquire the influence our Lord expects from me.—I'm sorry that you're not feeling as well as you should be. Above all, remember, preserve your peace of mind and tranquillity, even when your work doesn't go well. Only one thing is essential, that our Lord should grow within us and unite us to himself by and in conformity with his will. I pray that he may grant you all the interior joy and physical strength that will help you to radiate your influence for the good of the Institute. I'm writing today to Mme Parion. Devotedly yours,

PIERRE

---

[1] Headquarters company.

I'm answering your letter of the 12th January immediately, because tomorrow we're starting a pretty lengthy move on foot that may well make letter-writing difficult. We have to expect a week or so on the road. At the end of that time, I shan't be far from the place where Gabriel was stationed recently. This peaceful little journey isn't completely unattractive to me— except that it puts off still longer the day when leave will be granted, at the same time as it brings me nearer to you. Anyway, there's no danger for me, either on the way or when we get there. I'll try to write to you while we're on the march. My position as ' unattached stretcher-bearer ', i.e. ' chaplain—other ranks ' is still as it was the day before yesterday, that's to say I haven't yet joined my new company. I am quite sure that with God's help I'll soon be glad I made the change. In spite of everything, you can't imagine how much more readily, with my character and my way of looking at the relations between natural and super-natural, I can accommodate myself to a more complete incor-poration in military life than to this partial emancipation. To get back to your last letter, I must confess that I was a good deal surprised at first (less so, on reflexion) that Emm. de M. should take such an intellectualist attitude to the war question. The fact is, that's the great danger for him with his very proud and very lucid mind: he can't admit that anything is impatient of his penetration and analysis. Everything can be reduced, with nothing left over, to ' language '. That's exactly what Berg-sonism most objects to. I find this concept of the world so impoverished, so empty, so trivial . . . I, too, would very much like it if we could meet soon and have a few good hours of real conversation. That must be when God pleases! Meanwhile, I'm so glad that our Lord is keeping you in peace, in spite of your cares. I have just offered up my mass, to thank him and to dispel the latter.

The Allies' answer to Wilson, to which you refer, is surely excellent, for no cupidity ' shows through ', but simply love of justice. Let's hope this goes for the basis too. I see this document above all as a moral manifesto, something like civilized peoples' tables of traditional law. Germany must in the end declare her war aims too. And then she'll have to make her confession of practical faith in some sort of Nietzscheism, and so it will become abundantly clear that the present war is basically a struggle between two moralities. But if the Boches really have a perverted moral sense, they will be incapable of appreciating the force and beauty of our arguments and our claims, and that's somewhat disturbing. Who can judge? The United States? History? The Pope?—God, at any rate. It is the Vatican which will, I hope, be most impressed. It's Christian justice that we're fighting for. (Even to the ' Moor ' whom they want to deport!)

Ever yours,

PIERRE

[*Avrainville, Haute-Marne*] *18th January 1917*

I'm writing to you on the evening of our second stage. So far it's been a picturesque and very pleasant journey. The cold isn't too bad, and the snow most beautiful, thick, white and powdery. For the last forty-eight hours we have been crossing wide empty uplands, partly clothed in great forests; we're moving from east to west. Today we crossed the Marne. Comfortable billets, too. Last night, an aged and fatherly *curé* gave me a vast bed, in which lurked a stone hot-water bottle, and today some excellent country folk have prepared a similar treat for me. In fact, I'm getting soft. In my new job, everybody is so kind to me. Pray that with the help of all this sympathetic co-operation I may be able to make what's needed of my position. For in my case, it's a question of literally making it. There's nothing in fact to guide me, or oblige me, or direct me. What upholds me is the thought that I'm now—what I must be above all—the point through which our Lord communicates himself to the regiment under the forms and to the extent that seem good to him. It's indeed a fine office, this—most solid and real—and one that impels me to great union with our Lord in all things, and to a great kindness, and to great disinterestedness . . . I rather regret not having sufficient time to write these days, other than short notes. I seem to have quite a number of fruitful ideas these days—I hope that they will ripen profitably in the course of the long marches that await us . . . I always think that there's a way of being very detached by so attaching oneself to that element in the world that breaks away and becomes divinized. And I think it also so necessary to the love of God to base oneself on the pursuit of some great *tangible* interest, that it may really nourish *all* life.

God keep you. I don't forget you. May our Lord keep you in peace. Kind messages to Mme Parion.

PIERRE

Address me: 4e mixte T.Z., Cie H.R., S.P. 131.

[*Séjour*] *21st January 1917*

I'm taking advantage at dawn on a one-day break, near Brienne, to send you some news and to thank you for your letter of the 16th. My pilgrimage still goes pleasantly, although we have left the wild uplands of the Meuse for a low and damp country-side, full of poplars. We passed from one to the other through an odd district of which I was completely ignorant, the Der. It's a huge old forest, as old, no doubt, as Gaul itself, of which there are still some fine remains. Montier-en-Der, in the middle, stands on the site of an abbey founded by St Berkaire, still represented by an extremely beautiful church, in which a romanesque nave is attached not too happily to a pure gothic choir. The forest seems to have pretty well isolated the people and preserved their traditions: Thus at Christmas they carefully make cakes shaped like an X (called '*queugneux*'), quite possibly Celtic in origin. All this druidic and monastic past, in the appropriate setting of a sombre mass of wooded hills, is good to see and breathe. There one forgets the restless anguish of the war and lets oneself relax in the security and peace of things that are stable and deep-rooted. In this atmosphere of ancient France and civilizing Catholicism, I felt real emotion at saying mass on St Berkaire's altar; and you it seems to me, in particular, I did not fail to remember. Tomorrow we continue our march to the north-west. And I hope that when we arrive, there'll be leave waiting for us! In this routine of regular marching, I still can't judge very well the advantage or inconveniences of my change of office. What is certain is that I meet with great kindness. I can't foresee exactly what my position will be in the lines, for it will vary greatly according to circumstances; but there's no doubt that it will be then that my freedom to accompany whichever battalion needs me most, will mean most to me. I don't think I'll be appreciably less in danger.

Today, Sunday, we had a pretty successful high mass, thanks to the assistance of the Zouave battalion, the best part of the regiment and that which I still know least. A good chance for making contacts! Your letter of the 15th interested me greatly, in its comparison of the thought of Schopenhauer and Blondel. It confirmed me in my resolve to write something on the aspiration of the individual to complete himself by something that is all. Isn't that precisely the basis of Catholic dogma, whose whole system and theory are aimed at furthering and explaining the union of creatures in God through Christ?

I leave you now to give Benediction. I shared your distress in ' thanking ' your unwanted collaborator. You acted quite rightly. But, judging by myself, you must have had an awkward moment. May our Lord make it up to you for that and those tedious letters, by an increase of peace in his will.

Ever yours,

PIERRE

I received Mme Parion's letter yesterday. Thanks. Yes, a couple of pairs of socks would be most welcome!

[Bagneux, Marne] 25th January 1917

We've reached the end, at least for the moment, of our pilgrimage —a peaceful, fairly large village, a very, very, flat countryside, flanked by a marshy river. The front is a long way away, and I'm out of reach of Gabriel. To make up for this, I hope by this evening to have a little room in which I'll be able patiently to await developments. I do wish they'd give us leave at last: unfortunately there's nothing definite yet on that interesting question.—No letters, for the last four or five days. I rage against the post, and I fear that you will not have received the two little letters I wrote to you on our way here. Perhaps you don't even know that for the last week I've been tramping along the highways? I hope you do but don't feel sure of it.—The long march, just finished, was interesting on the whole and didn't tire me in the least. It was only the last day that the cold was rather too sharp. Even so, for marching, the dryness of the weather made it no hardship. I need hardly tell you that our future is still wrapped in mystery, not only for the simple *poilus* but even for the fairly high-ups. This would be the time, if ever, to give myself up to mental speculations. I don't know whether I'll be given sufficient leisure. All the same I'd like to put on paper a draft of some of the ideas I outlined to you at the beginning of the month. As time goes by, there's a danger they may become a bit 'faded'.

During our last days on the road, through a very bad country from the religious point of view, I had the opportunity, in talking with the people and parish priests, to gain a certain amount of human experience. You can't imagine the revolting state of selfishness, ill-nature, meanness and human pettiness to which these peasants are reduced, deprived of religion and educated on the state's republican principles! It's an unanswerable condemnation of *laïque* morality even from the natural and positivist point of view. I've never yet come into contact, so palpably, with the real decomposition of humanity that comes with the disappearance of religious feeling. One feels that one's in the presence of a veritable organic taint, as real as a disorder that attacks the tissues of the body. There's no doubt that morality has a 'biological' value much deeper and more profound than you'd suppose from reading the treatises and the sophisms of the Moralists . . .

I'm not writing a long letter this time. But that's because I'm worried at not having had your letters. As soon as I hear from you I'll write by return. There's a fine church here, and no priest. I have no difficulty in saying mass.

Ever yours,

PIERRE

I told you in one of my recent letters that I had Mme Parion's of the 17th. At last, I've just received your letter of the 21st and Mlle Tardieu's card. Many thanks.

[Bagneux] 29th January 1917

I'm still writing from my little corner in the Marne, where our position is still as uncertain and I believe as temporary. And it's still as cold. This last point doesn't trouble me much since there are at least four houses in the village where I am welcome to sit by an excellent fire, and at night I can treat myself to the luxury of a real bed. What I do rather miss, in all this lavish hospitality, is having no really quiet little corner anywhere, the ' *pensoir* ' that for six months I regularly managed to find in the Meuse country, at any rate in its forests. Another circumstance, of a higher order, deprives me to some extent of the tranquil recollection that I enjoy more than anything. I am, in effect, the local parish priest, and fate has decreed that the excellent old fellows of these parts should have taken it into their heads to leave this world during my time here. Hence, burials at awkward times that break into my day—not to mention the duty of holding devotional services, a thing I loathe (except when carried out with supreme dignity, a condition very difficult to

fulfil in a country hole).—For these various reasons, my mind
has continued for some time to be more distracted and stagnant
that I would have liked. It's not however for any lack of tempting subjects. It's that there's no way of focussing my ideas and
bringing them to maturity. You know better than I do, and
have for a long time, the misery of falling short of what one
might be, simply through circumstances.

By no means the least disturbing aspect of the problem of
evil, is this powerlessness of the world to develop successfully,
I won't say the best, but at any rate a good part of itself . . .
When you're confronted with this mystery, it's a good thing,
as you so well said, to abandon yourself to the masterful current,
as divine when it cancels out our efforts as when it carries us
forward. After all, what really matters is surely to be united
with God, and to fall in with the movements he imposes on us,
whatever they may be. And is it not as beatifying to feel the
influence of him we love exert itself to make us less (as his wisdom
plans) rather than greater?—to go back to Blondel's words that
you copied for me, ' the action of others on ourselves ' is more
clearly seen in sorrow than in enjoyment, and the same is thus
true of the resulting joy.

The general trend of what occupies my mind at the moment
is towards the sphere of morality, which I see more and more as
a direct extension of the biological and organic sphere. Morality
completes thought and freedom, as the latter form the term to
the psychological awakening of life. From a purely scientific
point of view one would have to put it that it's the moralization
of souls that carries on in the most direct line the work of
evolution. Thus the supreme duties of renunciation, of charity
(a virtue so fascinating in its mysterious charms that are so
difficult to define), all these are part and parcel of our nature.
You'll be telling me that I've discovered America . . .

Yesterday, Sunday, I had a very gay and pleasant day at the
neighbouring parish priest's, who had invited several priests from
our division. With them was a divisional stretcher-bearer, a
fine organist, a friend of Widor's, and a composer himself; a

man of great simplicity and distinction. He played and sang some beautiful things for us, which took me back into a new world, one I've almost left behind me for the last two years. I'll try and get Sergeant de Montrichard (that's his name) to come and sing to the men: They'll find it worth a sermon to hear him.

If only I could sometimes meet a couple of my Jesuit friends in the army like this! It's almost a year since that happened! And if only I could have a talk with you, too! That's a great privation that we'll both cheerfully offer up to our Lord, I'm sure. For there's still no leave in the offing, although there've been rumours of it.

I can't remember whether I told you that the socks from Mme Parion arrived, and her card. Thanks. I'll write to her.

Ever yours,

PIERRE

I've just had your card of the 27th. Thanks.

[?] *1st February 1917*

Since yesterday we've been back on the march; and we still have two stages to cover before we reach what must be just about the end to our wanderings (still well behind the front—and not far from you . . .) This evening we leave an endless, dismal, plain for the tall clay escarpment against which the German wave flung itself to death in 1914. Tomorrow, I'll be crossing, with all the interest you can well imagine, a corner of these historic parts that I still know very little, and that only from the newspapers. The grandeur of its memories will make me forget the long hours of marching.[1]—I wish you could see the picturesque village in which we're billeted this evening. Perched on the top of a chalk plateau it overlooks the monotonous plain stretching like a sea with just a slight swell, as far as Troyes. The

[1] The 1914 Marne battlefield.

177

neighbouring village huddles behind the vast structure of an old sixteenth-century castle (the Château des Pucelles) that mounts guard over the immense expanse of rolling plain. I think the country we're entering will be a restful change from the monotony of the last few days' march.—Kindly and hospitably entertained by the mother of the parish priest, who's away.— Tomorrow morning, the Purification and the first Friday, I'll say mass in the church (very magnificent outside, but very shabby inside). I shan't forget you, nor your Institute, nor all my kind friends there. May our Lord make of each of us a purifying leaven, in this universal, age-old, operation by which humanity is so mysteriously divided, through the activity of the Child-God, into the chosen and the rejected!—I've just been reading your very kind letter of the 29th, a great comfort at the end of a day's march. You can't imagine how delighted I am to learn of your scheme for ' evangelizing ' women, and even more of the growing enthusiasm you feel for this great task.—It's exactly what I envisaged for you in my dreams.—You can be sure that my prayers and my sufferings will be offered to God that he may deign to foster your efforts and make them bear fruit for him.— Carry on along this road, without any hesitation. You've found your real life's work.—I don't know what to say about leave. Next week, perhaps? . . . but I hardly dare ask you to entertain serious hopes. Did you know that I'm going to be attached to Olivier's formation?—We may perhaps meet.—Talking of books, I told my friend Baugeard, the Colonial troops' chaplain, that I'd give him a list of titles (novels, philosophy, history) of books that provide ' food for thought ' and stimulate one's mind (without being too hard reading). If you have a few titles and books (a couple or so) they'll be welcome.

Goodbye. I'll think over the question that closes your letter (how to make souls sensitive to religious considerations) and if I have any definite ideas, I'll let you have them.

Ever yours,

PIERRE

[? *Marne*] *5th February 1917*

As I wrote yesterday to Mme Parion, it really does seem as though leave is going to begin again. But don't rely too much on this pleasant prospect, for our hopes may still quite possibly be disappointed. And so, until, God willing, we can talk together once more in your little ' friends' corner ', I'd like to show you, in this answer to your letter of the 2nd, that paper and ink can still satisfactorily express much living thought and affection. I'm writing from a large village on the Marne, not far from Paris, where we arrived three days ago, after two stages of marching through country full of the great associations I spoke to you about. Many of the regiment had fought in this area in September 1914, and were able to tell tales of the struggle on the very ground they had fought over. Many graves, very well looked after, scattered about the fields and woods. But nothing at all to suggest the destruction and savagery of the present front, in sectors where you get the full intensity of war. In those days, fighting was the rifleman's job.

I'm very comfortably installed with an old couple, who look after me almost as though I were a son of the house. Only a part of the regiment is here, in the village down in the valley: The rest are billeted in enormous farmhouses on the uplands, as big as small villages, strung out over the monotonous Brie country. I've another very comfortable place up there too, in one of these farms where the owner has a drawing-room and dining-room and so on just like a country gentleman, and I make that my headquarters when I have to visit the battalions in the outlying billets, or take a service for them. To crown my good fortune, my friend Baugeard [1] lives in the same area as I do. In fact, I feel quite out of the war. The only thing I still rather miss is some really quiet corner, with no noise and where you don't have to talk when you don't want to. Because of the cold, it's almost impossible to go anywhere except to the only heated room in

[1] Chaplain to the R.I.C.M.—a regiment brigaded with the 4th Tirailleurs-Zouaves.

the houses, unless you take refuge out of doors, and it's not often you're alone in the chimney-corner.

I must say that you analyse the pain of forgetting those one loves very justly and with great insight. There's a whole category of strangely distressing feelings that I'm only beginning to define at all accurately myself, and the one you describe is among them: those that tear the soul apart by opposing its most vital determinisms to its most vital affections. Have you sometimes experienced what it is to be unable to love people by whom you're loved most touchingly and whom you want with all your power to love (you know well enough that I'm not referring to you here). It's happened to me—and I know no more exquisite pain. Then indeed is the soul sundered and torn by the action of the very forces that make it to be what it is and which are now seen to be endowed with a mysterious complexity—you are now experiencing, in relation to my uncle, a similar anguish: you are fighting against yourself. The true remedy, as you point out, is to turn your eyes towards our Lord, the centre of souls, and then, in a spirit of adoration, to bow before this inexorable law of Providence. What a domain, incidentally, there would be to explore, following up this problem of 'the soul in opposition to itself', for the psychologist or the novelist who could find his way in these dim regions.

I very much liked, of course, the passage from Sertillanges[1] you copied for me. I'd only add (what perhaps comes out in the context) that the incommunicable beauty and individual shade of every soul is not alien to Christ and is found again in perfection in Christ: for Christ is not only the supremely perfect individuality that has passed through our human society. He is also, in his mystical organism, the plenitude and form—fully worked out—of the *chosen* cosmos, so much so, that the beauties and individual gradations of souls acquire their *definitive significance* only as the traits and touches that make up the celestial visage of the great and unique ultimate reality. It is thus that

[1] The Dominican, author of an important book on St Thomas Aquinas, published in 1910.

we complete Christ ... The most exquisite distillations of knowledge, of the beautiful, of the good life, are needed to achieve this task of life. One by one, through human effort aided by God, souls are distilled, precious drops,—and the nectar which comes at the end has not the same savour as that which flowed first. Each has its own exquisite value. In that lies the meaning of human work, of the desperate search to master the secrets and energies (good and bad) of the world: to perfect, to purify, psychic life (individual and collective) so that types of perfection may ultimately be seen that ' centuries of centuries will never know if we do not give them to them '.— Sertillanges is utterly and completely right.—You see, the more I think of it (as I've done a great deal during these recent marches), the more I feel the necessity of defining and organizing the *total* natural human effort. Individual lives carry on from day to day;—political foresight never goes beyond short-term economic or territorial ambitions ... Every one, every life, proceeds *at random.* Christianity indeed contributes a common spirit and a common form: it makes souls cleave together by charity; it makes them adhere to the will of God; it spiritualizes them in desire and affection. But what positive, progressive, precise end are we to assign to human efforts? In what natural direction are we to advance? To what tangible end should we unite, *all of us?*

I can't believe that the world was given to man simply to *keep him busy,* as if it were a wheel to turn. There must be a precise effort to be made, a definite result to be obtained, and this must be the *axis* of human work and of the human lineage, serving as the *support* or matter of our fidelity to God, acting as the *dynamic bond* of our charity. Obviously, it's God [our Lord] who, ultimately, is all this. But under what human form, adapted to human becoming, does God offer himself, to be served, to be won? Detachment is purely negative and disintegrating (if it is not qualified); love of the divine will is a simple form that needs a support; charity is unifying, but, in itself, ' static ' ... It's evidently in the *natural perfecting* of souls, achieved by the *combined effort of all science, all aesthetic, all morality*, that we must seek a way to co-ordinate the dispersed effort of human beings.

Forgive this last page, still, like my thought, far from clear. It's not the first time I've taken advantage of you to clarify the glimmers that pass through my mind; you must take it primarily as a proof of my confidence and true affection.

Goodbye, just for a short time, *if* God allows it. In any case, I pray earnestly for you, Cécile, Alice, and my aunt.

Ever yours,

PIERRE

[*Pavant*] 15th February 1917

No news, I'd better tell you straight away, about leave. It seems to me more and more doubtful whether I'll be in the next party (if there is one). Besides, you'll have seen in the papers that 24-hour passes have been stopped. 48's have been so cut down as to be practically unobtainable. It's quite clearly as you wished to know it to be, necessity (an expression of God's good will) and not just incompetence that is keeping us apart. In this little thing, which we feel so much because of the loss it causes us, we should be happy to recognize the pre-eminence of God in all things. I assure you that the sacrifice we make in common unites us more than all the most delightful reunions.

I keep meaning to send you back Tourville and the two numbers of the *Revue des Jeunes*. The latter gave me real pleasure, as well as awakening a certain nostalgia for the intellectual current they stand for, and in which I would like, as soon as possible, to engage more actively. Not only in Père Sertillanges, but in the minds of all the contributors, too, you feel this concern, acting, I believe, as an emancipating force for our present age, to find in faith in Christ a leavening for man's natural activity. A whole movement is maturing, is getting to work in this direction. I'd like to feel that my activities were co-operating with it more effectively, instead of being wasted or known to only two or three people. Did you read, last Sunday, the long epistle in which St Paul says to the Jews: ' *Hebraeus sum? Et ego!* . . . etc.' For the new era that is now opening, has indeed already begun, I believe the best self-discipline and the most effective apologetic will, for the Christian, consist in being able to present the world, through the example of his own life, with this new challenge. You say ' *Homo sum* '—' *Plus ego* '. Shall I confess that my temperament carries me perhaps too far in this direction? In spite of the friendliness I meet with everywhere, in spite of the peace and freedom I enjoy more and more, I don't like my new position. It doesn't *carry me with it*, it doesn't *bear me up*. It's quite possible that I'll lose this feeling in the line, when I find that I'm needed, that I can give comfort and strength. At the moment I feel useless, a passenger. I assure you that I'd a thousand times rather be throwing grenades or handling a machine-gun than be a supernumerary as I am now. What I'm going to say may not be very orthodox—and yet I believe there's a core of truth in it: I feel that doing so I would be more a priest. Isn't a priest a man who has to bear the burden of life in all its forms, and shows by his own life how human work and love of God can be combined? I'd be interested to know how many of us soldier-priests think the same. . . . I have an idea that there's another deep current beginning to flow along those lines, too; at the moment it is chary of advancing openly, but one day it will triumph in a form blessed by God and the Church. I don't know whether I should react against this tendency. But I feel that I'm not being honest with myself unless I say what I think: if I said anything else, I'd be doing violence to my own self.—Fundamentally, however, since we seem to be approaching the end of the war, it's really an academic question. But if I had to start again, I wouldn't take the line I did in December 1914.

I'm telling you all this, because I need to explain it to someone. But don't let it make you think that I'm saddened or disheartened. The thought that, in spite of one's blunderings, one belongs to God, makes up for everything, and allows one to hope for every sort of compensation . . . Have you seen poor Duhem's [1] very flattering article in the issue for December 25th? I think you'll have applied to yourself the closing lines of the lecture: ' to give voice to the word of God ': that, strictly and properly, is the glory of the teacher's work. Tell me, in one of your next letters, how your plans for ' evangelizing ' girls are getting on. You know that they interest me greatly, as being your real line.

No change in my life here.

Ever yours,

PIERRE

Has Mme Parion any details of her brother's death? Tomorrow I'll be saying the mass I promised her. Olivier, did I tell you, left the corps just as I arrived. He's in sector 98, in the area where Marcel used to be . . .

[Pavant] 17th February 1917

Yesterday, I had your letter of the 9th, and today the two copies of the *Revue des Jeunes*. A first glance, as I looked through the latter with some eagerness, convinced me of the kinship between my ideas and those of Père Sertillanges (you'll have noticed the support he looks for in, of course, St Paul . . .) If only there were legions of us to conceive Christ in this immediate, practical and tangible form of ' the world's driving force '! Just turning over these few pages, I felt again a thrilling urge to think and write. If only peace would come! and with it the chance to re-form the fruitful contacts from which are born and in which grow the thoughts that make up for the sorrows of life!

To get back to your letter of the 9th, I must tell you I was

---

[1] Pierre Duhem (1861–1916), the physicist, whose most important book, unfinished at his death, is his *Histoire des doctrines cosmologiques, de Platon à Copernic.*

greatly touched by what you say about how much store you set by our friendship. I repeat: you must have no doubt, ever, of the joy and benefit it has been to me to know you, in the way we have for the last four years. I believe with all my soul that it's our Lord who has made our paths cross, or rather run together. And I needn't do more than just tell you, need I, that I regret as much as you do the difficulty we're having in meeting again. I'd be as happy as you if I could get a 24- or 48-hour pass, and it does something to me every time I see a Paris-bound train passing. But there it is . . . As I told you in my earlier letter, there are too many people here in the same boat. I don't like to keep on applying. For a start, when leave began again, I did all I decently could last week to work my turn to move up the queue. As I'm on the verge of being included in the next batch, I'll wait until next week to see if it comes off. If it doesn't, or if I'm not included, I promise you I'll put in an application to try to get a few hours at least. But don't count on its being granted. I fear you might be disappointed.—In any case, if I don't come, it will certainly be because our Lord has not wished it, for I'll have done all I can.—You see, if I really want to be a link between our Lord and the regiment, I have to be the most ready to accept the will of God, the most patient, the most mortified (without of course, being clumsily passive). And if I am to be all this, you must help me; you must share part of my burden, mustn't you?—And so we'll both be stronger and more united. More news, at greater length, soon.

PIERRE

I wrote to Mme Parion the day before yesterday.

[Pavant] 23rd February 1917

As I have to go tomorrow to a place some kilometres from here and have some teeth filled, I'm writing to you today—to let you know that I got back safely, and to tell you also, once again, what benefit and strength I derived from this last meeting. Once the slight melancholy of parting has gone, there remains only the satisfaction that comes from having at last met again and of having understood each other. May our Lord be ever more fully the centre and term of our friendship, a real friendship of brother and sister. The more we devote ourselves to making more room for him within us, the more we shall help one another, in a common building up of our lives. It was a real joy to me to see that every year your way of life is becoming more precisely directed towards action steeped in charity. Your plans to work for women and in education seem to me to answer your true vocation. I shall often pray God to help you to see them clearly and realise them.

On the way back, I read *Le Feu*.[1] There are scenes of impressive realism (the bombardment . . .); others seem to me rather forced (by piling up horrors that rarely coincide like that, (e.g. the attack, the scenes in the aid-post). Besides this, there are many half-wrong ideas—but deeply felt and disturbing (on evil, inequality, etc.); these, combined with an inability to understand Christianity that makes you despair (over-simplification, complacent acquiescence), will no doubt deter you from putting the book in your common-room library.—I think it's precisely in these impassioned errors that the work is a true and realistic expression of a mentality that is very prevalent and very deeply rooted in the ordinary fighting man's heart.

Reading these pages, coinciding with the frame of mind you know, has been like a crack of the whip to me. May God give us, and multiply their numbers, Christians who *in virtue of their religion*, will bear, more than any other human creature, the burden of their own time's aspirations and toil. Ah, if only we were able to instil into our charity an egalitarian passion for the people! . . . More than anyone, our Lord lived the life of men. We should be as he was. Without that passion (the passion for the human) we'll drift like broken ice on the current of our age! Don't you agree with me?

[1] Henri Barbusse's well-known war novel, *Under Fire*.

No change in our situation here. I can't get any news about leave.

Knowing that Mme Parion is travelling I'm not writing to her now. Every kind message to my aunt, your sisters, to Cécile, to Marcel and Robert.

Devotedly yours,

PIERRE

[*Pavant*] *1st March 1917*

I've just had your nice little card of the 27th. It's as good as a long letter. I hope Jeanne and Cécile will soon be quite well again—and Mme Parion, for her part, get safely through this term that's being so trying for her.—Nothing new in my affairs. Everyone is hoping for the arrival of the famous third leave period,—and we're still waiting. However, as I was telling you, it looks as though we'll be here for a good time still ... As things stand, I'd find it difficult to remain patient without our meeting a week ago.—And yet it's a very inconsiderable trial. On this point, in a matter that can't possibly do me any real harm, I'm interested at the liveliness of the feelings I'm experiencing in myself of injured ' *right* ', of the *injustice* suffered, etc. There must be many hearts in this world—legions of them—grievously torn by revolt; and it must be doubly intolerable to feel that no one cares, that you can't expect consideration from any one, that there's nothing you can do. What a burden it must be for those who haven't the comfort of resigning themselves to God while waiting for some slow, laborious improvement in men and their selfishness!

I'm reading and writing in the calm of my Pavant retreat. I've got down to writing the little essay (which I outlined to you in conversation) on the evil of the multitude. It's not going quickly, but even so I've got well into the subject. I'll need another fortnight at least to finish it. If I can do so, you shall have the first reading, as is only fair, and the essay itself, if you like.

Verhaeren's *Les Forces tumultueuses* contains some fine things, though in a rather monotonous rhythm and language. His inspiration is for a brutal realism, but I like it a good deal, for in it I meet again,—though unfortunately in a pagan form and with the impulse that might make them rise up to God stifled— many of the aspirations that are dear to me (because I look on them as essential to the human heart and as the only ones that have power to direct life). Christianity, of course, with its mortifications and its ' timid caresses ' is continually contrasted in these poems with the passionate blaze of real, human, life . . . Why can't I have a hundred lives and a hundred tongues to prove by my own example how empty is this sophism!

Père Sertillanges is certainly indefatigable in ramming home his point (about Christ and life). If you see the *Annales* for 25th February, you'll find an article on the cathedrals, ' works of vital synthesis and religious integration ', glorifications of human work, all marked by ' a universalist and naturalist tendency '.—There's evidently a line of thought there that would be most interesting to study,—even though it rested on a view of the divine in the world that is perhaps very extrinsic and intrusive. One of the gaps in my self-education is that I know too little about history and its sources.

Had a letter from Olivier, who, finding the war too quiet in his sector, is ' burying himself in his pre-war reading '. He tells me that he can't do much for Brunel, since the latter has already failed some time ago the entrance exam for Fontainebleau, and this disqualifies him from trying again. A pity.

Goodbye. Tomorrow, the first Friday, I'll earnestly pray to our Lord that he may take us very much for himself.

PIERRE

[Pavant] 24th March 1917

Many thanks for your letter of the 20th, the last page of which brings me such good news. I hope Père Mainage had a real influence for good on your former pupils and that you formed a useful contact with him. Tomorrow I'll offer this intention to our Lord, together with all your affairs, once again.—At the same time as this short note I'm sending you a note-book with my essay on the Multitude. Let me know whether you've received it. Its philosophical significance is obviously very roughly worked out, and may even seem Manichean. I've left it just as it is partly because I find it impossible to express myself better, and partly because it seems to me that under phraseology that may be somewhat erroneous or contradictory there lies a 'pointer to truth' that might be impoverished by language more strictly logical or superficially orthodox. All the same, I'd rather have had something more personal and more completely finished than this is.—Nothing new in my external situation. However, all indications seem to point to our having to anticipate an early move. I don't think, though, that it will be to a warm sector, but only a matter of bringing us closer to the lines. In spite of the charm of P. I shan't be sorry to get back to a more exciting life, freer from ordinary conventions. Once again, be sure that I'll keep you up to date with everything. I like to think that you, for your part, will be enjoying a fortnight's peace at Sarcenat or elsewhere. May our Lord be with you there.

Every kind message to Mme Parion. Always yours,

PIERRE

No news from Olivier or Victor.

[Pavant] Monday 29th March 1917

I think that, like all of us, you must be following with passionate interest the intoxicating course of events to the north of Soissons —puzzling, but with an intoxicating whiff of victory about them. You had been well prepared for it, by what you heard last Thursday . . . And now here are Olivier, and Marcel too no doubt, pushing on in the rear of the Boche. I wonder shall I be swept up in this advance? It might well be, since, as you know, my regiment's destination is not far from the area that has just been surrendered. Rumour, of course, is busy. Meanwhile, I'm still at Pavant in my comfortable family billet. If anything new turns up, I'll let you know immediately. When I got back here, I found your nice letter of the 3rd. And on top of that today your card of the 8th (addressed to Lyons) which was forwarded to me. Reading these brought back to my mind many of the things we said to one another during the pleasant hours of conversation we have had since then. And it only served to make me understand them better.

Yes, go out, with all your heart, to the students whom providence seems to send your way, not simply by chance meeting but as the fruit of a long preparation that is in fact the whole story of your life. Having known their difficulties and shared their way of living you can, more closely than anyone else, teach them to find all around them the God whom you yourself can now see more clearly in everything. I like to think that it is among them that you'll find your real sphere of activity, and also the gratifying consolation of feeling that many human beings have found warmth again in their life through association with you.

For my part, I told you the frame of mind in which I was going back to the front: more sharply aware that for the rest of my life my task is to develop in myself, humbly, faithfully, doggedly,—and at the same time to impart it as much as possible to others—the sort of mysticism that makes one seek passionately for God in the heart of every substance and every action.

Never have I so clearly seen how God alone, and no personal effort, can open our eyes to this light and preserve this vision in us. And never, on the other hand, have I understood so fully how much the practice of this particular science of divinizing life calls for the diligent co-operation of every form of activity I engage in. It needs the sacraments, and prayer, and the apostolate, and study: all these directed to the same concrete, very precise, end.

Pray to our Lord that this may be no dream, but a fruitful reality, and that he may help me to be of more real service than ever before.

I'm going on with writing my essay on the multitude. It's hard work alone. Even so, it won't be long before the end is in sight.

Goodbye. Every kind message to Mme Parion. She knows how much I enjoyed seeing her again.

PIERRE

[*Rocourt*] *31st March 1917*

I'm writing to you from our new quarters, closer to the front, this time, and less comfortable than Pavant—but more temporary, too,—where we arrived two days ago. As everywhere in the forward areas, the village I'm housed in is not very interesting: a dilapidated church, a dirty sacristy, a great many cars and lorries, few civilians and supplies, masses of *poilus* of all sorts. I've never seen these various factors so pronounced as in this area; it's literally bursting with troops. So the order to move on will be welcome; and I don't think it will be long delayed, whether it means taking part in the big show or simply being sent to hold some boring sector. I'm writing to you today to take advantage of the leisure I still have, and also to thank you for your kind letter of the 28th, which came yesterday. At the same time I'd like to assure you that I'll be thinking of you at the beginning of the days of prayer you've so happily chosen to spend at Paray. Among the things Blessed Margaret Mary relates, there's one that has always struck me particularly: I mean the vision in which she seemed to be an indeterminate atom striving to lose herself in the great centre of light that was the heart of our Lord, and unable to do so until the centre itself drew her in (which, in fact, is taken from the Gospel: *Nemo potest venire ad Patrem nisi ego traham eum ad meipsum*.[1] In this account I recognize the two elements which sum up life for me: *absolute dependence* on the creative and sanctifying energy of God, which alone can maintain rooted in us the passion for life, the passion for God;—and then, once this deep-seated attraction has been implanted in us, *an invasion by the divinity* of our whole environment, of all that we do, so that for us everything becomes the self-giving, transforming God.—While you are so close to our Lord, so responsive to the influence of his heart, you must ask him to give both of us a great love of his person, so that it may become the strength and joy of our life. Our Lord's heart is indeed ineffably beautiful and satisfying; it exhausts all reality and answers all the soul's needs. The very thought of it is almost more than the mind can compass. Why must this devotion be ruined by so much mawkishness and false sentimentality? ... I may be mistaken about this, I fear (for our Lord urged the love of his heart as something very popular, open to all, and therefore, like the Holy Eucharist itself, exposed to the excesses of false devotion) but my own natural inclination is to look on the Sacred Heart as an object of love worthy of such respect, so sacred, that it should be the centre of an almost esoteric cult reserved for those who wish with all their hearts to be real Christians, through and through. It pains me to see pictures of it scattered about here, there and everywhere and the devotion at the mercy of people who don't know even the A B C of their religion. But, I repeat ... fundamentally, the mistake may be mine. I always have this underlying, incurable, repugnance from anything in the way of pressure on souls or on freedom in religious matters. There's some truth in what

[1] John vi. 44.

I feel. But it shouldn't be exaggerated.—In the saints, love of God has always been found combined with a real passion for making him known.—So, we'll unite in prayer for one another this week, that the will of God may be realized in each of us, very perfectly and for great things if our Lord so please.

I'll let you know what happens to me.

Ever yours,

PIERRE

[Paissy] [5th April] Holy Saturday 1917

I've just received your nice card of the 3rd April. I hope that you, too, have had my letter of the end of March, sent to Paray.— I'm delighted that your first impression of your ' oratory ' was favourable. If only you knew how grateful I am to you for looking on yourself as to some degree taking my place there, and how I hope that our Lord has accepted the substitution! My Holy Week has really been very distracted, and I reproach myself for having failed to introduce in the atmosphere of toil and trouble in which so many men are busy around me, all the spirit of renunciation and compassion that, with a little faith, one should so easily be able to draw from these anniversaries of the Passion. It's always difficult to give spiritual realities a solidity, in our souls, that enables them to counter-balance the weight of tangible realities! Thinking yesterday, Good Friday, of the small number of *poilus*, out of the swarming masses that work here, who dream of offering to God their manifold sufferings, all they suffer from the mud, from the danger, from the unknown, from wounds . . . I told myself that perhaps God requires no more, if all this mass is to be sanctified and made to serve his ends, than the conscious oblation and sacrifice of a few more enlightened souls,—by whom the whole is leavened. Pray earnestly that I may meet God's wishes and be among the latter.—For reasons of security, I can't tell you anything about my external life. The sector's still comparatively quiet, and there are plenty of interesting things to see.

Tomorrow I'm expecting to say mass in a neatly kept cellar-chapel nor far away. There are several chaplains here: one of them typical, and touching: an old missionary, with a long white beard, a kind fatherly face, who leans on a six-foot stick, as patriarchal as himself.

Goodbye. Tell Guiguite that I've just had her long letter of the 3rd, and will answer her. My love to you both,

PIERRE

As noted in the foreword, letters written between the 15th April and the 10th June have been lost.]

[*Paissy*] 10th June 1917

Yesterday I received the little case of tinned food and today your card of the 6th. For the first, please accept a very hearty thank-you. As for the second, my letter of the 6th, and the one I sent Mme Parion the day before yesterday, will have shown you that you're worrying unnecessarily on my behalf—which is a great pity, seeing that you have plenty of worries already in your own life. Another time, remember that the Chemin des Dames is very long, and that only a small proportion even of the troops attached to a sector under attack is involved in it. It's not often, accordingly, that your anxiety needs to be determined by the gravity of the communiqués. I'll always let you know the truth, so far as is compatible with operational security. Apart from that, try to abound in the sense of peace and trust in our Lord. That will do most good to both of us.

I'm still writing from the village I mentioned to Mme Parion. There have been some flare-ups in the line. But here, it's out-rageously quiet, and I'm leading practically the same life I was leading a week ago at Serval. During the day-time, I have a room with a table at which to write. At night, I sleep on a comfortable bunk in a wooded grove. I've made several expeditions in delightful weather. So you see there's no hardship in my life. I don't know whether the regiment is going to occupy a sector, properly so called. If it is, I'll have no complaints: life in the saps and shell-holes has such a savour and tone that in the long run you find it difficult to do without it,—although, at first, when you go back to it again, you count the days and hours till your relief.—This morning, Sunday, there was a very fine 10 o'clock mass in the grotto-chapel. I don't know whether I'll be able to say it on Friday. In any case, we'll be united in prayer on that day, won't we? and if I can't say mass, your communion will be for both of us.

I told Mme Parion, I think, that I've met a Jesuit here, in the heavy artillery. Like every good gunner, weight of kit is no problem to him, and so he is well supplied with periodicals, including *Études*. In one issue, I saw that de Tonquédec has brought out with Beauchesne an *Introduction à l'Étude du Merveilleux et du Miracle*, which seems an original and solid piece of work,—and that there's a translation of Dante's *Vita Nuova* by Henry Cochin. Noticing this reminded me that one of the most interesting mystics to study from my point of view would, in fact, be Dante, so possessed by and passionately interested in the real. In any case I believe that there are few better examples than Beatrice to make one understand what is meant by the scaling-up (to the level of the universe) of the feeling nourished by a particular object (and of the object itself).—I'm continuing to improve and gradually give precision to the ideas and the scheme I spoke of in my earlier letters. I'm tending to give still more prominence to the realism by which mysticism lives,[1] and also to distinguish more sharply the alternating movement that carries the soul towards (and in turn drives it away from) the divine centre, homogeneous and essential, through the particular determined forms of the real that we have to know and love and bring into being.

[1] Anticipating *Le Milieu mystique*, completed two months later.

Leave is starting almost any moment now. So I'm not without hopes of getting away before July 15th. But will you still be in Paris then?... If not, now or never would be the time to get hold of a 24-hour pass for the end of June, so that we can talk of so many things that we've been writing about for some time.

Goodbye. I'm sending Olivier Robert's address.

Every kind wish to Mme Parion.

Ever yours,

PIERRE

[Ravin de Moulins] *17th June 1917*

Just a few words to thank you for your card of the 14th, which has just arrived, with Mme Parion's card of the 14th, and your two little cases of tinned food. You know how much I appreciate the kind thoughts of both of you. I'm writing from the bottom of my Boche sap, where it's nice and cool, unlike the trenches, which are rather too warm. The sector's still quiet, hardly disturbed by a few mortars. On our right, however, things hotted up yesterday evening. When they quietened down again, you can't imagine the intense feeling of romance that, with night hardly fallen, clothed this wild upland, still shrouded in smoke. Every now and again you could still hear the music of shells, hurrying over before it was too late, and from crest to crest, as far as Laon, many-coloured Boche flares rose up into the air.

This morning I went down to say mass in the village where I was a few days ago. I expect to start again the day after to-morrow. Meanwhile, I carry the consecrated host on me, for the benefit of some of the Zouaves. And so I spend my day literally heart to heart with our Lord. If I could but really profit from this privilege that only war can afford me!—So we're now not so far from one another. May our Lord grant that this prolonged presence of his may enlighten our eyes and heart a little, as you too wish, so that we may see him in all things, more completely and really.

Goodbye. I'll write again soon. Gabriel, the cable of whose balloon was cut by a 'kolossal' shell, has been moved a bit further back. But I still hope to see him again at the end of the month.

Ever yours,

PIERRE

I've had your letter (a long one) of the 9th and answered it (on the 14th, I believe)—you're quite right: for peace, as for the longing for God, we're completely dependent on grace. To me, it's like the state of an object illuminated by a searchlight: it can't force the beam either to fall on it or to continue to do so. —We, however, can ask for the light and, as you say, be certain that it will not leave us.

[*Montreuil-aux-Lions*] *Wednesday 25th July 1917*

I'm back in my room again, with my regiment still in the same place. There is no change on the horizon. There doesn't seem to be any further indication of our going back to the Aisne. I'm going to try to get down to work again once I'm settled in. You must say a little prayer that I may be able to straighten out my ideas as clearly as possible, and above all put them into practice: for it's not so much a theory as a plan of life (a plan, I might also say, for my apostolate). You know this, and you understand what I mean. For my part, I am telling our Lord that in everything I do from now till September I want him to see my prayer, a prayer that you may be given the vision of, the longing for, and union with, the Divine, in whatever form is determined by your own particular vocation.—Our friendship is precious. I look on it rather as a musical note that gives 'tone' to our whole life. May our Lord help us to make it such that it is wholly transformed into a force that leads us to him, with nothing wasted in fruitless mutual gratification (which would be a waste of energy and love).

I have no need to assure you of my very real affection. Kind messages to Mme Parion.

PIERRE

[Beaulieu-les-Fontaines, Oise] 5th August 1917

Yesterday I received your long letter of the 31st July. It was on the same day, I think, that I was putting into my letter to you almost exactly the same things as you say in yours. There's nothing tedious in such an identity of views: it shows, as you remark, how close we are to 'coinciding' in our Lord; and for that reason it is most valuable.

I find it quite easy to understand what you tell me about the ' chilly atmosphere ' you feel you're in. I hope that some of the sun that shines on the beeches and firs may have found its way to your heart. In any case, don't be put out, if you feel lost at Le Chambon, lacking as you do there the support you find in your own sphere of action and influence, which is centred on Notre-Dame-des-Champs. You haven't retired into the lonely countryside in order to feel yourself strong and a source from which strength radiates, but rather to forget yourself, to lose yourself, to remould yourself in him whose radiance shines on us through all creation, particularly, at some times, through its most majestic and silent manifestations. It's not a bad thing, at such times, to feel that one is of little importance. It's better still to surrender oneself to the domination of him who seeks only to give greater strength and to find his way, through us, to others. At the moment there is no better way in which you could help your family and console them—and also continue, from a distance, to sanctify and edify the work you have undertaken,—than to unite yourself more fully with our Lord in the austere calm of the mountains.—Don't let yourself succumb, I beg you, to the perpetual fear that you're doing nothing worthy of your life or commensurable with your wishes or God's grace. I believe that you're doing a great deal—much more than we can see. But is there any point in worrying about this? Isn't it enough to foster large ambitions within ourselves and try loyally to achieve them, to have the right to rely on God to grant them ultimate success? In every context, you must try harder, perhaps, to lose yourself in God,—so completely that you no longer even want to know whether you are doing much or little in this world—your sole happiness being the feeling that he is within you, at the beginning and the end of every desire and every act.

With regard to what you tell me about your dear father, I think your impression is quite right. Death *releases*, and if there were no death, the earth would doubtless seem a *stifling* place to us . . . You remember when we were saying that, overlooking the stream, before we came down again by the foxglove path?

We are still having continual rain, though it looks as though it may clear up today. This doesn't worry me much, since I have my room, in which I shut myself up for most of the day. Inspiration is coming more readily as the work progresses. I shall perhaps have finished my draft by the 15th.[1] It's disappointing to realize how impoverished and reduced your ideas become when you try to fit them into a common plan. Each one becomes a small stone, cut down and shaped, when it might be the kernel of a whole building . . . Just one reference, one paragraph, for what calls for a complete study . . .—In the end, I'll have put into 30 or 40 pages what I could spend my whole life talking about.—Mass every morning. It's my turn to take your place and Mme Parion's. Tell her so, and thank her for her card of the 30th.

Always yours—remember me to your family.

PIERRE

I'm in the village where Joan of Arc is said to have spent her

[1] *Le Milieu mystique* is dated 13th August 1917, from Beaulieu-les-Fontaines.

first night on her way from Compiègne to Rouen—by a rather roundabout route, presumably. You can still see a small brick building in which she is said to have been lodged. And the Boches, perhaps because of their dislike of the English, have left intact the statue of the saint which stands nearby. On the other hand, they have made in its shadow one of their cemeteries in which, under ponderously and meticulously incised gravestones, lie the dead of 1914–17.

[*Beaulieu-les-Fontaines*] *14th August 1917*

Yesterday, I sent Guiguite the *Milieu mystique* so that she can send it on to you when she's read it. I'd have liked you to have been the first to see it,—the more so that you're certainly the person who will understand me best. I thought I rather owed it to Guiguite to start with her,—apart from the fact that as you're going to keep the manuscript you might as well have it last.—You'll see that there's nothing very new in these pages. They're primarily a clarification of points that you're already familiar with; and in the end I can't help wondering whether they're really very intelligible to anyone who hasn't read the *Vie cosmique* and the *Multitude*. You'll probably find that once again I've compressed it too much. But if only you knew how difficult I find it to write at greater length without losing the general thread of my theme. And in essays such as this, it's the general thread that counts for most.

I'm experiencing a certain pleasure in feeling free now to start on some fresh subject, if any should suggest itself. No doubt, however, it will be my old hobby-horse coming up again in a different form.—For some time now I've been rather tempted really to get to grips with the problem of ' evil and progress ', not, of course, with the idea of reaching a final solution, but simply in order to force myself to make up my mind what exactly I mean. My interest in this, which is of long standing, has been reawakened by reading Vigny, and also by some of

Claude Farrère's *Histoires de Guerre*. There's notoriously a certain glamour about *daring* evil; the fact is that when it's successful it somehow seems to provide its own excuse. There must, one rather feels, be someone who devotes himself (if one may put it so) to upsetting conventional ideas which tend to make some faults *more vital than virtue*. There's an ' organic sophism ' in this, that cannot fail to impress one, and which, from my point of view, it is very important to clarify precisely and to expose.— If I find that I'm still unable to see my way clearly in this problem, I'll turn my attention, perhaps, to the aesthetics of war which we discussed. For this, however, I should go back and breathe again the heady atmosphere of the firing line.—As always after a long rest, I feel overcome again by nostalgia for the front.[1] And yet there's an uncommon charm about the corner we're now billetted in. Yesterday evening, again, I found endless delight in the absolute silence and strict solitude of these great expanses, all white with fragrant umbellifers, beneath the apple trees. To express what I feel, one would need Vigny's instrument—subject, I should add, to using it rather differently. I've been rather disappointed, I must say, when reading him, to find him so pompous, such a phrasemonger at times, so loaded with metaphor,—so much a slave to words, that too often they govern thought. My disappointment has to some extent affected my appreciation even of classical poetry. It seems to me a quite impossible task to force rich and flexible thought into a predetermined harmonious framework. With a song or short rhetorical piece, fair enough—(and this could justify the existence of certain poetic forms; various categories of feelings or ideas patient of falling into—though this is hardly to praise them—a definite verse form . . .). For the expression of other spiritual states, more complicated or oratorical, classical forms of poetry are a rough approximation which can never mould the thought, even if rhythms and strophes are combined. Every poetical work calls for its own particular rhythm,—a rhythm in the whole, a rhythm in the parts, and a rhythm in the paragraphs

[1] The title of an essay dated 20th November 1917.

and sentences. Regular line-cadence is good: but it's the infancy
of poetry: it checks poetry, and breaks it up into fragments.—
A literary piece, if it is really felt and expressed, should be like
a piece of music, with shades of emphasis, silences, themes, an
over-all harmony, etc. . . .—a completely individual typographic
arrangement. Don't you agree? But I'm not offering to
produce it . . .

My card of the day before yesterday will have told you that
I've received your letter of August 10th. Isn't it odd that both
of us, you and I, have the same weakness for the self-centred
life of contemplation, undisturbed by anything, and in which
no 'third party' (unless specially chosen for that purpose) is
unwelcomely added to the two essentials, the soul and God?
You're quite right: we should resist this weakness. But it's
still true that, speaking on a natural level, the 'other' (which
means everybody except the handful of human beings allowed
to move in our orbit) is an importunate intruder. At least, that's
how I feel sometimes. Instinctively, I'd much rather have an
earth full of animals than one inhabited by men. Every man
forms a little world on his own, and this pluralism is essentially
distasteful to me. We have to remember that we are in process
of becoming, and that all this multiplicity, through the charity
which our Lord asks of us, in spite of our natural inclinations,
will end by forming only one whole . . . It's no doubt an
increase of this unity, bought by our effort to get outside ourselves, that makes itself felt in us by a fuller development of the
interior life, resulting from the exteriorization of ourselves
through the charity of which you speak. At those times, as at
the times when providence sends us suffering, we become
strangely aware that our real strength is not in ourselves, but
comes to us from outside, when we surrender our freedom to
conditions of existence that have nothing in common with our
petty personal inter-relations. I don't understand the very
considerable success of (extreme) theories of immanence and
autonomy: extrinsic forces are so much part of our experience,
and so excellent!

I hope the sun has dried out your woods. Here, we're having downpours of rain every day. According to the latest rumours, we shan't be moving from here for ten days or so; but I'm not trusting much to that.

Goodbye, and our Lady's blessing on you.

PIERRE

[*Muret-et-Croutes*] *23rd September 1917*

I've just had your letter of the 19th, which gave me real joy. I thought indeed that the cloud would soon roll away, but I'm infinitely happier to know it for certain. What you must retain from this experience is the realization that once we have put ourselves in our Lord's hands we can expect that he will handle us with vigour—always, however, to make us advance a little further within him. What price should we not be happy to pay for such an advance and such a transformation! . . . As you asked me in your letter before the last, I ' offered ' you up, with all my heart, at mass—and do so every day, at the same time as I offer up myself also. I don't know whether you know this prayer by one of our sixteenth-century fathers; it's a little strong, but most beautiful, and I'm sure you'll be able to understand it in his own original words: *Tu Domine, include me in imis visceribus Cordis tui, atque ibi me detine, excoque, expurga, accende, ignifac, sublima, ad purissimum Cordis tui gustum atque placitum, ad puram annihilationem meam.* I am very fond of this prayer, and say it for both of us.

We're living a quiet life here. But the various companies are rather scattered and when I can get away I have no really quiet retreat, except the woods. I would rather like to be able to analyse and account for, briefly, this feeling of a plenitude of being and of something more than human that I've often experienced at the front and that I fear I'll miss after the war. I think one could show that the front isn't simply the firing line, the exposed area corroded by the conflict of nations, but the ' front

203

of the wave ' carrying the world of man towards its new destiny. When you look at it during the night, lit up by flares, after a day of more than usual activity, you seem to feel that you're at the final boundary between what has already been achieved and what is striving to emerge. It's not only that activity culminates in a sort of intense but completely calm paroxysm, dilating to the scale of the vast work in which it is playing its part,—but the mind, too, gets something like an over-all view of the whole forward march of the human mass, and feels not quite so lost in it. It's at such moments, above all, that one lives what I might call ' cosmically ',—aroused intellectually as much as emotionally . . . I don't yet know whether I could deal with this theme properly in a few pages.

You were quite right to send Guiguite the *Vie Cosmique*, although I had asked you to have it typed partly on purpose to save her the trouble. Still, since she's anxious to have it . . . But I'll call on you for the typing, all the same, when the time comes.

I wrote to Mme Parion yesterday.

Always yours,

PIERRE

[*Muret-et-Crouttes*] *25th September 1917*

Yesterday, with the same pleasure as I always have, I received your letter of the 22nd. You are perfectly right, I think, in what you say about the necessity and difficulty in influencing souls from within. What gives me great satisfaction in this, so far as it affects you, is to see that you are being led by the necessities inherent in your life and the duties of your position to fall back on the *Milieu divin*, and to seek union with God as the first, and almost consciously experienced, condition for action. It is thus, through a sort of deep rift, that God enters into the tangible reality of all that is most human in your life;—and once he has made his way in, he will never cease, you'll find, gradually to extend his dominion until he invades anything. Thank you for reminding me that the Institute's retreat begins on Friday. Should God spare my life and things work out favourably, I think I'd like to give that retreat one day.

I'm still in the same quiet billets. Our future continues to be pretty vague, both as to when and what it will be. What the future imposes on our present existence is not exactly a feeling of depression;—it's rather a sort of seriousness, of detachment, of a broadening, too, of outlook. This feeling, of course, borders on a sort of sadness (the sadness that accompanies every fundamental change); but it leads also to a sort of higher joy. I should be inclined to think that during these periods of waiting, a slow but continual process of adaptation is going on, at the end of which the soul finds that it has been raised up to the level of the great duties that await it. In this connexion, the idea I mentioned in my last letter is becoming clearer in my mind, and it would be worth my while, I think, to get it down in writing, even though briefly. I'd call it 'Nostalgia for the Front'. There is such a feeling, without any doubt at all. I'd like to describe it shortly, and give some reasons for it. The reasons, I believe, come down to this; the front cannot but attract us, because it is, in one way, the *extreme boundary* between what one is already aware of, and what is still in process of formation. Not only does one see there things that you experience nowhere else, but one also sees emerge from within one an underlying stream of clarity, energy, and freedom that is to be found hardly anywhere else in ordinary life—and the new form that the soul then takes on is that of the individual living the quasi-collective life of all men, fulfilling a function far higher than that of the individual, and becoming fully conscious of this new state. It goes without saying that at the front you no longer look on things in the same way as you do in the rear: if you did, the sights you see and the life you lead would be more than you could bear. This exaltation is accompanied by a certain pain. Nevertheless it is indeed an exaltation. And that's why one likes the front in spite of everything, and misses it.

That's rather the sort of thing I want to express. I don't

know whether I'll be able to achieve sufficient clarity of thought and language to do so.

Yesterday I had a long letter from Robert, full of ideas—very well thought out, it seems to me—about the Americans. He seems very happy. Olivier's written to me, too: still near Avocourt and expecting leave.—I'm awaiting with interest and high hopes the result of Victor's exam.

Goodbye. Every kind wish to Mme Parion. May our Lord be with you more and more.

PIERRE

[*Muret-et-Crouttes*] *4th October 1917*

Your letter of October 2nd came yesterday. You should have had a line from me the next day. But, if I'd thought of it, I'd certainly have written for your beginning of term. I thought that that wouldn't be until about the 4th. In any case my mass intention this morning was that the year that's now starting may turn out well for the Institute. I like to think that gradually, instead of being weighed down by your external cares, you'll feel yourself to some extent *carried* by them towards God, by the need you feel, in your love, to *do* something for him and your inability to do anything worth while except in close union with him. Prayer and action should nourish one another—that goes without saying.—On this feast of St Francis, I didn't fail to pray to our Lord to give us, you and me and all of us, if possible, the vision of and delight in, his divinity present in all things, which we long for and whose need we are conscious of,—don't you agree?

I told you that I had sent Père de Grandmaison my ' *paper* '.[1] Before that, I had read it to my friend Beaugeard, in a colonial regiment, and to a captain I'm friendly with, who liked it. I'll let you know how *Études* receive it. By an odd coincidence, three or four days ago, two of my comrades (of very different

[1] *Nostalgie du front.*

206

moral calibre), invalided out because of wounds, confessed to me that the thought of the front made them feel homesick. This shows that the feeling of nostalgia that I've tried to analyse is very real and deep-seated.

You can see, from the tone of this letter, that we're still resting in the rear areas—in almost exactly the same conditions as a year ago. The anticipation of something happening fairly soon (though nobody here has any precise information) arouses in me the impression (whose importance I can't yet judge exactly, but which is certainly coming to occupy a large place in ' my universe ') of the ' consistence of the future ', which each time impresses me more forcibly. I experience a sort of peace and sense of plenitude at feeling myself advancing into the unknown, or, more correctly, into what cannot be determined by our own means. So long as we live in the context of factors that depend on our own choice or that of other men, we have the illusion of being self-sufficient, and it seems to me that the sphere we then move in is one of great impoverishment. But the moment we feel ourselves dominated and tossed about by a power that nothing human can master, I have an almost physical sensation of God catching me up and clasping me more closely—as if, with the road ahead disappearing,—and men, beside us, fading away powerless to help us effectively (I'm not, of course, speaking of friendship and prayer that shields one, as yours do: for they are one with God)—as if then only God were *ahead* and *around*,—*thickening* (if I may use the word) as we advance.

My days couldn't be spent more pleasantly. When I'm not writing, I talk with Beaugeard, who lives the other side of the square, or else I go for a walk along the dry hill-sides or in some wood. This life, a little cheerless in itself, is made interesting, or, if you prefer it, takes on a savour from the prospect of the weeks to come.—I've been reading Léon Daudet's *Salons et journaux*. There's a fiendish vigour in his writing, but it's still terribly superficial as the picture of the period the author attempts to give. What interested me most in the book was its very sincere expression of the joy of living in a chosen circle of 'cultured friends' at the heart of events and ideas. So long as they don't turn into little Capuas or ivory towers, such coteries of artists or intellectuals are, I believe, most effective organizations, in which it must be very pleasant to experience the joy of creation. The ideal thing for a man to do would be to spend six months in such a group and six in the austerity of research and conflict.

Indeed I recognized the gentleman you mentioned to me. It's Comte Bégouën. In 1913 [1] his sons found, at the bottom of a cave on his estate in the Ariège, some clay models of bison, whose discovery caused quite a stir. He and his two sons [2] (particularly the elder, who was wounded back in 1915) are men whom it's a delight to meet and to live with, for we all share exactly the same tastes. In Bordeaux's *Les Derniers Jours de Vaux*, at the end of the book, there are a good many quotations from the younger son's field-diary.

Goodbye.—Always yours with affection. Kind messages to Mme Parion.

PIERRE

[*Muret-et-Crouttes*] *8th October 1917*

Mme Parion's letter, received yesterday, has reassured me about the fate of my correspondence. You must have had two letters from me since September 25th, reassuring you about my own fate. Thank you all the same for your short note, so full of

[1] In fact, on 10th October 1912.

[2] Max and Jacques Bégouën had been posted to the regiment of Moroccan colonial infantry (R.I.C.M.) which was brigaded with Père Teillard's 4th mixed Tirailleurs-Zouaves. Marguerite Teillard had met Count Bégouën through their common friend, Emmanuel de Margerie. Twice, during the summer of 1915, Count Bégouën had been given permission to visit his two sons serving on the Ypres front, and it was then that he had the opportunity of meeting Père Teilhard again in the Moroccan brigade. It is to these meetings that Père Teilhard is referring.

solicitude. Certainly, I know indeed what you are to me, and I feel it. This letter, again, will not add anything to what you know about my position. We're still resting, and waiting. What I object to most in such times is the uncertainty that makes one shrink from tackling any considerable work, for lack, as far as one can anticipate, of time—and then one ends up by having very long periods of leisure on one's hands. This situation has one advantage—that it makes me bear in mind how much more important it is to realize in practice the views one has acquired than to confine oneself to speculations, working them over again in one's mind and giving them greater subtlety . . . This present spell, I feel, is for me a time of choice, if I really wish that for me the world should become Christ. As I said to you in my last letter, it is unbelievably good to bury oneself deep in God, recognized as the fundamental element that controls our movement and forms us.

I must tell you that yesterday I had a brief preliminary word from *Études*. Père Grandmaison says that at first glance my ' little article seems most original and interesting '. So apparently it'll be published.[1] Besides this, when Guiguite has finished a copy of the *Milieu mystique*, I propose to send it to one of our fathers at Lyons [2] of whom I spoke to you and in whom I have the utmost confidence. I'll do the same, I expect, with a copy of the *Vie cosmique*. When I get back down the line, if God grants me the time, I have almost made up my mind to make a start on an essay in philosophical synthesis (you'll smile to hear this ambitious plan) called *L'Union créatrice*.[3] I think this essential if I am to make myself understood by those before whom I shall sooner or later have to defend my ideas or forward them.

With all this, I haven't thanked you for your parcel; the two tins of food will certainly come in very useful up the line: heartening both physically and spiritually.

[1] The reference must be to *Nostalgie du front*, printed in *Études* for 20th November 1917. Cf. Claude Cuénot, *Pierre Teilhard de Chardin*.

[2] Père Vulliez-Sermet, s.j.   [3] Written a month later.

Goodbye. It's very seldom that I pray without remembering you.

PIERRE

[*Muret-et-Crouttes*] *13th October 1917*

Contrary to what I told you in my short note of yesterday, it looks as though we're still going to be here for some time. The wind and the rain no doubt have a good deal to do with this delay, which on the whole is not much to our taste. Yet should we not see God in the elements that make up this world, however contrary they may seem? Yesterday I had your long letter of the 8th–10th October. From it I saw, with a great deal of satisfaction, that your kindergarten is developing along Catholic and modern lines, and that (as is quite right) you're devoting yourself to it because you see it as a vast horizon opening out beyond the heads of these little tots. You may be sure that if my life, these days, can have any merit in the eyes of God, I want it to serve to bring success to your educational efforts.—What you say about the need to work on something real, to *make* something real, has illuminated a corner of my own self. Be careful to preserve this salutary desire, but without causing yourself worry. It is without any doubt one of the deepest roots that the love of God can implant in your real, practical life. Can't we see that he alone can give *real existence* to what our actions produce? And is he not therefore, *ipso facto*, one of the very *conditions* of our appetite for activity? I think that it's through these sorts of vital urges, much more than by abstract logic, that God commands our faith. That's exactly Blondel's point, too, isn't it? And so I hope that our Lord may be always increasingly loved by you, as the source which makes your activity real.

I've begun to read *La Chartreuse de Parme*, lent to me by a lieutenant, a great devotee of Stendhal. As a picture and example of the novelist's craft, it's obviously a very rudimentary effort. The strict austerity of the style and psychology, however admirable and formative it may be, doesn't seem to me to justify the cult that some people have for the author. No doubt I suffer from not being sufficiently familiar with the history of the French novel, and in particular with the weakness of earlier novels. What interested me most was to see what view of the Church could be taken a century ago by an ardent admirer of the Revolution. It's very gross in its calumny and contempt; but some forms of contempt are most revealing as symptoms.

More news soon.

Always yours.—Kind messages to Mme Parion.

PIERRE

[Muret-et-Crouttes] 16th October 1917

In case I may find it difficult to write to you these days—(we're always more or less on the point of moving off)—I want to do so once more in complete peace,—and tell you how much you are, and will be, present in my thoughts, whatever happens, as a source of strength and protection.

Things are still quiet with us. But any moment could bring a sudden change. Well, you know in what frame of mind I'll go up the line again. I feel that I'm held between two mighty powers: the power of God, which in some way draws me into the creative atmosphere of the furnace, and the power of my country (though to say ' my country ' still leaves much unsaid . . .) which drives me forward, like a little fragment representing her. Anyone who really felt the pressure of these twin powers—one at his back, animating him and dedicating him, and one ahead of him, loving him and absorbing him—should go forward with enthusiasm to scale the ' high places '. Pray, I beg you, that it may be so with me. You may be sure that I'll do nothing needlessly rash; but you can be quite certain, too, that, to do what must be done, I shall, in my mind, be relying on your encouragement.

I haven't yet heard any more from *Études*. I expect the next thing I'll get will be the proofs to correct. In case you should read the *Nostalgie du Front* before I have a chance to send it to you, I should warn you that in the paragraph referring to a certain inability shown by those in the rear to understand us at the front, there's no question of you or people like you. With you and me, we have never ceased to see into each other with increasing clarity.

Kind messages to Mme Parion.

Always yours,

PIERRE

[*Letters written between 16th October 1917 and 9th July 1918, like those for 15th April–10th June 1917, have been lost.*]

[*Forêt de Compiègne*] *9th July 1918*

Just a short line today. This morning we were withdrawn a little to the rear, to the other side of the river, that is, in the forest of Compiègne. We're living under canvas, among the great beeches. So there's no change in the external comforts of my existence. It simply means that we're, to all intents and purposes, out of range of shell-fire. And quite apart from that, it would be ungrateful of me to complain about our situation: in this lovely weather, life in the woods has a real charm. The only drawback is that saying mass and writing are still not easier than in the forest of L.[1]

Yesterday I sent you a notebook containing *Le Prêtre* (in the second part of the book, the pages at the beginning have been used for personal notes, more or less tentative, which I won't inflict on you). Tell me what you think of it. When you can get me a notebook I'll make another copy for Père Vulliez-Sermet,[2] and, I expect, for Guiguite.

[1] Laigue.

[2] Novice-master at the Jesuit house of studies at Sainte-Foix-lès-Lyon.

I have a few other fragmentary ideas in mind at the moment, I'll tell you more about them, if they take shape, once we're settled in.

Always yours,

PIERRE

[*Vauciennes*] *12th July 1918*

Received your letter of the 8th yesterday.

I'm writing on the morning of a rather sudden move that will take us 50 kilometres to the south without bringing us appreciably closer to the lines. Nobody knows quite what this move means. No doubt we'll have a shortish spell of rest. But there are also rumours going about, of various changes in store for us. And we're wondering, too, what point at the front is our final destination. I'll let you know about this, as I find out myself. In any case, I doubt whether I can expect a return to leisure.

What is certain is that we're going to leave the forest: and I foresee that I'll miss its enveloping shelter which makes me so tangibly and immediately aware of our immersion in a tangle of living entities. The forest of C.[1] is even more finely wooded than that of L.[2]: one can wander for hours on end through an endless colonnade of straight, smooth, tree trunks, treading on a carpet of dry leaves, under regular vaults of greenery.—You couldn't imagine a better temple of recollection.—I have often found, as you have, that nature is disturbing rather than satisfying: it's so obviously the basis of *some thing*, wears the face of *some one*, that you can't define: and you can find no rest in it, at least so I feel, until you reach the ultimate term hidden in it. But, unlike you, I'm so fascinated and intrigued by the riddle that I find in it a *sufficient stimulus* to search and thought. Perhaps this peculiarity of my sensitivity derives from the fact that things in the cosmos and in life have always presented themselves to me as objects to be pursued and studied,—never just as material

[1] Compiègne.   [2] Laigue.

213

for contemplation.—The lack of satisfaction I find in nature,—to the point where it causes me physical suffering,—is chiefly the inevitable *superficiality* of our experience of it here below. Anything *new* we can contrive to discover or extract is contained within a zone limited beforehand by our faculties. As soon as we reach a certain depth, we're down to rock: we're ringed in by a barrier that we can't break through, that can only be broken through by some *complete organic transformation* such as death alone can bring about. Nature makes us want to die, so that we may see what lies within her—(to die by the death which is the *term* of life brought by providence *to its maturity*, one should add, if one is to follow the direction given by sound reasoning and experience)—: there, it seems to me, you have the final development of the emotion aroused when you look at things. Somewhat to my surprise, I found this view expressed by Baudelaire, somewhere in the *Fleurs du Mal* (a little corrupted by dilettantism and pessimism, of course): *To die, so that one may at last find one's way to something new.*

What I've just been saying about the present impassable barrier to our experience, doesn't at all mean that I deny to primitive consciousness the power to give us *some absolute*. On the contrary, I'm firmly convinced (—and in fact could any other philosophy be christianizable? . . .) that the substance of our states of consciousness—which is the stuff of the universe in so far as it is *experienced* by us—represents some absolute. The absolute isn't to be found only in the perception of truths and principles: it's primarily in the vital current we feel within ourselves, modified and moulded by the impact of countless phenomena.—This absolute, however, we can attain only in a way that is limited and determined by the organic stage of spiritualization we have reached: and it is in order to reach a new *level* of knowledge of the absolute that we have to throw off our present physical form.—I very much liked your quotation from Ravaisson [1];—I've been greatly struck by noticing that

[1] Félix Ravaisson- ollen (1813–1900), archaeologist and philosopher, a noted commentator on Aristotle.

everyone who thinks is forced to reach the same concept of gross multiplicity passing gradually into spiritual and divine concentration. The particular slant of our present thought (a refashioning no doubt of some Greek thought, but wider in scope and more emphatic) is no doubt to seek in this gradual progress not only a *stable* and harmonious *distribution* (order= *kosmos*), but a road for life to follow, the shape of the individual and collective being, in *course* of formation.—Ravaisson's sentence could appear as a note in the *Union créatrice*. I'll only add that nature isn't simply the lower pole of our *experience* (consciousness): it's that of the *development* of the universe, too; and hidden in the depths of the elements into which it is still broken up, lies a spark of the absolute (participated) that converges on God at the same time as we ourselves do.

I think you're right about the masculine inability to handle sentiment. That's an idea that might be followed up.

Goodbye. More news soon. I'm glad to hear that you're tackling your work with relish. I pray for you.

PIERRE

[*Vauciennes, Oise*] *14th July 1918*

Although I may be much too early, I'm writing this letter for St Margaret's feast (the 20th, isn't it?). You'll know that on that day,—at my mass, if I'm able to say it,—and in any case before our Lord,—I'll be remembering you, with very deep affection, and in the firm hope that our present friendship is only a beginning compared with all the goodness and strength that is still to come from it, for us, and for many others, in God.

The change of which I was speaking in my last letter, has now taken place. We're no longer actually in the forests, but not far from them; and I can assure you that their thick fleecy mass of foliage is a lovely sight when you see it silhouetted, five or six kilometres away, beyond a veritable sea of yellowing corn. After some weeks deep in the woods, the spirit finds a new youth with which to appreciate the charm of these wide horizons. We're in very good billets, in houses built for the workers at a sugar refinery that's been evacuated recently. It's a great pity, in one way, that Gabriel's on leave. I reckon his P.C.[1] isn't more than an hour's march from here. By the time he's back, I fear that we'll have left. Whatever plans they have for us are still wrapped in mystery,—the more so that the division has been in the line for the last two months. However, the chances are that we won't be left to vegetate here. I'm a little sorry about this, for I have a room, a mattress, and a table —and a church a quarter of an hour away. I was able to say mass this morning (the third since I was at the Institute). I didn't forget you.

Morally (and physically) I'm very well. If it weren't for the disturbance of all this moving about, I think I'd be in a suitable frame of mind for thinking out a number of points and getting a clearer view of them. I expect you know what it's like to feel that there are tendencies within one, impressions, still half-formed, that only need to be given definite shape and intellectual precision. That's what I am experiencing at the moment.—For anything to emerge from these still infra-intuitive elements, I'd need, I expect, some conversation, some opposition, something to read, that might give me a foundation to work on or another point of view to demolish. But war offers few such opportunities.

I'm going to tackle the *Divine Comedy* again, of which I've only read half. To go back to what I was saying a moment ago, I think that I should now, when talking with people who don't agree with me, distinguish just what are the points, in my way of looking at things, where I differ essentially from them and can, in some way, supply what they lack.—In my own mind, the old and the new, the *philosophia perennis* and my own individual impulses, run together in the end, so that I fail to distinguish as clearly as I should the important points to stress and dwell upon.

[1] Command Post.

I hope that the changeable weather we're having now won't turn into bad weather in the Cantal. I'd like this month of July to be a real rest for you and Mme Parion (who's written to me from Royan), a time given up entirely to the claims of friendship. I wish you joy in the light and peace of our Lord.

Always yours,

PIERRE

[*Morienval, Oise*] *24th July, 1918*

Just a word to let you know that since this morning I've been relieved and am out of the fighting. I'll send you some details tomorrow about these stirring days, when we're finally billeted. Had your letter of the 17th yesterday. I pray that you may have peace and the joy of life in God our Lord.

Always yours. Kind messages to Mme Parion.

PIERRE

[*Morienval, Oise*] *25th July 1918*

Yesterday's short letter will have reassured you about my fate. We arrived at our rest-billets only this morning, so that I can't write at any great length today. All the same I mustn't wait any longer to tell you something about what's been happening to me these last ten days.

While you were thinking that I wasn't engaged in the last offensive, I was in fact in the place of honour; the division formed the first assault-wave, in the Villers-C. area.—For once the secrecy of the operations had been admirably preserved, so much so that when we suddenly received the order to move off we thought at first it was an appeal for reinforcements from Epernay, and didn't guess the truth until, under cover of night, we saw a mysterious column of tanks entering the woods with us.

What the papers reported about the battle seems to me pretty well the truth. The beginning was a real surprise for the enemy, whose line was broken without resistance;—and then, after two days, the operation turned into a bitter hand to hand struggle. I've never been present at so tremendous a battle before, indeed, has there ever been such a battle? . . . You can imagine the vast uplands of the Soissons country dotted with groups of men advancing in single file,—then halting and taking cover. On all sides, great bursts of smoke appeared, white, black, and dirty grey, in the air and on the ground. Over all this there rose the sound of a continuous light crackling, and it was a shock to see among the ripening crops little blotches that lay still, for ever. Here and there a tank slowly made its way through the tall corn, followed by a group of supporters, like a ship sailing the seas. Too often, you'd see that it had been hit, and was burning in a thick cloud of black smoke. In our corner there were at least ten tanks stranded in the middle of the fields. And then, high above all this turmoil on the ground, groups of aircraft flew overhead, sometimes coming down very low to machine-gun, seemingly at random. With them, too, as with the tanks and the sausage balloons it sometimes happened that it all ended in a great mass of flame and smoke. There was something implacable about all this, above all; it seemed *inanimate*. You could see nothing of the agony and passion that gave each little moving human dot its own individual character and made them all into so many worlds. All you saw was the material development of a clash between two huge material forces.

We had the Americans as neighbours and I had a close-up view of them. Everyone says the same: they're first-rate troops, fighting with intense *individual* passion (concentrated on the enemy) and wonderful courage. The only complaint one would make about them is that they don't take sufficient care; they're too apt to get themselves killed. When they're wounded, they make their way back holding themselves upright, almost stiff, impassive, and uncomplaining. I don't think I've ever seen such pride and dignity in suffering. There's complete comradeship between them and us, born fully-fledged under fire.

We were relieved by a very fine Scottish division. That week was a revelation to our men of what their allies mean to them.

On the first day, I had no precise duties and what I did have wasn't anything out of the ordinary. Later, I had plenty to do in bringing back the wounded, which I liked and which was good for me. I must tell you that during the night of the 21st and 22nd, I spent some minutes that were among the most dramatic in all my life. Crossing the huge fields of corn in 'no man's land' I lost contact with the main body of my stretcher-bearers. After a long way, we—there were three of us—came upon two wounded men (they'd been lying there for two days) with no stretcher; meanwhile the Boches, hearing the noise (for the wounded men were talking and groaning) began to spray the field with shell- and machine-gun fire. How could we leave those two poor fellows, half-mad with strain, and yet how could we get them away? . . . It's terrible, I can assure you, to be faced with so nerve-racking a dilemma. Finally, we managed to carry them on our backs, to the shelter of a stranded tank, while, to crown everything, an artillery barrage was in full swing and aircraft were dropping bombs. Before daybreak I was able to collect two complete teams, who finally brought them in. Yet how many other casualties were left lying, lost in the middle of those great corn fields, between the lines . . .

More than ever, perhaps, during those days, I felt that I was living in another world, superimposed on the surface of the other, shaping it, and yet so different!—It was still roads, fields, ripening corn.—And still—what irony!—in front of us, menacing and impregnable, rose the wooded ridge on which last October I used to walk. But the whole wore a different face, compounded of horror and something super-human. You'd have taken it for a place where what lies before death was in the *very act of passing into* what lies beyond death. The relative proportions of things, the normal scale of their values, were altered, ceased to apply. All the time I felt, very strongly, that my own turn to die might come:—a thing that never happened to me at the beginning of the war.

I came back from the front rather tired, but in good moral and physical shape. Starting tomorrow, I'll be able to say mass again. You know how constantly the memory of you is with me, and how dear to me it is. I, too, thought of those days in 1917, when we were together.

Whatever your inner state, have complete trust in our Lord, won't you? The work he does within us is more precious than any success, however conscious we are of it and however satisfying it may be.

Another letter soon.

PIERRE

[*Trosly-Breuil, Oise*] *28th July 1918*

I've had your cards of the 20th and 22nd, and Mme Parion's letter of the 23rd.—Thank her very much for it. I'll be answering her.

We didn't stay long in the village from which I wrote last time. Once again, we had to make a move. Now we're resting (though rather impermanently) in an evacuated village on the edge of the forest. As a residence, it's not very luxurious. But we've learnt not to expect too much; and, so long as we're left alone for a fortnight (which we'll need to pull ourselves together again) there'll be no complaints. I have a comfortable mattress to sleep on, and I can say mass. Our mess is running well, too, That's as much as we need to satisfy the spiritual and physical demands accumulated during the last ten days. I sleep like a log and eat like a horse.

The great advantage for me of our present billet is the nearness of Gabriel. He's only a dozen kilometres away and I've already been able to see him for a few minutes yesterday. He told me that he'd just seen Victor (now a Second-Lieutenant), whose battalion, arriving from Verdun, has just been billeted for a few

days in the very place where he, Gabriel, has his headquarters.—
It's a wonderful piece of luck.—Victor must have moved up
into the part of the line from which I've just come down. He
must certainly be glad to exchange the shell-holes of Verdun
for open country: but I fear he'll be in a very dangerous area.

I'm very anxious to have a long letter from you, telling me
something about what you're doing and thinking. Above all,
I hope you're having a rest, and getting back your strength, and
that you're enjoying the friendship of Mme Parion again, undisturbed by administrative cares. Couldn't she visit Sarcenat
when she leaves Le Chambon?

So far as I'm concerned, the recent interior turmoil hasn't
died down sufficiently for me to be able to see whether these
new shocks have stirred up anything new in me. My morale is
good, and my eagerness for God sufficiently keen, but they're
not yet focussed on any really exact point. However, I'm
finding pleasure in going over again the ideas that I tried to
clarify in my last essay. And, then, this fresh experience of the
imminence of death, real and personal, makes me still more
conscious of the need to put into practice the ideas that attract
me, but which so far, perhaps, I've developed only as theoretical
points of view,—and not sufficiently as attitudes to be adopted
in concrete reality. This might perhaps be the time to devote
more attention to interior work, after having principally
thought . . .

Various subjects for study tempt me, more or less vaguely.
I'd like to show [to analyse] under some such title as *Diversity*
the necessity for particular individual vocations, and for alternating phases of conquest and renunciation in one and the same
life; I'd also like to study to what extent the single unique
world breaks down into as many worlds as there are souls, each
one sanctified [beautified] to its own particular measure, each
with its own Providence, under appearances common to all.[1]
From another point of view, I feel the need to prove to myself,

[1] Anticipating, apparently, *l'Ame du monde*, written during this same
year.

and to others, that the Christian ideal in no way makes a man less ' human ' (not only in the sense of causing him to have no interest in certain essential tasks, but even more in the sense of *failing to develop in him certain moral forces [preoccupations]* that everyone today is agreed in admiring). I believe that unbelievers are mistaken about the value of these new *human virtues* that they prefer to sanctity, or at least that in imagining that they can cultivate them outside religion, they set humanity an impossible task. But at the same time I think we Christians, for our part, have a great need to ' humanize ' our sanctity—without, of course, doing violence to the dogmas we hold.

However, for all this, I'd have to have a lengthier period of tranquillity.

Good-bye. You know how much you mean to me.

PIERRE

[*Trosly-Breuil*] *30th July 1918*

I've just had your two cards, of the 24th and 25th. I'm glad that my last letters have reached you so quickly.—I feel that it won't be long now before I get a real letter from you. You know how much I enjoy those big sheets of yours and how much good they do me ... I like to believe that writing them isn't a waste of time, even for you, because they force you to give more of yourself and ' define ' yourself more clearly.

I'm still writing from the same little village, which, as you can imagine, seems more and more pleasant to us the longer we stay in it. If it weren't for the semi-desolation of the evacuated houses and the ugly muddle of lorries and supply-trucks, this site of ours would be admirable. The river flows, slow and deep, between two ranges of flat-topped or rounded hills, covered with thick forest. As you look upstream or downstream you see a whole series of wooded ridges, every shade of blue in the mist, reflected in the still waters, thick with waterlilies.

In the cool of the evening, the peace and poetry of the place is entrancing. I wish I could show it to you.

So far, my days have been something of a muddle—much occupied by necessary contacts. Moreover, I have no quiet corner—except the countryside itself—where I can think and write.—So I don't anticipate that this spell of rest will be particularly fruitful.—Still, God has made me feel, these days, that joy in him and in all things is more alive within me. I notice that after every period when I find myself torn away from quiet meditation on the truths and 'points of view' (at first sight rather out of the ordinary, esoteric and complicated) that you know so well, I come back to them more easily and with more pleasure each time, as to an environment in which my thought feels more at home and can see more clearly . . .—It's a sign, no doubt, that I'm advancing along a road that is not going to peter out.—I should add, too, that the whole of my thoughts and tastes, developed throughout so many pages of writing, seem to me more and more to be concentrated on one point, or one attitude, both extremely simple and fruitful: they come down in the end to a very small thing—and it's a thing that brings me a solution and consolation for everything.—There's a prayer I'm fond of saying now, because it sums up what I mean: '*Jesu, sis mihi mundus verus.*' May all that is elect in the world, Jesus, be to me a channel for your influence, and be increasingly transformed through my efforts into you.

For the last couple of days, I've given some thought to what you said about how Christianity must not to allow itself to be eclipsed by certain human virtues but must assimilate them (since they, too, are equally incapable of flourishing without implicitly basing themselves on Christ). It seems to me that if a man of our age is convinced that there is nothing beyond the earth, it gives him (1) a concrete and direct *compassion* for other men, (2) an *eagerness* to work, (3) a *disinterestedness* in his work . . . which makes up the moral ideal of our time.—Conversely, there is a danger that belief in God may (by a distortion, of course, but the danger is still there, in fact) make us lazy, preoccupied with

our own 'petty salvation', charitable only as a matter of form
. . .—The remedy, I believe, for this slackening of the Christian
effort, is always the same: to understand that God is obtained
by carrying through our task as men,—that Providence in no way
dispenses us from effort,—that our neighbour must be loved in
himself through love of God.—When I try to analyse myself, it
seems to me that my own individual hopes of a heavenly reward
do not prevent me from devoting myself to this world's tasks
with the same feelings of conviction, and ardour, and renunciation
that I would try to have—that I imagine I would have—if I had
no faith.—But I owe this to the particular view I've arrived at
of the relations between the fulfilment of this world and the
kingdom of God . . .

Did I tell you that the Moroccan colonial regiment has left
our division? With it went its chaplain, my great friend Beaugeard, and for me he's quite irreplaceable. So again I'm a little
bit more on my own. But if only you knew what a joy it is
to me to feel that I'm being led by God!—In just following this
divine guidance, there's an overwhelming compensation for all
the pain it brings . . .

I haven't seen Gabriel again yet.

Goodbye. Thank Robert for his letter. They want a lot
of interpreters for the Americans, these days.

Always yours. Remember me to Mme Parion.

PIERRE

[*Forêt de Laigue*] *4th August 1918*

The day before yesterday I had your nice long letter, in which
you tell me what you're doing, and in particular about your
taste for Plato. Nothing could give me more pleasure—although,
to my shame, I must confess that I know that splendid thinker
only at second hand. When things quieten down somewhat,
I'll have to try and get hold of some of his dialogues to read at

the front. Your friend Z.,[1] I expect, will be able to help you much better than I could in your study of Greek philosophy.— About ' becoming ': I'm just wondering at the moment whether the ' individual ' should not be looked on as an element of fixation, or stabilization. In that case, movement, evolution, would be realized in a sort of surround, a sort of ' sheath ', enveloping and giving birth to, individuals . . . the truth would lie in a synthesis of fixation and movement.

I'm writing from the same forest as that in which, a month ago, I wrote *Le Prêtre*. In fact we're going up the line to hold the same sector as we were holding then. Don't be frightened. It's a quiet corner and we're sent there as a rest . . . Even so, we'd have been glad of another week in our village. But for the next three months we mustn't count on such strokes of luck as that. I'm sorry to be going further away from Gabriel, and I fear I may find myself unable to say mass for some considerable time. Once I'm settled in, I'll write to you at greater length and fill in all the details.

Yesterday I had long letters from Sarcenat. Through Gabriel I've learnt that it was Victor's division that took Grand-Razig last week. I'm rather worrying to get news of the latter . . . [. . .]

I've been reading, these last days, an interesting book by Mâle[2] on French and German art. His thesis is that in the Middle Ages the Germans didn't initiate anything at all, either in art or architecture. I can't, of course, judge whether he's impartial or not; but it certainly seems convincing, and it's most interesting to read in this corner of the Ile de France, so full of churches (terribly ruined!).

I also found, in an old number of *Deux Mondes*, an interesting study of a young American poet killed in the war (Alan Seeger), whose *Juvenilia* seemed to me to be shot through with the fire of a real ' cosmic passion '.

[1] Léontine Zanta, who had greatly distinguished herself in her oral examination on her philosophical thesis for the Sorbonne.

[2] Emile Mâle (1862-1954), art historian, specializing in religious art of the twelfth and thirteenth centuries.

Goodbye.   Tell me if you're beginning to see your way to some solution of what to do during your next year.   I pray a great deal for you—Remember me to Mme Parion.

Always yours.

PIERRE

[*Forêt de Laigue*] *14th August 1918*

Yesterday I had your card from Vic-sur-Cère.   Thank you, and Mme Parion, for remembering me.   I'm still writing from the same forest, and in more or less the same military situation.   So long as the Lassigny Massif hasn't fallen (if, in fact, they really want it to fall) we shan't move from here, I think;—and, if it does fall, the Boches will retreat of their own accord, as we did on the 11th June.   Meanwhile, we're living a half-peaceful, half-alert existence, which is really rather tiring because it's neither inaction nor movement.   My days are spent rather aimlessly and in useless goings to and fro, so that I don't think this spell in the forest has the fruitfulness (immediate or felt) of my earlier one.   Even tomorrow, on the Assumption, I shan't be able to say mass.   I'll try to make up for it by a little more recollection;—and my meditation on our Lady will be accompanied, as always, by a very warm remembrance of you.   As it says in the gospel for the feast, we'll try, both of us, to attach ourselves ever more firmly to the possession and, in a way, the indwelling, of the ' *unum necessarium* '.   I've been rather struck for some time by the sort of *double* necessity that determines our progress.   Below, there are the lower demands of material life, of the body, of bread, of our country to be preserved in its physical integrity . . .—and, to this fundamental necessity, that none can escape, we must add that of ' sacred unity '.

Above this, however, there is another necessity, one that is spiritual and truly sacred, a goal to be reached, and an ideal. About that necessity, there's disagreement, ' *freedom* (of conscience) ' is accepted;—there's hesitancy, indecision . . .—Yet the lower necessity is in some way inert, serving as a foundation. The higher necessity is what stimulates progress.

Isn't it odd to note this dispersal and dissipation of effort, as soon as it seeks to go beyond the material or organic stage that has been achieved, and rise to a higher level?

I had a line from Victor the day before yesterday, written on the 6th. At the time, he was still in the line, on the Vesle,—after twelve hours of attack. He had been given the Croix de Guerre on the field of battle. It won't be long, I think, before he goes on leave.

Goodbye.

Always yours,

PIERRE

[*Forêt de Laigue*] *17th August 1918*

I shan't write you a very long letter today, for the double reason that I'm not allowed to say much about what's happening here, and that I suspect the postal authorities will want to hold up this letter for some considerable time. Even so, I want to let you know that I'm thinking of you, and also to thank you for your letter of the 11th, which served so well to fill out for me all that you said in the *Véroniques*.[1] Your explanations told me what I wanted to know, at the same time as they enabled me to understand you better. I'll send you back your manuscript, with two or three notes, as soon as things are quieter and a bit more settled. I'll be glad to read your stories, and I'm sure I'll like the ideas behind them. I'm really delighted indeed to see that you're getting down to writing and thinking, with some confidence in your own powers.

In spite of the continual turmoil I've been in for the last month, I can see that various ideas are quietly continuing to work themselves out in my mind,—both about the nature of 'the human virtues' and the ' human moral ideal ', which seems

[1] These essays have been lost.

to be the preserve of the stoics and of those who close their hearts to all personal hopes of heaven,—or about the sort of divineness of the future,—the future that is made up of terrifying inevitability, of no less frightening renewal, and at the same time of benign Providence that can make itself manifest and modify itself in proportion to the intensity of our faith. In this latter group of ideas particularly (the future) there are, I think, many things to be said and discovered, which can help us *to reveal to ourselves* the deep-seated centre of our emotions and fears, and which have the power, in consequence, of revealing God to us.[1] I'll tell you about this as my thought takes final shape. Meanwhile, pray for me, won't you? I count more than ever on your remembering me.

Tell me something about your plans for October. Remember me to Mme Parion (if she hasn't left yet) and to all your household. But did I thank Robert for his letter? ... I think Alphonse[2] is over towards Rheims.

Always yours,

PIERRE

[*Carlepont*] *23rd August 1918*

I wasn't intending to write to you until we'd been withdrawn a little to the rear. But as our time in the line is being extended (and things are becoming increasingly quiet, which doesn't promise a speedy relief) I've decided not to wait any longer. You can't have failed to realize, from my postcards and the communiqués, that we've again being taking part in an attack,—which the high command, I expect, decided on after the success at Amiens,—and which very greatly altered the character of our ' rest sector '. I'll let you have more details later: for the

[1] A first statement, apparently, of the themes treated in *La Foi qui opère* and *Forma Christi*, written in October and November 1918.

[2] Marguerite Teillard-Chambon's first cousin, Fr. Alphonse Teillard-Chambon, O.P.

moment I'll only say that we had the satisfaction of repeating, exactly and completely, but in the opposite direction, the course of our retreat on June 10th. I'm back in exactly the same place as I was in May,—in the very same dug-outs. The only difference is that there's a great deal of Boche material, and more destruction too, the work of our guns. The two rather tough days were the 20th and, even more so perhaps, the 18th, the day on which the regiment, as a preliminary to the attack, captured an awkward hill. On the whole the operation, in this corner, wasn't such a tremendous affair as that of July, but it was highly successful. On the 21st we occupied the area south of the Oise without a shot fired. I don't think we'll be put in to attack again. We may well, however, have to hold the sector for a few days longer.

Naturally enough, in the turmoil of these days, I lost some of my recollectedness and of my awareness of my own interior life. However, when things settle down, I may perhaps, with the help of God, find something new. For, even if I was in no serious danger, I was pretty deeply conscious of a number of impressions and a number of things that revolted me. I'll tell you more about all this when I'm more at peace and can see things more clearly: but I'll have to pull myself together somewhat in prayer. My yesterday's mail has been held up, and won't arrive until the evening. I don't mind betting that there'll be a letter from you! It will be most welcome.

Meanwhile, you know how much I'm thinking of you. Every kind message to all of you.

PIERRE

[Carlepont] 28th August 1918

I've just had your letter of the 26th (?) which gave me, I don't know why, a special pleasure, no doubt because I can see you more and more clearly in the hands of our Lord, who brings you consolation after the trial. No, indeed, you were not wrong in writing to me on the 19th about the distress you felt within you. Our friendship derives a great deal of its strength from our each being able to call on the other for assistance in all circumstances. Each of these spiritual reversals has its own significance, its own value, and enables us to know ourselves better. You know that nothing could make me happier than to know that I had really helped you to be a little more for God and in God. And I'm glad to know, too, that your interior peace is accompanied by a relish for thinking and writing.

We've still not been relieved, and in spite of our losses (many wounded, few killed) it looks as though we'll be moving on again towards N.[1] (to hold ground, I don't doubt, rather than to fight for it). Meanwhile for the last two days I've been back at the regimental aid post, which is more or less a rear area. I'm living a very quiet life there, and sleeping very well. However, I haven't yet been able completely to regain my interior recollection,—even though I feel, rising to the surface of my soul, the taste and desire for the divine. I don't even find it easy to say mentally the ' mass on the altar of all things ' that came easily to me in June when I was in the tall woods of Laigue. However, when I can do so a little, I can see the sense of communion growing still sharper and deeper. I'll have to write something about that, even more fully worked out than Le Prêtre.[2]

I shan't tell you much yet about the last fortnight. I'm waiting until it's all over before judging it as a whole. In brief, I was in no serious danger this time, and did nothing outstanding. That's probably why I was more vividly aware of the ' shadow of death ', and the formidable gift that existence presents us with: an inevitable advance towards an inevitable, sentient end, —a situation from which one can emerge only through physical dissolution . . . I believe I've never felt that to be so real . . . And then I understood a little better the agony of our Lord, on Good Friday. And the remedy seemed clearer to me, always the

[1] Noyon.
[2] To be realized later in The Mass on the World; written in China in 1923. cf. Hymn of the Universe, Harper, 1965.

same: to abandon oneself, with faith and love, to the divine future (the becoming) which is ' *the* most real ' of all, ' *the* most living',—whose most terrifying aspect is that of being the most renewing (and hence the most creative, the most precious of all). Yet how difficult it is to fling oneself into the future: inevitably our sensibility sees in it only a dizzy void and restless fluidity: to give it solidity, we must have faith, mustn't we?— Let us pray for one another.

Forgive this shocking writing. I'm sitting on the edge of a table;—and then I've written so little these last ten days!

I'll be thinking with pleasure of you at Sarcenat. In spite of the ruins, and shell-holes, and the torn trees, the country here is still delightful. The nights fall over our forests, clear and lovely, with the owls calling, just as in Auvergne.

Goodbye. Always yours.—Tell me where to write to Mme Parion.

PIERRE

The regiment has had its fourth citation (for April—yellow lanyard [1]), and a fifth (18th July). Perhaps there'll be a sixth for this show. But I doubt it.

[*Carlepont, Oise*] *31st August 1918*

This is to tell you that I'm still very well, and to prevent you from thinking that the capture of Noyon was our work, a success that might have caused you to have some fears for me. The town fell to a khaki division, sister to ours: we only looked on, or gave a hand from a distance. As we are on the pivot-flank and the regiment, moreover, is in reserve, I didn't move, and won't, perhaps, until we're withdrawn for what will probably be a short spell of rest in the rear.

[1] Referring to the coloured cord worn round the left shoulder by unit cited in general orders.

231

I was glad to learn that you're going to spend some days at the Polignacs' with your friend Zanta. Life with an ' élite' (which one must learn to do without in order to have the courage to plunge into the ' masses' and work among them to form other ' élites') is no doubt one of the great human joys, a salutary and necessary happiness, like a breath of mountain air. I pray to our Lord that he may help you to draw from these pleasant hours the strength he has hidden in them for you. Once again, you must, for this, have trust—you must *believe*,—when you're faced with an agreeable future just as much as when it's worrying. What is said in the Epistle to the Hebrews, ' *fides substantia sperandarum rerum*', may, I think be translated so: faith is the element that stabilizes and divinizes our future,—it creates it, for each one of us, to the measure of our own salvation and our own particular chosen destiny.

For the last three days, I've been able to say mass. I go on doing so with a great sense of fulfilment, and at it I never fail to remember you.

Always yours,

PIERRE

[*Moyvillers, Oise*] *8th September 1918*

Your cards of the 5th and 6th reached me together, today. I'm glad that the visit to Sarcenat of Joseph's ' betrothed' resulted in your prolonging your stay at Polignac.[1]

I greatly admired the view of the castle you sent me. It seemed to me like a proud affirmation of the need for an ' élite', which is, I believe, one of the most decisive and permanent convictions I've acquired from my experience in recent years. None but a race of men, strong and conscious of having outstripped their fellows, could have conceived and built those towers, proudly poised on the rock, overlooking the torrent.—The whole difficulty (and secret) of real democracy is to encourage

[1] The Château de la Voûte-Polignac, near Puy-en-Velay.

the renewal and the recruitment of the élite, and to make inclusion in it as universal as possible. But *in itself*, the mass of humanity is profoundly inferior and repulsive. Don't you find it so?—Only yesterday I found myself in agreement on this problem with an officer newly arrived in the regiment, a chance meeting with whom showed immediately that we had a great deal in common. He's a Jesuit ' old boy ', who has, unhappily, ceased to be a practising Catholic but still retains true ideals and a great loyalty of soul. Talking with him, I appreciated once again the great wrong done to Christianity by believers, and by priests in particular who are insufficiently ' human '—whose religion, I mean, does not, as its first effect, make them more faithful to the duties and problems of *their own day*. Pray to our Lord that in the many contacts I have and am making with people of unorthodox views, the dominant influence may be *his*.

I'm pretty well settled in here, now. I have my own corner, and my own table. I'm still rather short of leisure (this evening I have to go seven kilometres to bury a poor old woman). But by tomorrow I have every hope of being able to get down to clarifying, in a notebook I've got hold of, the fragments of ideas I've been collecting for the last two months.

I feel that I've seldom had so conscious and clear a faith in the future.

Goodbye. Today I said a special prayer to our Lady for you. I know that you'll have done the same for me.

Always yours,

PIERRE

[*Moyvillers*] *12th September 1918*

I've just, with all the pleasure you can imagine, received your long letter of the 9th. But I'm sorry that my frequent short letters haven't been reaching you more regularly. I made the mistake of sending them all to Le Chambon; and I may be equally wrong in addressing this one to Polignac. However, they'll all turn up in the end and bring you proof of my constant thought of you.

I was most interested by all you told me about your life at Polignac. I greatly hoped that this stay would bring you the fruits of rest and instruction (moral and supernatural) that you have in fact derived from it. You can't imagine how happy I am to see your love of our Lord find such nourishment in the most diverse human hopes and so gain the power to influence others for good. I pray that our Lord may use you to foster and develop a *real* Christianity in your two friends, whose souls are so open and so loyal;—both of them, perhaps, threatened, at different levels, by the same danger of dissipating their powers in a too facile and popular success.—Oh Marguerite, do you realize what a grace God has given you by depriving you of so many things you would so have liked to have? . . . I'm most anxious that you should finish the two stories. Balzac was right when he said that when the inspiration's there, you must get to work straight away 'like a miner in a fall of rock'. In the case, at any rate, of a mind that continues to work and evolve, a few months, sometimes, is enough to prevent it from continuing to see things in the same way;—for each phase in the progress of thought has its own particular freshness, which nothing else can replace. You should fix at least the essence of the vision you now have.—I'll send you back the *Véroniques* shortly, with some notes. I'm taking advantage of the profound lull, whose value I feel so intensely at the moment, to do some work—quietly and for my own satisfaction.—I'm setting out in a notebook various thoughts, that gradually fall into groups around several main centres. I still think that my first essay will attempt to define my views on the constructive (creative, I might even say) properties of hope. (1) I shall begin, I imagine, by expressing as vividly as I can our situation in regard to the future: flung into existence, we are forced to advance into a future which terrifies us by its novelty and disheartens us by the 'chance' that seems to govern its development. We suffer equally from the *determinist* processes that involve us in their various phases, and from the forbidding indeterminism of chances whose multiplicity and slenderness make it impossible for us to control them.—(2) Following upon that, I shall put forward (without proving it except by its effectiveness in action and its compatibility with dogma) a particular concept of faith. If the future seems to us so uncontrollable—both in its causal sequences and its capriciousness—it is because we are afraid to plunge with it. Once we have faith (in the vigour of our spirit, and in the powerful goodness of God) then the *future* will submit to control, and lose its terror. First of all, ' chances ' will give way to our personal effectiveness;—and then there will emerge, from the strength developed by our own faculties, a freedom we have never dreamt of. The creative power somehow needs our faith on which to rest its advances. The world will achieve its fulfilment only to the extent to which we commit ourselves more confidently in the direction of what has not yet taken shape —confidence *forces the barriers* of determinism and *brings order to chance*.—(3) This is not to be understood as a sort of ' *faith-healing* ', as in Christian Science. It is in the supernatural sphere that the world is now being created.—And it is therefore above all to an *achievement* of *sanctity* that the sum total of the chances that punctuate the whole course of a believer's life will directly co-operate. The same group of events represents as many independent Providences as there are individuals. The more the individual has confidence, the more will his Providence (his own individual universe) lead him to God. All this can come about without any *particular* determinism of the world being modified by faith (Providence is for [looks to] *the whole*).—At the same time faith has an even wider function (in the supernatural order), than to triumph over chance: it really enables the soul to attain new stages of being. It doesn't simply ' order '; it creates new powers.—Idealist philosophy (and Christian Science) seem to see the supreme liberation of being as a deliverance from the necessity of death. That is a mistake. The more one changes, the more one dies. Trust in God (and in the being which is maintained by him) does not, then, do away with death: but it makes death such that it opens the way to greater fullness of life. There are, of course, as many *deaths* as *lives*: the greater the faith with which one allows death to carry one off, the more will death introduce one to some individually heightened form of existence . . .—In short, we may say that the more we believe in life, the bolder we are, the more the Universe is able to build itself around us *in its mystical reality*,—of which all that has already taken shape makes itself manifest then to our *vision in faith* (inseparable from our *action in faith*).—Don't try to examine these sentences in detail. My thought is feeling its way, and once again I'm trying to clarify it by talking to you.

I've chosen for my abode a little room in the presbytery. Ideally tranquil—the first touch of autumn gives the countryside a slight air of melancholy. It's odd how sensitive I am to the rather sad charm of this country, almost like Picardy, dotted with copses and ponds that reflect the rain-swept sky. I've always been particularly fond of autumn. And then these surroundings bring back to my mind vague memories of England,[1] or even of the old estate at Hornoy.[2]

I've come across some odd numbers of the *Revue Hebdomadaire*, containing the end of the *Lord of the World*. I was delighted by the exact way in which Benson describes pantheistic mysticism and the possible unification of the ' great monad '. At the same time I was very aware of all the difference in point of view that separates me from Benson. I certainly don't agree that enthusiasm for the ' spirit of the world ' is confined to the Antichrist. Side by side with the purely natural and exclusive type of God that Felsenburgh[3] ascribes to the cult of the world, there's room for a love of the earth based on God-the-Creator. I dislike Benson's view of Catholicism in its last days, not because it's persecuted and humiliated, but because it seems to me unjust,

[1] Ore Place, Hastings.

[2] The estate in Picardy of Père Teilhard's maternal grandparents, the Dompierre d'Hornoy.

[3] A character in R. H. Benson's *Lord of the World*.

anaemic, and anti-natural (almost as much as supernatural). Goodbye.

Always yours,

PIERRE

[*Chavannes-sur-l'Etang, près de Montreux-Vieux*]
20th September 1918

I can't refrain from sending you a short line to tell you what a charming little corner I've landed up in after yesterday's march. The place we left was gayer and more populous than this, but its very busyness destroyed the poetry that nature and history have given to these parts; moreover the rolling character of the ground prevented one from obtaining as extensive a view as one would have liked;—and, finally, it was misty or even raining. Since yesterday evening, the clouds have dispersed and it's in a limpid, clean-washed atmosphere that I can admire the little village on the Upper Rhine in which I'm living, and more particularly the wide panorama it offers. The view as I come out of the house is a constant delight to me. To the right, and behind me, the mountains Emm. de Margerie is so fond of, reveal the tops of their wooded slopes, bounded by steep cliffs. But to the left and in front of me, especially, there's a really glorious sight: the velvety blue of the jagged mountain barrier, rising up from the emerald green of the marshy plain. It's not the panoramic view you get from Sarcenat, but rather the view you have of Mont-Dore rearing itself aloft from the Rocquet uplands.[1] And the purity of line and colour is nothing beside the wealth of memories, the intense air of strangeness, that cling to these peaks or rise from the plain stretching away to the distant east! Indeed, my contact with this countryside, so mixed up with my childhood memories (our first governesses came from these parts) and with so many things I've since read or heard, has made a deep impression on me; it's almost as though it was

[1] The family estate of the Teilhard de Chardins.

237

giving me back my youth. To cap it all, it turns out that the presbytery of this out of the way village used to be a Jesuit house in the days of the old Society (1720), dating from the time when our houses were multiplying in these parts to combat the Lutherans. Everything in it is ' ours ', from the date over the door (from which you expect to see the head of a grumbling porter emerge) to the situation of the building, conveniently close to the church, and its vast proportions, very countrified and practical. You can't believe the pleasure it has given me to come back ' home ', and in what a powerful and warm atmosphere of the past I'm enveloped, in spite of my apparent isolation. Like the men who lived here before me, I am committed to God's work, in itself and as adapted to my own time, and I have the feeling that a whole accumulated store of strength is around me, within these walls. There—that's what I felt I must tell you this evening. Ahead of us, at any rate, the front seems extremely quiet. It's possible that they may ' turn us out to grass ' there. That would be a wonderful rest, in this weather.

Always yours,

PIERRE

Could you (if it is not too much trouble) have a copy of *Le Prêtre* typed for me ? I'd like to have one for Beaugeard. If you can't manage it, I'll ask Guiguite.

[*Chavannes-sur-l'Etang*] *27th September 1918*

If I'm still writing you such a small missive, when circumstances would seem to allow me to spread myself somewhat, you must attribute it to my being rather absorbed in writing and copying out *La Foi qui opère*.[1] I'm now copying out my rough draft again, and hope tomorrow to send you the manuscript,—as usual. I think I've nearly succeeded in saying what I wanted.—

[1] cf. Letter of the 17th August 1918.

It's interesting to note in oneself how much words, while they impoverish living thought, at the same time give it a strength that completes it, and sometimes surprises it.—Another thing I noted again—but with a more lively awareness than before—is how much the effort of composition (at least when the subject is something by which the mind really lives) enriches one's understanding, and even one's power of expression, and makes it more lively.—You know that in my case, at the moment, the source that enriched this liveliness (which extends to the whole supernatural world, of course) has been the natural beauties of the setting in which my present life is spent.—I'm under no illusion about the basic value of this present facility. But I'm trying to take advantage of it.

Yesterday, I received your long letter from Sarcenat, which gave me very great pleasure. I found in it a wonderful clarity, and a remarkable coincidence with my present state of mind, which confirmed me, most forcibly, in my faith in ' union through the spirit '. This gratifying experience came on top of another very different one I had just met with (it arose out of some things said to me in confidence) concerning the troubles entailed by the contrary approach; and these made me feel, with superabundant clarity and decisiveness, how much the world demands that ' those who see ' should commit themselves integrally, whatever they may sometimes experience themselves or learn by hearsay, to the side of the primacy of spirit. I know few things that impel me more powerfully towards an exact care for sanctification and a passionate (I'd almost say desperate) reliance on our Lord's strength, than this awareness of the need for the treasures of this world to be purified,—and the feeling, too, of the present struggle between the two ' principles and doctrine ' of union, through matter or through the spirit of our Lord.

Tomorrow, I presume, you'll be in Paris. You may be sure that I'll pray faithfully that you may be given the grace to summon up your strength again. If I have one piece of advice to give you, it is this: to contrive, in your daily time-table, a few minutes of morning meditation, so that you may *regain contact* with the mystical environment in which we both wish to live and act.—And, secondly, don't be *shaken* by any weakness or stagnation of spirit: but believe all the more firmly in our Lord's help and his providence for you.

Things are still quiet with me. I left my ' residence' the day before yesterday, but only to find a still better one. I'll write to you at greater length the day after tomorrow and tell you how I'm comfortably installed, this time in real Alsatian country.

Every kind message to Mme Parion (whose letter I've had).

Always yours,

PIERRE

I'm glad you saw Antoinette.[1]

29th September 1918

I'm writing on a quiet Alsatian Sunday morning, a little misty, unfortunately, but how peaceful! In the house next door, the fatherly parish priest is teaching the blond, well-behaved, children to chant the psalms. The bells are ringing to call a faithful population to mass. It's a fine, robust, country, stamped with all the goodness of German piety—Let's hope we don't spoil it, with the restless fire of our French spirit!

Yesterday I sent you (as I said in my letter of Friday) my latest essay.[2] I'm rather beginning to wonder whether I shouldn't, once again, offer it to Léonce with a view to publication (in *Recherches*, for example). I feel that my own too individual ideas are represented in it only by that side of them that is generally applicable and certainly sound,—in a form that minds in sympathy with mine will recognize, without others taking alarm. But once again, I've become so accustomed to living in ' my

---

[1] His brother Joseph's fiancée.
[2] Presumably *Mon Univers*, dated 14th April 1918, from Ay (Marne).

own universe' that I haven't much idea of what's strange or familiar to others. You must tell me what you think.

The result, as is natural enough, of the work I've just done in writing the essay, combined with my present physical fitness (autumn has always been the best season for my soul) has been to make me feel, with even greater sharpness and conviction, what has become my fundamental passion (or my faith). I can see, in sudden, clear, vivid, impressions, that my strength and my joy derive from seeing in some way made real for me the fusion of God and the world, the latter giving ' immediacy ' to the divine, and the divine *spiritualizing* the tangible. Seeing this, I can assure you, brings me real ' beatitude ' because it is this, I feel, that I have always tried to express for myself, and it's this that enables me to take hold of and finally to achieve (in accordance with my own particular destiny) the fulfilment of the Beautiful and the Good. I can now say that I feel my action is based on an unshakable foundation (with God's help, of course) and a real conviction. I told you, in my last letter, how prominent a part in my life is now being played by the truth (a very elementary one, you'll say . . .) that I must live only to develop *spirituality* in *immediacy*,—and, at the same time, by the assurance that the spirit must win, and has hidden within it a power that will ensure its victory. *Faith in spirit.*

You're quite right in your letter (written from Sarcenat) in saying that the masses can only apprehend what is concrete. But you show how well you know me when you suggest that I may have an instinctive predilection for collective entities (no —*not* abstract!) in some way ' immediately apprehended '. After all, isn't our Lord ' humanity ', or even ' creation in *person* '? and isn't the particular attraction of his being precisely the uniting in him of the centre and the sphere,—if I dare say so?—About what Pascal[1] says, you know the only sense in which I'd allow it (which is by no means, perhaps, Pascal's); geometry is not the term of our intellectual effort, but is ordered towards *divinizing us*, by developing the spirit in us, and can

[1] *Pensées*, 72 (ed. Brunschvig).

therefore be directed ' religiously ' not only ' by intention ' but by reason of the work it performs in us. Isn't it Plato who says θεὸς ἀεὶ γεωμετρεῖ [1] (*Deus semper 'geometres est'*)? (I should warn you I've never seen these words in their context.)

After all this, I haven't told you where or how I am. You'll have learnt from my last letter that I've left (not without some regret) my Jesuitish abode. They made us move fifteen kilometres to the north. In the end, although close to the lines, we landed up in a more populous and comfortable village than the one we'd just left. The parish priest (a perfect example of the pastor who's all-powerful in his own domain) immediately offered me a little room (with a real bed) and every facility for saying mass. I'm right opposite the church—which is clean, painted, polished, big, and in excellent taste.—From the material point of view our mess is functioning well (and in fact I'm even having to act as housekeeper). So you see everything is going splendidly.

What makes it a real rest, as you can imagine, is never to hear gunfire, and to live among people peacefully busying themselves with cutting their cabbages and digging their potatoes. And for me personally there's also the real relaxation of gazing at a beautiful countryside and a lovely horizon. The mountains are some fifteen or twenty kilometres to our left, but in between there's only a gentle marshy dip, so that the range, seen three-quarters face, rears up its whole height in front of us. In clear weather or when there's not much mist you can pick out the various layers, the valleys, even the trees. At other times, all the details merge into a deep unbroken blue. Closer at hand, the country is remarkably green. You'd think that it had been ruled off, almost regularly, into woods and meadows, with church towers, sometimes pointed, sometimes rounded, rising up pretty well at equal intervals—following a pattern that tells you you're close to the Rhine country. In fine weather, if you look south, the horizon is marked by high ridges, sometimes jagged—over towards where Mme Parion has her hermitage.

[1] Plato, *Theaetetus*, 162.E

It makes one feel rather ashamed to be enjoying all this, while France's battle-front is ablaze.

I need hardly tell you how closely I'm following all that's happening these days, one thing on top of another. If Bulgaria really folds up, it's the end.

Always yours. Be of good heart for the new school year.

PIERRE

[*Chavannes-sur-l'Etang*] *3rd October 1918*

Four days already, since I wrote to you! Time goes so quickly in the profound peace they're leaving us to enjoy. I've just had your first letter from Paris (the 29th). In spite of the pleasure it gives me to feel that you're at Le Chambon, or with good friends, I too, you know, like to know that you're in your own home in the Rue Montparnasse. It's there that you seem closest to me—a natural feeling, since it's there that we've known one another best. I'm thinking, this time, of taking a few days' leave in Paris,— among other reasons, to see Père Léonce. It'll be so good to meet again. But when is this famous leave going to materialize? . . . It seems to me that it will be difficult for my turn to come round before they call on us, somewhere or other, for another effort. At the best, I'm not counting on getting away before the end of the month.

I was glad to hear what you have to say about the notes I made for the *Véroniques*. You keep your independence, and you have appreciated the ' jealousy ' of my regard for you. I had indeed thought that the *Revue des Jeunes* was the obvious place for you to appear in. I didn't tell you that Guiguite wrote to me to say that she was very pleased with what you read her of your stories; it's a good sign. Go right ahead, and ask our Lord to help you to find your way to him in an abundance of light.

The day before yesterday, I had a letter from Père Chanteur[1]

[1] Provincial of the Lyons Province of the Society of Jesus.

in which he writes about *Le Prêtre*. Once again,—and unlike
Père V. S.[1]—his reaction is primarily one of anxiety. He's
obviously afraid (though he writes most affectionately) of seeing
me fall into pantheism. This friendly criticism has had the
salutary effect of making me face the difficulties of practical life,
and, incidentally, the slavery imposed on us by a certain group
of accepted scholastic formulas (in particular those relating to the
various forms of causality). Evidently I must find a certain orthodox way of putting things if I am to get across my 'experience'
without distorting or *weakening* it. The important thing,
fortunately, is that, intrinsically, the experience is orthodox;
that, it seems to me, I can be sure of since, in June in particular,
I was told so again,—and because I have St John and St Paul on
my side,—and have moreover, a whole mass of postulates and
interior satisfactions that can hardly, I believe, be misleading,
so deeply rooted are they in my life. All the same, I've been
anxious to let you know about this new warning I've had, so
that you too may not engage yourself in a situation that may
prove rather hazardous—or at any rate delicate. If you can
have the essay typed, as you say, send a copy all the same to
' M. l'Abbé Beaugeard (chaplain to the regiment of Moroccan
colonial infantry, S.P.112)'; there's no awkwardness with him.
I'll be very glad to have the Platos you say you're sending.

I've taken advantage of the wonderful weather these last days
to spend a long time wandering in the woods. The trees are
far from being as fine as those of the Oise and Aisne; but even
so I prefer the tangled forests of these parts to the tidy plantations
around Compiègne: you get more of the feeling of age-old
nature, and you seem to be very close to the mystery of the
Hercynian forests. Every time you come out on the edge of the
woods, it's a new marvel to see the Vosges or the Jura or, right
in front of you, the ridges of the Black Forest. The only drawback is the multiplication and apparently meaningless confusion
of the wire fencing. Here and there you meet crafty old territorials (reservists) skewering huge mushrooms that they then

[1] Père Vulliez-Sermet.

sell for vast sums to the messes. All this is most restful. Even the Boche aircraft, in this privileged area, drop only pacifist leaflets instead of bombs.

As you see, I'm still lucky enough to have my room, my bed, and the church close at hand. The *curé* has called on me to speak on Sunday (Rosary Sunday) to his faithful congregation. From the ' thinking ' point of view, I'm hoping to get down in a few paragraphs, as an appendix to the *Union créatrice*, the various new points that have taken definite shape or fixed themselves in my mind during the last year,—for my own benefit, of course, and with an eye to future critics,—and not for general publication. I'll let you know more about this later.

Goodbye. We must pray that our Lord may really be all to us. Remember me to Mme Parion.

Always yours,

PIERRE

[*Foussemagne, Haut-Rhin*] *11th October 1918*

I've just received your Plato, and even looking through a few pages has set my feeling for the spirit ' vibrating ' within me. I feel that during the last four years I've been really beginning to understand what it is to have ' a faith ',—what bliss it means for the man who has it,—and what power it exercises over the multitude of souls who are asleep or hesitant. The effect of the war on my own personal fortunes will have been to give me a faith. Until now, zeal has always been for me something artificial, applied from outside one, something forced. Now I can understand a little what sort of passion it was that inspired the apostles. But it's most remarkable that this feeling began to arise in me only when religion became illuminated [was given life] for me, by a ' personal ' way of looking at things, a ' personal ' taste. No doubt there's some general psychological law at work there,—even though in many cases it may be difficult to verify it.—In one sense, mightn't you say that everyone has to have *his religion*, grafted on a particular natural passion??—all these particular religions converging on the same Jesus Christ . . .

I take the attitude you suppose to the cares of which you tell me in your letter of the 6th. I like to think that you find pleasure in withdrawing into the ' *milieu mystique* ' and that you succeed in doing so. Since to be able to do so is a gift from God, I pray a great deal that our Lord may allow you to find your way to him, more and more as your normal refuge, and there find continually greater peace. For the rest, try to go forward bravely through the tangle of briars that seems to you to have been barring your road this year. You'll find that they'll disappear.—Don't forget that you're not engaged on any trivial task, but on a work of real sanctity; and so you have a double right to count on Providence.

Nothing new in my external existence. It would be humiliating if the end of the war found us here, and I'd be sorry not to have had my share in the emotion of the final triumph. But are we there yet? . . . Wilson, meanwhile, is rising to the stature of a Felsenburgh. And, indeed, he seems to me to have a serenity and an idealism that make me feel, with new conviction, how essential it is to Christianity not to allow the ' sap of the Earth ' to drain away from it. One very clever thing in the President's answer—and probably not a matter of design—is that it doesn't make him appear to refuse peace. The French soldier is not, so far as I know, so intoxicated with victory that he'd resent anyone who prevented him from dealing the final blow (it may be a different matter for the Americans and English). He'll drink his fill of victory, but only if he's forced to go on fighting.—I'm beginning to think that the Germans will make up their minds to evacuate the territory they invaded.

You ask me for my notes on what I said for Rosary Sunday. I haven't any, and moreover, I didn't follow up my line very far. This was my idea: (1) To recall the historical development of the rosary, showing that it is no more than a development, an extension of the angelic salutation (the rosary is an expansion, a further explanation, of the Ave Maria). (2) To describe the parallel development of the Ave Maria in each individual's religious history. The Ave Maria is first of all a manifestation, primarily instinctive, of love for our Lady, a manifestation that is often ' interested '.—It turns into a need to know our Lady better, to ' sympathize ' with her: in some way the heart of the Blessed Virgin becomes transparent, and in it we relive the mysteries,—so that the whole of dogma becomes familiar, concrete, and real, in *Mary*. Finally, we understand that the mysteries have their parallel and their extension in the alternations, often indeed mysterious, of our own joys and sorrows. So our whole life is Christianized, in a way, in the development within us of the Ave Maria . . .—You can see what I was getting at.

With the continual calm, which allows my dreams to run on unchecked, I am ' continuing to make progress ' along various lines of which I'll tell you. Anyway, I've given up for the moment the appendix to the *Union créatrice* about which I wrote to you. There would be too much to say; I'd rather wait until some new central aspect emerges from the various components. —The different reactions of Père Ch.[1] and Père V.-S.[2] are more easily explained than you think: I realise that the tricky part in my writings is not the blunt correction of formulas (easy enough to look after) but the inspiration behind them and the general tendency.—Pray earnestly that it may always be the *good* spirit that animates me.

Thank you for sending the copy to Beaugeard. You'll have realized that the cost should come out of the money I sent you in September.—Don't forget to buy the books that you'll enjoy. —I've written to Robert.

Always yours,

PIERRE

P.S. I've just had your letter of the 9th.—Thanks. I'll send you the outline you ask for, when I've turned it over in my mind (with great pleasure)—the day after tomorrow, I expect.

[1] Père Chanteur.   [2] Père Vulliez-Sermet.

[Méricourt, Haute-Saône] Monday 4th November 1918

Thanks to a lift in a car belonging to a friend of mine, a captain, who was, like me, catching the 8 o'clock express, I got back to the regiment the same evening at 7.30. We're on the move again, on foot so far, for no one knows where. I'm still, for the time being, quite close to Gabriel, but without his being aware of it, and with no way of letting him know.

So I had an excellent journey, and comfortable, spent in thinking over all that we said to one another, and reading Schuré.[1] The introduction really aroused my enthusiasm. By contrast, ' Rama ' seems to me terribly fanciful, and scientifically more than outmoded. But, as you said, it's Schuré's soul that's interesting, at least as much so as that of his initiates.

Finding myself in a favourable psychological atmosphere, I've finished drawing up a plan for my next essay, *Forma Christi*, and decided on the lines of my wedding address [2] . . . I'll write again about all this.

I found here your welcome letter of the 15th, telling me of your scheme for the 21st [3]. You'll have appreciated, I don't doubt, how deeply I shared your joy and how much at the same time I feel that our union was being made closer ' *in Xto* [*Christo*] *Jesu* ', in whom union never stands still, but progresses indefinitely, in intimacy and fruitfulness and beauty.

You're quite right: there is no interior change in anything in life through such an act, but the whole profundity of things takes on new life from it. It's the ' *milieu mystique* ' manifesting itself.

Think, in the presence of our Lord, of the second promise of which M. V. spoke to you. I believe that there too there's something to be done, for the joy and unity of life. Perhaps, though, you might develop the implications of the sentence:

[1] Whose best-known work, *Les Grandes Initiés* (1889) went through several editions.

[2] For the marriage of his brother Joseph to Mademoiselle Antoinette Levert.

[3] See Preface, page 9.

'... so long as it is manifestly the will of God to bind me to educational work. ...' It may be that this act will mark for you the end of the internal dualism you suffer from ... I pray a great deal that our Lord may be the joy and unity of your life.

Goodbye, and, more than ever, I am always yours. Remember me affectionately to Mme Parion.

PIERRE

[*Citers*] *Thursday 7th November 1918*

Since my letter of three days ago, we've been continuing to make our way on foot northwards, through lovely country, quite new to me. We're advancing leisurely in short stages. No one here has the least idea what they have in store for us.

All the time we're on the road, marching through the leafless woods, I continue to think of you and of all that makes up our common interest. I was able to say mass this morning, and did not forget you or your preparations for the 21st. It's real heaven on earth to see so many things ready, for us and through us, to be divinized. Never forget to guard jealously in your soul this fundamental joy or passion, above *everything*, even above success and immediate, apparent, personal achievement. Only one thing matters, and should nourish our taste, our passion, for living: to feel that God is realized everywhere, in us and around us. So long as this fundamental transformation continues to operate in our lives, what matter the annoying or discordant details that still, no doubt, persist—and which we have to fight against—but which can themselves serve to bring about the substitution of our Lord for ourselves? This is how we now want to be happy, don't you agree?

I suppose that you've taken up the burden of your educational work again. I hope that the number of your pupils and the good health of your assistants may be a consolation to you, and enable you to find leisure for your stories.

For my part, I'm wondering when I'll be able to get down to

putting on paper some ideas that are nearly matured. All I can do now is to turn them over in my mind as we march along. I think that, thanks to the talks we had which made us think things out, I'm beginning to have less vague ideas about the Resurrection, and the essential role of the flesh of Christ. This will form the last paragraph of the essay I have in mind,—in which I shall deal particularly with the question of the attraction we feel exerted upon us by our Lord (a question which is fundamental to the apologetics of ' immanence '), and of the comparative value of attachment and detachment.—I'll talk to you about all this when the time comes, of course.

Always yours. Remember me to Mme Parion.

PIERRE

[*Docelles, Vosges*] *13th November 1918*

The news of the armistice pulled us up short as we were speeding up an advance that was taking us, I imagine, pretty well straight to the capture of Metz. For the last two days we've been waiting for orders in the little village where the new order of things came upon us unexpectedly. The place is rather crowded with Chasseurs Alpins (a training battalion) and the situation moderately pretty (we've left the pine country for one with big bare, cold, hills). By good fortune I've landed up in a hospitable presbytery, where the *curé*'s cousin (he's in the army) lodges me and looks after me like a mother. In these conditions I can look forward to, and indeed would like to have, a few days in which to recollect myself and determine my attitude to what's been happening. For the moment, of course, it's impossible to make any definite plans. But one must attune one's mind to an effort ' to be applied in time of peace '. That's what I was saying to you the day before yesterday. I already feel, and I'll be feeling it more strongly, something of the impact of the feelings I anticipated in the last paragraphs of *Nostalgie du Front*. The atmosphere I feel around me is going to become more oppressive and more uninteresting. What I have to do is to master this external sense of flatness by a more intense than ever interior life and vision. This calls for a new adaptation, a preparation, to which I want to devote these last weeks of independent and solitary existence. However, don't imagine that, in spite of various little sacrifices I'll have to make if I'm to accommodate myself to ordinary life, I feel any disinclination for the tasks I can see around me. I'm emerging, as I told you, from these four and a half years of retreat, with a store of fresh energies and a precise Christian ideal, which I am anxious to test and use. Besides, for some time I've been feeling that the war itself had lasted long enough for me and was not bringing me anything worth while; it was time either for the war to finish or for me to change my circumstances. On top of all that, it's useless for us to want or regret things over which we have no control. Once again it's God's will manifesting itself; all we can do is to abandon ourselves to it in all peace and openness of heart. Pray that I may take the right road in these opening hours of the new life that is soon to begin for me. And pray still more that the passion for living and spiritualizing, which is my only strength and which you help me so much to keep burning, may never cease to glow. What you tell me in your letter of the 7th, about the increasing importance the idea of sacrifice is taking on for you, has been a great joy to me, because I think that this shows that you are making your way into the final circle of divine union, and that you are doing so after having been through the circle of human attractions and having thereby strengthened both your power to give and your capacity to achieve detachment. For those in whose eyes God has become the supreme reality in the universe there can logically be no more stable and more profound happiness than to feel this reality painfully taking the place of their own being—in so far as that being has been faithful in shaping and developing itself. It's an intimate happiness that nobody can appreciate who has not been the object of this precious transformation. I pray to God with all my strength that he may make of you a most pure and docile instrument for his action. When once one has begun to see people and events in this particular light,—one can only be terrified at the crying need for purity the universe suffers from, and almost beside oneself with longing to do something to supply it. What a wonderful object on which to focus our interior efforts, don't you agree?

I've had your card of Saturday. Once again, we've been experiencing things *together*.

Tell me what you're doing, and what's happening to your *Contes* (and the *Véroniques*) and the Plato courses. The gnostics ought to be studied not by a critic nor a philosopher, nor just by a theologian,—but by a mystic. I fear you may not meet with one.

Always yours,

PIERRE

[*Lapoutroie-Hachimette, Alsace*] *17th November 1918*

I've received your little note—such an affectionate one—written on Armistice day, and it touched me deeply. If anything makes me appreciate God's allowing me to emerge safe and sound from the last four years, it is indeed (together with the hope of working for him) the sweetness of a friendship such as yours. During these last days of November I've been thinking very particularly of you, and I'm trying to be a little better in everything for your sake,—so that God may find you worthy and take you within himself for ever. I expect I'll have a line from you to say whether you're definitely deciding on the 21st November or the 8th December. In any case, my masses (if I'm able to say them) will be said for you on both those dates.

We're still continuing our march along the main roads, and shall be doing so for a long time yet, I fear. In the end we were sent due east, so that I'm not without hopes of reaching the Rhine in ten days or so. At the moment we're still in France, but tomorrow, I expect, we'll be going over the passes and beginning to drop down into reconquered territory. The higher we climb, the blacker and grander the forests become, flung like fleeces over rounded peaks, in outline not unlike those of our own in Auvergne. But the colder, too, the weather becomes, and the more icy the meadows in the bottoms, under their few bare trees. I'm beginning to get impatient to reach some permanent station where I can settle down and read and write. Just think of it—since we left on November 3rd, I've never been more than twenty-four hours in the same place! Even so, I'm feeling ready to get something written,—a new summary, reshaped and refocussed, of my old ideas.—As for Schuré, I still haven't got beyond Rama.

I've just been reading a number of the *Action Française* that takes an extremely pessimistic view of the threat contained in the German bloc that's in process of consolidation. But what's the remedy? . . . It looks as though the whole history of recent times, while it illustrates the grave danger of large racial agglomerations, at the same time teaches the impossibility of preventing ' natural ' combinations. I simply cannot see how one can prevent German unity by force . . . My only hope,—though it would make the pundits smile—lies in some transformation of the Boche soul. What is certain, is that the future of centuries to come will be at stake in a month's time at Versailles, and that we must pray, *with faith*, that Providence may guide our modern prophets. There we have a fine, comprehensive, intention at hand, to wish for and use for our sanctification, don't you think?

Goodbye. Let's meet again in Christo.

Always yours,

PIERRE

Remember me to Mme Parion.

[*Illhäusern*] *18th November 1918*

This time I'm writing to you from well inside reconquered Alsace. At 8 o'clock yesterday morning we were crossing the col du Bonhomme, in a wonderful setting of pinewoods; and this evening we're in the plain; twenty-five kilometres from the Rhine, north of Colmar. We were rather wondering what sort of welcome we'd have. On the whole, it was touching and even enthusiastic. All along the Kaisersberg valley, through which we reached the plain, the villages were decorated (with flags prepared under the noses of the Boches before they retreated), with a triumphal arch at the entrance and crowds everywhere in their best clothes throwing flowers and greenery. In the first place of any size we went through, Alsatian women in white, with their national headdress, handed out a pleasant light Rhenish wine, in buckets. These demonstrations made us sorry not to be entering Colmar today (a treat reserved for the Messimy division . . . politics again!); it appears that the municipality had voted 30,000 francs for doing things in a big way;—that the general was to be received by a body of 800 Alsaciennes in national costume, etc. All the local people would be turning up to watch as on a public holiday. It was rather different for us; we made our way to humble billets in a little village on the Ill, where hardly anyone speaks a word of French and where the Boches were still installed at mid-day yesterday. So the celebrations have been on a much smaller scale, though there's a friendly attitude to us. I think we'll be here for forty-eight hours. After that, I'm not sure whether we go on to the Rhine or back up towards Strasbourg. You see some odd sights here: Rumanian ex-prisoners,—Alsatians serving in the German army, coming back from Russia or Berlin, still in uniform, with tricolour cockades on their grey tunics . . . Not much abandoned supplies. From this point of view, our entry into Alsace at this part on the front where the war was dormant, is turning out rather flat. However, this lack is made up for by the charm of the countryside. I've seldom seen a more picturesque little place than Kaisersberg, in its setting of tall black mountains, with its castle perched on a spur of rock,—its massive bridge,— its narrow streets of ancient houses decorated with wood carvings and elaborate coats of arms,—and the whole hung with tricolour

flags (just as in Hansi's drawings). I can really understand now
how people could have been ready to dedicate themselves to the
restoration of Alsace to France. The population has suffered
a great deal in the war; they've been reduced to eating an
unspeakable black bread. Our ration loaves, our rice and coffee,
arouse general enthusiasm. We're obviously providers of food
as much as liberators.

This is a terribly 'superficial' letter. But I thought you'd
like to hear about all this.—You know that all this coming and
going doesn't stop me—far from it—thinking of you,—particularly at this time.

Always yours,

PIERRE

[*Illhäusern*] *20th November 1918*

I received your long letter of the 15th the day before yesterday.
Don't worry: your great joy at the news of the armistice didn't
seem at all selfish to me: all it did was to touch me deeply, sure
in my knowledge that your joy was not preventing you from
guessing all that I might be feeling side by side with the relief of
having finished with the painful aspects of the war.

We've made no move since my last letter, but by tomorrow,
it appears, we'll be off again. There's more and more talk of our
going to Strasbourg. That would indeed be an honour for the
38th division! For the moment I'm lodged as comfortably as
can be with the *curé* of Illhäusern, who is completely friendly and
a complete Francophil. Would you believe it—in this fortunate
parish one-third of the men (beginning with the mayor and his
assistant) are Franciscan tertiaries!—It doesn't seem to stop them
from being efficient citizens and farmers. I have a bed at the
presbytery, and a huge room, carpeted and heated, to work in.—
If only I can find a similar retreat when we finally take over
garrison duties on the Rhine,—though, to tell you the truth,
I can't be sure that that's our destination. I can't say anything

for certain about what we'll be doing later or when my class will be demobilized. What I do want to avoid is being taken away from the regiment *before* demobilization, to moulder in some depot. I'll have to play my cards carefully if I'm to avoid that catastrophe. Meanwhile, I'm still impatient to reach some place where we can settle down. Yesterday, sitting by the stove, I jotted down in a notebook a lot of notes that I must now make an effort to put into order. And then, I haven't yet properly begun the wedding address![1]—I've also been reading Schuré, who's obviously a great mental tonic: he makes you feel and think, in the order of realities that interest us both. It's a pity that he's unfortunately so fanciful and, what's more, that he gives you so little chance to check what he says. Reading him, I've appreciated once again the great danger that threatens naturalistic mystics of looking for mysteries (and their solution) in the plane of our own experience and of our own sensible universe, and not within a circle of the universe that lies deeper than our world. This fault in outlook gives to even the finest insights an infantile air or a note of illuminism from which they should at all costs be preserved or released.—Real esotericism, the real *gnosis*, have no impact on the scientific order, and (unfortunately) do not allow us to make the exasperating veil of phenomena fade from before our eyes. *For every circle of the world, mystery lies in the next circle:* that's the principle that should protect the mystic from every fanciful dream and from every absurdity.

I understand perfectly (from having experienced them myself) the two feelings you have, of rejuvenation when you immerse yourself in an atmosphere of thought,—and of ' lack of interest ' when once again you have to teach children literature. The first of these experiences shows that you need intellectual nourishment and that, if you are to be true to God, you must seek it as much as possible. The second should not upset you: Providence may well have good reason to run counter to our tastes. I wonder whether, to give new life to your teaching,

[1] cf. letter of 4th November 1918.

you should,—not try to force yourself and create for yourself an illusion of interest in the *matter* you expound,—but allow yourself, by careful reflexion, to be possessed by the 'philosophic' and heavenly grandeur of the *function* of even elementary teaching. By so doing, even if the things you're explaining leave you cold, your heart at least will be afire to speak, when you consider that it is your vocation, or at any rate your occupation, to mould the spirit, so far as you can, for eternal life;—there are few more effective ways of collaborating for the fullness of Christ than working upon the souls of children,—don't you feel that?—And even though, in its results and its chances of enduring, the Institute may not realize your ideal, it will still have been one ' moment ', one ' form ' in the vast history of Christian education. How strong and confident you can feel in this secular framework of your own personal effort!

I still don't know whether the 21st—tomorrow,—is the day you've chosen. Perhaps I'll hear from you this evening. In any case, I'll carry on as though it were. And that won't prevent me from being more united with you, if possible, in our Lord until the 8th.

Always yours. Remember me to Mme Parion.

PIERRE

I am saying mass for Uncle Cirice [1] and for your family.

[Wolfisheim-Strasbourg] 27th November 1918

I don't know whether you'll have had my cards of yesterday and the day before. Until tomorrow, we're serving as an isolated detachment of the regiment, which means that we're not having any regular mail. No letters since Saturday. On Saturday I still thought that we'd be spending several more days at Makenheim. And then in the course of the day we were told that the regiment is to be represented on the 26th at Strasbourg for Pétain's entry (I

[1] Marguerite Teillard-Chambon's father.

had been detailed to form part of the detachment, as an old member) and that we leave on Sunday morning. A hurried departure. Everyone was leaving his things in rather a muddle, expecting to be back on Tuesday. Then on Monday it was announced that the division is being moved to Strasbourg, or near it, which means that they're joining us on foot. And so here I am for the last three days, cut off from all resources, hoping that my things will catch me up without too much lost,—installed in a little village four kilometres from Strasbourg, where there's unfortunately no *curé* and no regularly served church. It's the other side of the medal,—but it doesn't matter much compared with what I've gained by coming here: a chance to see a wonderful town at one of the finest moments in its history. You can readily imagine that it's a most unwelcome task to take part in a military parade. Apart from the physical fatigue (which doesn't really matter) you only see a small section of the troops marching by, and always the same ones; you move on quickly, without being able to see or enjoy the interesting places; in my case, I was at the tail-end of the regiment, which itself was at the tail-end of the 38th division, which meant that I arrived to find a crowd already hoarse from cheering the brass-hats and the colours. All this was an accumulation of unfavourable circumstances, to which was added the fact that we weren't the first troops to enter the town. Even so, we had a welcome that I, for one, will never forget. There was the external setting—most attractive—of the old gabled houses and ancient churches we saw as we crossed the multiple lines of forts, redoubts, and ditches that form a ten-fold ring round the city;—then there were the infinitely graceful ranks of hundreds of Alsaciennes, in their national head-dress and multicoloured skirts, who lined the pavements and were gathered in the squares;—and above all there was something you so seldom find, the confluence and meeting of countless spiritual energies,—the whole soul of a country that finds itself again, to join up with that of another country. Side by side with my own positive and conscious participation in this awakening (which was strong enough) what

I experienced most of all was a lack in my power to feel ... I had not allowed the passion for my own country to grow sufficiently strong within me, the Alsatian problem was too foreign to me, so that I couldn't fully immerse myself in the spiritual current that I nevertheless felt flowing around me—without being able to plunge into it, to ' communicate ' with it ... It's an odd feeling, this, of its being present and yet at the same time outside oneself. If it hadn't been for the oppressive concourse of *poilus*, respectful but noisy, crowding round the clock (to see the twelve apostles appear when it strikes) I'd have been much more moved and felt it more deeply when I made my own personal visit to the cathedral yesterday. I had seldom realized so fully what spiritual power is concentrated in a church loaded with whole centuries of prayer,—and which emanates from the beauty of vault and glass. As a result of repairs that hide the great rose-window and obscure the choir, there are many blemishes on the beauty of the interior, but they are soon overlooked. And then, adjoining the great austere aisles, and sharing their majesty, there's the chapel of the Blessed Sacrament,—and that (a double one) of the Sacred Heart and a Pietà chapel (very old indeed, hung with cloth of gold and jewels and in spite of these trappings very moving) which are perfect gems, full of warmth, of gothic art (geometrically foliated ribbed vaulting) and of the best modern German statuary. The postcards I'm sending and will be sending later, will give you some idea of the fineness of the carving on the outside of the church, still as fresh as ever on the fine red Vosges sandstone,—which is as tough, and how much gayer than our Auvergne lava or the grey stone of Notre-Dame. Our Lord favoured me here with a happy encounter. While I was watching, in front of the square, a group of young Strasbourgers proceeding quietly but methodically to shut up a Boche beer-house and tear up its flagstones,—I noticed, enjoying the same scene, my old friend Decisier, chaplain to the 18th infantry Chasseurs, whom I hadn't seen since 1914. We flung our arms round one another, and for two hours we gave free rein to our memories, our plans and our ideas. I've not often spoken to you of this friend of mine,—but he's one of my most vital and dearest friends,—feeling essentially just as I do, but working primarily in the practical sphere of social groups. I found him full of praise for the clergy of Alsace, and particularly for the part played by the Church in Strasbourg, where the big seminary is a real centre for the whole life of the city. And we deplored the lack of organization and the feebleness of the French clergy. And we lamented the religious ' extrinsécisme ' from which Catholics suffer. And with all this there was the wonderful joy of feeling that we were one of a number, united in our approach to a fine task.

I hope that tomorrow we'll be moved into permanent quarters, where I can settle down to some regular work, close to a church. Only one month until Joseph gets married! I'm still not quite certain that I'll be able to get to it. But in any case I really must get down to writing my address.

Always yours in Christo.—Remember me to Mme Parion.

PIERRE

[*Hönheim*] *2nd December 1918*

We're still detached from the regiment, and so we still have a poor postal service. I'm writing, accordingly, without having had your news. I hope this state of affairs will come to an end tomorrow, and that I'll be able to find my various papers again. Meanwhile I've no cause to complain about my time at Hönheim, the suburb of Strasbourg we've been stationed in since Friday. I told you in my last letter that the *curé* was entertaining me with charming hospitality. Since then he has passed me on to the Sisters who run his school—excellent Alsatians of the Ribeauvillé congregation—who can't do enough to spoil me. I live surrounded by eiderdowns, cakes, flasks of kirsch and Alsatian wine —not at all, as you know, my style. Still, it's amusing to take it by the way. And most of all, there's something very touching in this so disinterested solicitude. I hope that our Lord will

reward these good souls, so honest and simple.—A more important advantage is that I have a desk in a quiet room, where I can
settle myself in. If we stay here, I'll be well placed for doing
some work; but I rather think we'll be off on our wanderings
again, this time perhaps into Strasbourg itself. Without my
notes, I haven't been able to do more than almost finish the
wedding address (except for the paragraph for Antoinette: I'm
still waiting for Joseph's answer); for the rest of the time, I've
been several times into the town. Now that the shops are open
again, the streets of the old city, at once picturesque and modern,
are extraordinarily gay and animated. The Boche is lying low,
and in any case he's closely watched. Faithfully each time, I pay
a long visit to the cathedral and beneath its dim vaults I try to
introduce a little more order into the world of aspirations—
still, in spite of everything, very confused—I feel within myself.
I try to do something to harmonize them with that intensely
powerful current of practical and mystical life from which
emerged the pillars, ogives and stained glass that surround me
like a miniature universe. Why was the spiritual drive of the
middle ages pulled up short? Was it only because a great influx
of new elements cooled a fire that in extent covered hardly more
than half Europe?—or, was it also because the religious world,
as seen by our ancestors at that time, was placed by them on too
immediate a plane that failed to allow the natural universe its
own proper scale of grandeur and its own particular development? . . . I can't help wondering how in these days we should
envisage a cathedral.

While awaiting the arrival of Georges[1] and Poincaré,
Hönheim had its own little celebration, the day before yesterday,
in honour of the new civil authorities of Strasbourg who came
to visit the municipality. A procession immediately formed, in
the regular Alsatian style, the same wherever I've been. First
of all, young people on horseback, with tricolour scarves; then
three Alsaciennes, hand in hand, in full national costume;—then
the band, solemn and intent;—then the fire brigade, in dazzling

[1] Georges Clemenceau.

helmets;—then three more Alsaciennes;—then the officials;—then the veterans of 1870, the municipal council, and a crowd of good people in top hats; then a flock of colourful Alsaciennes, arm in arm. Reception by the mayor, the *curé*, the Sisters, little girls in big bows.

All this concourse serious and laughing at the same time. It was a very artless and pretty scene.—The French have a great deal to learn from the Alsatians, that's sure.

So, everything is going well for me. I hope it's the same at the Institute. During this advance, I'm feeling that since the Incarnation is taking on a continually more real, universal and living meaning for us, we should try to arouse in ourselves a very ardent desire to see Christ achieve all his fullness in the world. We'll join together in this intention—I'm counting on this—in front of M. Denis' picture.[1]

Remember me to Mme Parion. Always yours in Christo.

PIERRE

[*Strasbourg*] *8th December 1918*

I'm writing before my mass, which I'm going to say at 8 o'clock in a neighbouring parish, St-Louis. I feel that, on this day, this is a good time to talk to you; and I feel, too, that nothing could prepare me better to receive our Lord shortly than to place myself again in the atmosphere in which we both wish to be in him. You know what, particularly on this feast, is my dearest wish: that God, through our Lady, may grant us so to share in her purity and to have so ardent a passion for her, that we may really be able to serve, in our own small way, to regenerate the world. We must have absolute faith in the power of this divine virtue to transform souls and spread itself; and we must see to it, too, that the greatest interest of our life is to feel that we are growing a little more within her, and are serving to radiate her influence.

[1] The painter Maurice Denis.

I've had your letter of the 29th. I'm glad that in return for your offering our Lord has given you that longing for a certain isolation and interior silence. As you know, the more I feel that he is taking you for himself and absorbing you, the more I shall know that we are together—united again where union grows endlessly closer and knows no more what it is to be separated.—I can't help being a little sorry that you've had to add to your work. Try, as soon as you get the chance, to make a little time for yourself and for your own personal spiritual nourishment. Meanwhile, you're quite right: everything must be sacrificed to the clear duty in which God manifests himself. Whatever appetite we may experience, and cultivate, for any task that leads towards what we feel to be the fulfilment of our nature, we must have within us a much more fundamental appetite: that for feeling God grow within us through the universal and dominating action of his providence. And I really do believe that this appetite can ultimately replace all others, by which I mean that it can make us find life passionately interesting even in the most commonplace and tedious setting. The real substance of even such circumstances is divine.

We're still at Strasbourg, and I've fallen into a regular and studious routine of life which in some ways reminds me of my time in Paris. Except at night-time and for meals, I spend my time in the seminary by the cathedral where a room has been placed at my disposal. I'm working on *Forma Christi*. I'll tell you about it later. Today, of course, I'll be at the services in the cathedral. Tomorrow, Poincaré's reception.

Goodbye. I'm off to St-Louis.

I must tell you again how much, in a few minutes time, I'll be united with you, when I make my offering, and that of all things, to the divine holiness, through our Lady.

Always yours in Xto.

PIERRE

I wrote to you the day before yesterday; but since then I've had your long letter of the 5th. Yesterday, moreover, was Strasbourg's great day. So, for both these reasons, I must send you a word today. I'm delighted to agree that this year our common intention should be the one you suggest: to work and pray that our Lord, at the dawn of this new world-cycle, may descend among us ever more and more living. In fact, this agreement between us will not mean much of a change of orientation in my inner attitude,—but I feel that it will give it reality and stability: when there are two of you, you're much stronger; and, most important of all, the *exteriorizing* that such an association gives to a state that was until then interior, endows it with a completely new solidity.—This concern (as you, I'm sure, understand) to make God reign over all things must be not only an intention, a more or less extrinsic object of desire,—but also an *habitual guiding force* behind all our actions (even the most trifling), which are then made as perfectly as possible in order that God may dwell more intensely in our souls and, through them, in everything else too. This habitual awareness of a *vast concrete aim* behind our least actions is a source of the most profound peace and satisfaction: a source, too, of tremendous strength when faced with all sorts of temptations. In one sense, it's true to say that you can conquer the world only by using the world against itself.—With regard to what you say about Thomist piety, you know how much I agree with you. There are some things that force me, when I come up against them, to summon up all the great incentives that urge one towards peaceful tolerance, if I am not to give way to irritation. At the moment, the Church, or rather its administrators, have no understanding of what real life is. To do my own small part to create in her a movement towards progress, would seem to me an excellent use of the period that's just beginning.

And now for Poincaré's reception. The papers will be spreading themselves, I expect, in recording the enthusiasm of the people of Strasbourg. And they'll be justified. It was a wonderful celebration, quite flawless.—As the barracks were closed in the morning, I stayed working at the seminary, so that I missed seeing the official procession (which I'd have liked to have witnessed, for the sake of the crowd's ovation). In the afternoon, however, I was at the ' civil ' parade, which was an extraordinary sight. For over an hour and a half, through streets black with people and hung with flags, musical societies, co-operatives, employers' associations, congregations of men, deputations from Alsatian municipalities, each with their own emblems and banners and costumes, marched by in a continuous stream. At the head of each musical society, the vice-president carried across his shoulders an enormous silver-mounted horn, that serves both as a trumpet and a drinking vessel. The mayors, in tricolour sashes, and sometimes the *curé* or the Sisters, accompanied the people from their parish, who, for the most part, wore their ancient regional costumes. Apart from the popular big bow, the Alsaciennes wear many other head-dresses: sometimes a close-fitting cap in gold, with a wide starched brim of embroidery, sometimes a tiny bonnet worn over a little bun—sometimes a mass of ribbons on the side of the head—according to the particular locality. Thousands of these Alsaciennes had come in lorries from the most remote villages, with their men in wide felt hats or otterskin caps with green silk lining. All this world marched by in a long column, a medley of bright reds and greens, arm in arm,—sometimes at a quick step,—sometimes, with delightful spontaneity, to a farandole rhythm. Occasionally there'd be a hold-up: and then the whole undulating mass flowed back, still dancing and waving handkerchiefs, but all in the most faultless taste. I've never seen anything like it. What was most impressive in this celebration, and moved some hardened *poilus* to tears, was the presence, beneath this popular gaiety, of a very deep, somewhat ill-defined but still real, feeling. It will be a long time before such a scene is witnessed in Alsace again; for it was *natural*, in no way organized or artificial. You can't give orders to the soul of a people (even less than one can to one's own). And yesterday it was the whole soul of a province that was profoundly happy and gay.—On such occasions, however little one consciously looks for it, one *feels* the reality of the extra-individual world, of the world which takes shape through a union of souls. The feelings you experience and that animate the crowd with one mind, are definitely of a higher order than those experienced in the private life of an individual. You would have to be blind not to see that such an expansion is possible for our own individual souls, and what hopes it opens up for us. I can assure you that yesterday, in the presence of [within] this unanimity, I really understood heaven better, and 'yearned' for it.—At the same time, I saw more clearly than ever that in the great concrete human emotions there is something for which there can (generally speaking) be *no substitute* for arousing and moulding our hearts. Our religion must integrate this or become ossified.—And a final thought that came to my mind as I watched Alsace march past: this people is astonishingly organized and disciplined, beneath its completely French spontaneity and lightheartedness. If only that quality of theirs could spread to us too! . . . To wind up the day yesterday, there was a torchlight procession. The main streets were packed with people. You could have seen me, arms linked with a warrant-officer and a sergeant, following the torches, in a crowd of people arm in arm. It was most amusing to see all this slightly crazy exuberance, with lots of troops making their way through the throng, their *képis* crowned with oak-leaves and their tunics swathed with the tricolour.

You won't mind my telling you of nothing but the celebrations, while you have no lack of cares at the Institute. You know how much I think of you for that very reason.—Remember me to Mme Parion: will she soon be able to go to Switzerland? Always yours in Christo.

PIERRE

Have you the copies of the *Union créatrice*? Anyway, keep them by you.

[Strasbourg] *13th December 1918*

I'm writing to you today, because tomorrow I have to go to Haguenau (to see the wife of one of our captains, killed in July), and on Sunday my morning will be taken up by a high mass.

Well, what have I to tell you since my letter of two days ago?

First of all, I've finished writing and copying out *Forma Christi*[1]. It makes twenty pages, very close-packed with thought, which seem to me to be an advance on what I've written so far (from the point of view of the picture I give our Lord in this world). You'll be the first, of course, to read it. I'll bring you the notebook at the end of the month, if nothing crops up to stop my going to Joseph's wedding. I'm all the more pleased to have finished this new essay, because, having been in preparation for a long time, it was beginning to lose its freshness for me and was stopping me from turning my thoughts to other matters as I should have liked.

Now, I've been able to get back to Schuré, from whom I've had great, but rather complex, pleasure: the joy of finding a mind extremely sympathetic to my own,—the spiritual excitement of making contact with a soul full of enthusiasm for the world,—the satisfaction of realizing that the questions I'm concerned with are indeed those that have animated the deep-rooted life of humanity,—the pleasure of seeing that my attempts at a solution agree perfectly, on the whole, with those of the ' great initiates' without doing any violence to dogma, and (because of the integration of the Christian idea) have at the same time their own very special and original slant. You can readily appreciate that it's a great pleasure and encouragement to me to see so clearly what I can use, and what on the other hand is artificial or unsatisfactory, in Schuré's vision: it makes me feel twice as strong.

Reading this book (which I haven't finished yet) has greatly strengthened, I feel, my conviction of the necessity for the Church to present dogma in a more real, more universal, way

---

[1] cf. Claude Cuénot, *Pierre Teilhard de Chardin.*

—a more ' cosmogonic ' way, if I may put it so. Human consciousness and the very nature of dogma demand this. I've also felt that the problem of creation, looked at not in its present (evolutive) phase but in its first (involutive), is taking on increasing importance in my mind. What is the origin of the lower multiple? What ' need ' is filled by the fundamental fragmentation of being—driven from its source before returning to it? Until this problem is more or less coherently cleared up, one can't, I think, understand the worth of souls and the value of the incarnation ... Apart from this question, which has become more important for me and more exactly defined, I was able, in reading Schuré, to put my finger on the mistake of false mystical systems that, confusing the levels, look for mystery at the phenomenal level,—forcing external realities to their own imagination,—confusing ether, the ' astral medium ' and the *real* mystical medium. I've almost made up my mind to write something on ' mystical science ', to defend from such abuses and place in its real light (glimpsed by Schuré, but with serious errors in perspective), this science of sciences which is also the supreme art and the supreme work. On a first reading, then (for I haven't yet read that chapter thoroughly), I was surprised at the narrowness and incompleteness of Schuré's view of Christ: about the incarnation, the Eucharist, the mystical body —that marvellous temple of esotericism—he has nothing to say!—Whose fault is it if our religion is still, in its most living profundities, unknown to men who claim to have examined all religious revelations in turn?

Side by side with so many flashes of illumination that I do really believe I can find in things—in proportion, I should say, with them—I sometimes feel myself overcome by my powerlessness to make others see them and so spread their light. Where can one find the souls that have vision? How can one bring them into being and associate them, hampered as we are by the countless ties of modern conventions and regulations? ... Not one of my best friends, so far, understands me fully. (Thank God I have you!) To set oneself up as misunderstood seems ridiculous and conceited. And yet, in truth (without, I think, the least touch of conceit) I do believe that I can see something, and I would like that something to be seen. You can't imagine what intensity of desire I sometimes feel in this connexion, and what impotence! What keeps me calm is my complete confidence that if there is a real ray of light in ' my gospel ', somehow or other that ray will shine forth. At the worst—of this I'm sure—it will reappear in another heart,—all the richer, I hope, for having been faithfully guarded in me.—The only wise and Christian attitude is obviously to wait in all loyalty for God's own hour—if it is to come.—I am counting more than ever on the influence of your prayers that I may never fail the light.

In my outside world, no news. I'm continuing to become more and more of a Strasbourger. A calm and happy period, in short. I wish you the same.

Goodbye. Always yours in our Lord.

PIERRE

Strasbourg, 1st January 1919

When we parted yesterday, at Saint-Germain-des-Prés, we forgot only one thing, to wish one another a happy New Year. Now I am sending you that wish from the inmost depths of my heart, and I am charging it with all the fullness of desire, of ambitions and prayers of which I am capable. I would so much like to feel that you are growing more and more within the embrace of ' the one thing that is necessary ', there to find enduring peace! ... In spite of the inevitable ups and downs that you're bound to meet, I believe that you are making progress in this happy direction. I pray that our Lord may light up for you all the heavy clouds that seem to gather almost everywhere on your horizon! and that after having stabilized, this year, the inner side of your life, he may now allow a little unity to spread over the visible matter of your existence!—that was what I asked of him this morning as I said mass, praying that he might sanctify and make use of our friendship more than ever.

I reached Strasbourg yesterday at one o'clock in the afternoon, in lovely bright weather, thanks to which I was able to admire the descent to the Rhine, which is most picturesque: the desolate marshy uplands of Sarrebourg suddenly give way to deep valleys, dug between tabular walls of red sandstone, through which you drop down gently to the plain of Alsace. As I got out of the train I met Beaugeard, also just arriving from Paris but moving on to Mulhouse. I had time to look round the town with him and show him the cathedral. He expects to be demobilized in less than a month's time (his regiment is going to Morocco). Once again we swore not to forget one another after the war. Oddly enough, he's a great friend of Stanislas's present superior, a Breton, as he is. So there are new ' possibilities ' coming to light.

To round off the day, I met Emm. de Margerie at the *Terminus*, where we talked for a long time, with great pleasure on both sides, I think. We discussed everything, science, Alsace, the Church, Rome . . . He brought up the question of the Institut Catholique himself, and promised to go and see Mgr Baudrillart when he gets back. I didn't hide from him that if the place had any interest for me, it was primarily as a ' platform ' for intellectual activity;—and he seemed perfectly happy about that. I think we'll be meeting again before the end of the week.

From what I've told you you'll see that the 4th mixed regiment is still at Strasbourg. It looks as though we still have another week here. Meanwhile, I've gone back to my life at the seminary, though after tomorrow, when the students return, it may not be quite so pleasant.

I didn't want to spoil Wells by reading him in the train. But this morning, just turning over the pages, I came upon sentences like these:[1] ' One's individual existence is not so entirely cut off as it seems at first; one's entirely separate individuality is another, a profounder, among the subtle inherent

[1] *First and Last Things*, by H. G. Wells, book II, section 8.

delusions of the human mind' (in italics).—'Between you and me ... there is *something*, something real, something that rises through us and is neither you nor me, that comprehends us, that is thinking here and using me and you to play against each other ...' 'I think this real solidarity of humanity is a fact that is only being slowly apprehended, that it is an idea that we who have come to realize it have to assist in thinking into the collective mind ...' 'I see myself in life as part of a great physical being that strains and I believe grows towards beauty ...' Wells recognizes that this whole concept underlies all his novels and is developed in them (I must say that I've recognized it in him and felt it to be there, for a long time, as in Kipling and Benson) ... very, odd, isn't it?

All these convergences of view, and the popularity of this new (and very ancient) gospel, are dazzling flashes of illumination for me, and at the same time make painful impact upon me. That, and much more than that, is what I'd like to say (and it's *that* that *must* be said to the world of today, if it is to be saved). Will anyone ever listen to me?

Goodbye. Tell me everything that happens about the various matters that call for your attention: Robert, Mme Parion, the question of the will etc.—and may our Lord be your solid and universal joy.

Always yours in him,

PIERRE

Strasbourg, 5th January 1919

The day before yesterday I received your note of the 31st, the pictures (which are excellent), and the Psalter (which I've started using). You mustn't regret the shadow of sadness that came over you during the days we saw one another. First of all, what I like more than anything is to see you as you really are. And then, these limitations that Providence often imposes on our dearest joys are God's most effective way of reminding us of, and intensifying in us, his presence: this is a thing we must never forget: the life of our Lord never triumphs more within us than when we suffer diminishment [when we feel diminished] within him. Don't forget, will you, to keep me informed about your various worries?

Since my last letter, I have to tell you that I've spent a day at Colmar with Emm. de Margerie—such an excellent person. It was a real delight to have a few hours with him. The only pity is that Colmar, in spite of its old-world Alsatian charm, is so poor in geological material and sights. We were only just able at the last moment, by climbing up on to a footbridge, to make out the panorama to the east: the volcanic massif of the Kaisersfuhl, rearing itself up from the open plain, on the right bank of the Rhine,—the Black Forest,—and, right in the distance, the Swiss Oberland silhouetted against the clear sky like a huge jagged saw. Emmanuel de M. has a really prodigious store of learning, and it's almost exhausting to feel how much above one's head is his familiarity with Alsatian problems. I found him quite determined to support regionalism in the field of scientific institutions. But he seemed to me terribly sceptical about the chances of progress open to the human species. If so, I don't at all see what can maintain in him his zest for research, and a sort of patriotic fire.—One more reason why we should both of us interest ourselves in him.—When we parted, he told me again that he wouldn't delay in seeing Mgr Baudrillart.—About the success of that step, I really don't know what I think or want in my heart of hearts. I see that the attempt should be made and that there would be great advantages if it were successful. But if it fails, I shan't more than half regret it. I am confident that our Lord will guide me.—What seems to me increasingly clear is that I shall be able to carry my gospel only ' to those who seek ' and only by urging them to ' seek still further '. I shall say so in so many words to my superiors and those who have influence on the external development of my future. At the moment I'm collecting, under the title ' Notes towards the evangelization of new times ', the views I've expressed here and there in my various essays: it will make a brief plan for an apostolate or, if you prefer it, a manifesto, which I'll show to my friends in the hope of initiating a movement and bringing into being some schemes for practical institutions.

On the whole, they were happy days, those of the war, when I lived and thought as though there were no one but myself!— I feel a certain nervousness as I see the time approaching when there'll be conflicts, frictions, disappointments ... But that, after all, is the law that governs all effort.—To create anything at all, you have to stand up against inertia, or even worse than inertia. It means more than ever to me to feel that you are close to God, and with me.

I've been looking through Wells again. It's often rather an annoying book, because of the complete ignorance of Catholicism he displays. Wells attributes ridiculous views to us, and he has no understanding at all of the real interior life of the Christian. All the same, there's much to be learnt from his accusations, for they show us what we can look like (partly through our own fault) to outsiders.—What is really interesting, in the book, is the development in Wells of a real mysticism of human effort, the phases of which, he explains, are recorded in his novels. As a writer, there's nothing of the dilettante about him; he's a man who all his life has sought for the truth.—Have we a single novelist like him in France?

Goodbye. You know how much I am yours in Christo.

PIERRE

Strasbourg, 8th January 1919

I've let myself get a bit behind-hand with you because of drawing up my little ' manifesto ',[1] which I've almost finished today. Here and there, I've used rather forceful language, but I believe I've never said more than I sincerely believe, nor written without

[1] ' Notes towards the evangelization of new times ', written on the Feast of the Epiphany at Strasbourg.

an over-riding love for the Church that alone can assure us the joy of possessing our Lord. What I have primarily tried to do, is to make myself understood by friends: and so I've sought above all to be straightforward and clear. I'm thinking of sending the thing first to Père Léonce, with a letter explaining it. I trust him to guide me, to suggest practical methods (if occasion arises) and also at the right time to influence my superiors' decisions. Don't forget to pray a little for me, will you?—I'm particularly fond of this Epiphany season. Doesn't our happiness lie in being present at a revelation of our Lord in all things, and isn't it our dearest wish to spread abroad that vision? I pray specially for you, at my mass, that we may always be more at one in this light and this zeal . . .

I'm thinking of you as being alone now, coping with the immediate cares and the grim outlook of a difficult term . . . I'd so much like to be able to help you a little, and make you see how fundamentally divine is your monotonous and exacting work. I haven't heard from you since the 31st; I'm not surprised, because I know how busy you are and how irregular the mail; but I'd like to know what's happening to Robert, and Mme Parion and the others. Keep me up to date, won't you? No news here for the last three days. I've discovered the excellent Cottreau in Strasbourg, a tower of strength in the museum's laboratory, and mad about sea-urchins,—at the moment a second lieutenant in the territorials. Tomorrow we're going to renew our youth by a visit to the university collections.

Goodbye. Just a short letter, this time, but you know how much I am thinking of you, in Christo.

PIERRE

Strasbourg, 11th January 1919

I've just had your long letter of the 9th (after your brief line of the 5th), which confirms in me the anxiety about Robert that has been difficult to keep at bay for the last three months. What

can I say to you that you don't already know about the really
brotherly share I have in your distress, and about the wishes
I entertain for you? I am praying, of course, a great deal for
the health you hold so dear. And I am offering an equally heart-
felt prayer to our Lord that he may give full reality to the mystery
you glimpse in the shadows that now surround you. While
neglecting nothing that may assist the cure we must believe to
be possible, abandon yourself to the power of him who, in
order to have you for his own, uses the effect on you of a painful
and *ordinary* trial, as he has so often already allowed to happen
in your life. In spite of the fundamental, prime, importance
I've always been led to attribute to human effort and development,
I realize that the soul begins to know God only when it is forced
really to suffer diminishment within him. So abandon yourself
to our Lord and let yourself be borne up by him, won't you?
Beneath what seems empty and menacing, you'll find a solidity
proof against all the ups and downs and sorrows of conventional
life,—you'll attain the unique reality, that replaces everything
else.

I'm glad you had such a frank talk with M. V.[1] That's what
I expect of you in many things.—About my *Note sur l'Apostolat*,
I sent it yesterday to Père de Gdm.[2] with a very frank letter.
(You won't be annoyed that I didn't give it to you first, will
you? It wouldn't have told you much that you didn't know
already, and in any case I'll be showing it to you.) You might
perhaps have found in that *Note* too explicit an expression of
what I think, but I felt it was better to speak frankly in an explanation that amounts, in fact, to a disclosure of conscience. Before
sending it to any one else, I'll wait to see what Père Léonce
thinks about it.

I'm still reading Wells with interest. A whole section of the
book[3] is a sincere, but very bitter, criticism of the Christian
God, a criticism that might have a very unfortunate effect on
an untrained mind. I told you before that Wells's judgment of

[1] M. Verdier. [2] Père Léonce de Grandmaison, s.j.
[3] *God, the Invisible King.*

275

us (he knows Christianity only through Protestantism) is most unreasonable. But even when he exaggerates he's instructive, because he shows us what we look like to outsiders, and what, at the present moment, are the unforgivable 'faults against the world or against humanity' that a religion can be guilty of. Apart from these 'impieties' (and there's no doubt they're both distasteful and—since we ourselves unfortunately lend them some colour of truth—plausible), Wells's religion is extremely noble, and instils virtues of work and renunciation that are completely admirable and in harmony with my own ideal. It's odd to note how the Trinity, so fundamental a dogma for Schuré, is a red rag to a bull for Wells, even though at bottom Wells and Schuré are 'of the same mind'. This paradox is explained by the radical agnosticism Wells professes about the creator of the *whole universe:* Wells refuses to take any cosmogony seriously and confines himself to the future of *mankind.* His religion, in short, is an anthropogony. However, within this (quite arbitrarily so, it seems to me) restricted field, his feelings are completely those of a pantheist,—with this capital difference that according to him the God in whom we struggle and are absorbed so that he may be fulfilled is a personal being, distinct from us.—Wells says that one could almost always substitute 'Jesus Christ' for his 'finite God' (with this difference, that he cannot say whether the finite God is subject to or in revolt against the Veiled Being creator of the world . . .): he doesn't realize how much truer this is than he thinks.—For the existence of his God, Wells adduces no proof other than the religious experiences of 'conversion' and of 'the feeling of a presence', and the fact that there exists a 'consensus' universally reached in men's souls, that assumes some God similar to his own. In other words, he falls back on intuition. Aren't we all forced to do more or less the same with *faith*?

When I've finished the book, I'll send it to you, with some comparisons between Wells and Benson. On the whole, reading it has again confirmed me in what I suggest for 'the religious needs of new times'.—I'm often astonished at the timeliness with which books that are 'musts' come into my hands at just the right moment. And it gives me great pleasure to note that these gifts of Providence come to me through you.

Good news from Sarcenat [. . .]

No news so far as I'm concerned.

Always yours in Christo.

PIERRE

Strasbourg, 14th January 1919

I'm sending you by this same post that very good and very bad book, Wells's *God, the Invisible King*. Right up to the end, in spite of the 'impieties' it's littered with, I found a strange kinship with my own aspirations. Isn't this an odd situation that I'm in, of being reckoned (and in fact being) among the orthodox, and yet feeling with the heterodox? I hope that this dualism is allowed by our Lord in order that I may be able more easily to act as a link between the two. But you can well imagine that it doesn't make for interior tranquillity.

You asked me to make a rough parallel between Wells and Benson. This is how I'd compare them:

(1) As I understand them (and feel them) both have the basic vision of some immediate and universal divinity. It is this that feeds their deep-seated passion. Both, no doubt, have at some time experienced the natural ' revelation' (described at length by W. James in his *Varieties of Religious Experience*) of an omnipresence in the world. (Wells, pp. 27-8,—Benson, *The Green Robe*, and in *None other Gods*: the morning ' scene '.)

(2) Both, then, try to transfigure (intellectually, in their perception of things,—and actively, in their work) the face of the universe by ceaseless activity. For Wells, the whole effort lies in human will. For Benson, a providence controls, integrates (without cutting across) the forces of determinism (*None other Gods*), or the soul is seen as a ceaseless worker, with the power to influence the universe (*The Convent Chapel*);—the soul, absorbed

277

because ' busy inside ' (*None other Gods*)=for both of them, the supreme human happiness (exactly ' on the lines of W. James ') is to *work upon* (*operari*) the world.

(3) Starting from this basic attitude, common to both of them, Wells and Benson then part company completely.

(a) Wells confines himself strictly to humanity. His ideal, his God, resides in ultimate human success—(actually a very vague objective)—certainly, in Wells's mind *super-human*,—that in any case rules out every sort of selfishness or holding-back.

In his pursuit of this ideal, Wells shows completely individual preferences that another person (even if he shared Wells's ideas) might well contest. Wells (although extremely ardent) is concerned exclusively with *external* activity, and *never* treats anything emotively. Like William James, too, (who's very hard on St Aloysius Gonzaga, for example) he doesn't understand that interior recollection, a certain ascesis, are matchless forces, even for natural human development. This is an Anglo-Saxon shortcoming. Wells's religion is too exclusively a ' sacred ' dusiness.

(b) Benson is quite the contrary. He sees the new universe emerging *from the ruins* of the old. *Christ in the Church, None other Gods, Lord of the World*, are typical of this view. The kingdom of God is won by *human failure*.—The divergence from Wells is widened still further by Benson's *personal* character, for he is notoriously *emotive* in his mysticism.

—*The Lord of the World* provides an interesting comparison between the two writers. Felsenburgh's reign is fairly close to the divine kingdom that Wells hopes for (except, of course, that the realization is still much too human, and that rather too much stress is laid on the actual cult—see Wells, Chapter 5). Wells certainly sees the kingdom of God as taking the form of a state (Chapter 7, para. 5) such as that realized by Felsenburgh. Benson rejects all that, and yet at the same time he paints much too vivid a picture, to my mind, of the world's humanitarian enthusiasm, not to have suffered ' the temptation '—by which

I mean, not to share Wells's fundamental attitude, as I said at the beginning. In several passages, it seems to me, of the *Lord of the World*, Benson has not been true to himself.

For my part, I believe the truth to lie between the two of them, by which I mean that one can conceive the kingdom of God as cutting across the kingdom of man, going beyond it, integrating it, *without destroying it.*

Kipling seems to me a third ' harmonic ' of the same basic note, just as Wells, in his various novels, is the scientific citizen of the physical and biological universe,—Kipling is the English citizen of the inhabited living world. Without actually presenting in his books any definite philosophy or theology, in practice he *feels with the whole earth*: his books make you live with animals, they make ships and locomotives speak, they make you feel with the eastern soul, give you an insight into a theosophical existence, send you on a voyage through all the countries of the world.—He has a way of talking about the desert and the joy of being alone and free in it, that rings true. Practically speaking, his moral attitude is the same as Wells's: his religion is that of human effort.

In short, Benson, Kipling and Wells seem to me to be three different forms of the same profound feeling for the universe [of the same profound awareness of man's immersion in the universe] [and of the possibility of human action on the universe] (in Kipling's *The Light that Failed*, a story about an artist who loses everything, including his sight, one might find a pendant to *None other Gods*: Kipling's hero, with his whole world in ruins, kills himself, on his camel in the middle of the desert. There's a sort of grand, stoical, surrender to fate in his suicide which isn't as different as one might think from the final scene in Benson's novel.)

Yesterday I began to work at the Strasbourg Mining Institute. Since I can find books there of the same sort as those at the museum, the illusion is complete. The only thing is, you're not at Strasbourg! . . .

Everything goes as it should. I think a great deal about

you, and most of all in our Lord.   Write to me,—and particularly about your worries.

PIERRE

P.S.—A final word about Wells's book: you couldn't, I think, imagine a more touching call towards some divine *immediacy*.

I enclose a photograph of Alsatian costumes that you probably haven't seen.

Sarcenat, 1st February 1919

You must be finding me rather silent.   However, I've had your last little note, in which you tell me about your various troubles. I pray that the shadows that lie over your soul may soon be dispersed, and allow you to see in all things, brighter than ever, the light of our Lord,—to whom you are being brought closer, borne on the monotonous waves of day to day commitments.

I'm glad that we'll soon be able to talk together.   I expect to be in Paris on the 6th or 7th, for a day or two.—No news about my affairs.   I've written to M. d'Alès, asking him to try to have some useful tips to pass on to me as I go through.   Fundamentally, I'm quite easy in my mind about the result of the line I'm pursuing—as much for logical reasons as from inclination.

Although one battalion of the 4th mixed has crossed the Rhine, I believe the bulk of the regiment has remained at Strasbourg, and it's there I'll spend my last fortnight in the army.   I'll be demobilized on February 27th, probably.

My life here is still just the same: in the chimney corner at Guiguite's, when I'm not in Clermont.   I don't have much time for thinking of many things that come to my mind: but the conversations I'm having, particularly with Père Treuvey[1] (of whom I think a great deal, and who is very fond of me—though yesterday we had to agree that we really don't think along the same lines)—these conversations are forcing me to clarify a

[1] A fellow Jesuit.

number of points in my mind and are suggesting quite a number of questions I'll have to work out in writing . . . What makes me easier in my mind at this juncture, is that the rather hazardous schematic points in my teaching are in fact of only secondary importance to me. It's not nearly so much ideas that I want to propagate as *a spirit*: and a *spirit* can animate almost all external presentations.

[. . .]

Goodbye. You'll be very much in my prayers tomorrow. May our Lady help you to bear as bravely as she did a heart full of cares.

Thank Mme Parion for her note from Guétary.

Always yours, in our Lord.

PIERRE

[*Goldscheuer*] *12th February 1919*

After an excellent and comfortable journey I rejoined the regiment on the other side of the Rhine. So goodbye to city life. I'm in billets 8 kilometres south-east of Kehl, right in the Baden country, and in other ways I've really nothing to complain about. On the recommendation of a *curé* (no fanatic, I may say) I've found a lodging with two good old pious peasants, who are completely devoted to me;—religion, with them, being combined with a sort of obsequiousness, as with all the local people. It's completely flat country, abounding in hares and pheasants, of which we get our share. The Black Forest is only some twenty kilometres from us, but so far it's been hidden by a light mist. The village consists of neat little houses in rows, each standing in a garden full of fruit trees. Yesterday evening, with the moon shining, and snow on the ground, and lights in the windows, it was like looking at a huge German Christmas card. So now I'm cut off from Strasbourg and the university. I'm not sorry. These last three weeks in the regiment will be more pleasant and profitable for me, I think, if they're spent in the peace of the fields. It was with real pleasure, though with some sadness in it, that I rejoined my old 4th mixed. Of course, this sort of life couldn't go on ... Still, the war brought me, in the regiment, a group of unassuming and open-hearted friendships, in an atmosphere of complete disinterestedness and devotion, that I doubt whether I'll ever find again. And then there was the life of adventure and freedom from care that will be gone for ever next month. It's no wonder if I regret it a little. As the 13th area is being demobilized almost at the end of the formation, I won't get away before March 5th—which is only a week later than I expected. I'm hoping to get some writing done in between, as I told you. At the same time as this letter to you, I'm sending one to Lyons, giving my plan for study during the coming months. I'll probably have an answer before the end of the month.

And now, as you know yourself, there's no need for me to tell you again how much I enjoyed the days we've just spent together and how much I am hoping that, in one form or another, the friendship that we both need so much will continue to grow and sustain us. It's quite true: you were given to me for the war. But what we both gained during those five years should still be put to good use. Moreover, what can divide those whom the love of our Lord makes one? As I've said before, I'm sure to need you very much, to tell you what I'm feeling and doing. As the time approaches when decisions are implemented one's difficulties seem to become greater and one's hopes fainter. And that's no time to withdraw the help we can give one another.

I pray that the shadows that surround you and enter into your soul—particularly these recent ones—may soon disappear. Never let these periods of darkness dishearten you. Now that you know the right direction, press on unshaken. The light will shine again closer at hand. Again, as we were saying, foster a great love for him who, when seen by the eyes of faith, animates the whole complex of exterior events and interior experiences. Is there any better way of understanding and enjoying intimacy with the divine than the knowledge that our Lord is at the heart of all that moves us? Have unbounded trust, and may all your thoughts and searchings end in a feeling of complete abandonment to the infallible and loving guidance of God. And, that this may be so, reject every other feeling and even every other personal pseudo-evidence.

I hope this letter will reach you quickly. Give my very best regards to Mme Parion. I'll write again soon.

PIERRE

Goldscheuer, Saturday 15th February 1919

I'm writing on my return from a walk through the marshy meadows that border the Rhine. There's any amount of hares, pheasants and ducks, and I watched a number of successful shots and still more misses. The mess larder's well stocked. This evening, the wintry fog dispersed with the thaw and there was an excellent view of the Black Forest, which, for a Frenchman, has even more glamour and romance than the Vosges. In the distance you could make out, between the poplars, the tall spires of Strasbourg, with which there's no doubt many of my most pleasant memories are associated.

You see that country life has sent me back to walking and the open air. Even so, I'm still doing some work, particularly in the mornings. I haven't yet got down to the Essay you're thinking of;—but I'm devoting a few pages to clarifying some ideas that occurred to me last week, in discussions with the de Margeries. I'm trying to express clearly what *remains to us* from the war effort among the disappointments of peace,—and I'm trying to show that it's the awareness we acquired, for a moment, of the spiritual strength contained in unity. I'm calling it ' *Terre Promise* '.[1] I had thought, at first, of writing it for Père de Grandmaison;—but now seeing where the argument led to logically, I think that the manuscript will go to the same

[1] cf. Claude Cuénot, *Pierre Teilhard de Chardin.*

283

place as *La Grande Monade*[1]. At any rate, I'll have clarified one more idea. Your little letter of the 12th gave me great pleasure, as you can imagine. The day after I'd written to you, I had a line from Monsieur Chauvin[2], in reply to my first letter (written from Clermont). He sees no objection in principle to my going to the Institut Catholique, and even recognizes that it might be the best thing for me. But the real point will be what he thinks of the plan for a doctorate. The more I think of it, the more I feel that the Institut Catholique will fall through. This prospect doesn't disturb me in the least. I feel that I've completely made up my mind to follow what I increasingly believed to be the logical course, and seek my home in the ' *milieu mystique* ' . . .

For this, and other reasons, the vicissitudes of the new armistice leave me pretty well unmoved. It's almost a pity that my demobilization will come round so soon! I'd have had a chance to see a little more of Germany.

Goodbye. Forgive me for writing rather briefly. It's the fault of this evening's shoot. Kind messages to Mme Parion, and always very much yours in Christo.

PIERRE

Goldscheuer, 19th February 1919

I've just had your nice letter of the 15th. Thank you for what you say. Your friendship will always, indeed, be very dear to me. I'm still living in my quiet village, where I divide my days between writing and, sometimes, walking. For the last few days, I've been deserting the Rhine to go eastwards, to various villages in which our battalions are billeted. So I've been into

[1] Written 15 January 1918, from Vertus. cf. Claude Cuénot: *Pierre Teilhard de Chardin.*

[2] Père Chauvin, s.j., Provincial of the Lyons Province from September 1918.

the neutral zone, which doesn't of course differ outwardly at all from the rest of the countryside, though you can't help feeling a particular attraction in taking a walk through it. A final sentry-box marks the spot where the occupied zone ends. It seems that even beyond this the natives aren't lacking in obligingness towards us. I had the advantage of taking these last walks in extraordinarily clear, even though rainy, weather, which allowed me to enjoy an admirable view. The Black Forest stood out like purple velvet against a rain-washed sky. You could distinguish all the peaks, the perspective, and sometimes even the contours of the woods; and the mountainous ridge stretched away as far as the eye could reach to the south. I have an idea that a month from now I'll be cherishing the memory of my present life and freedom ...

I must tell you, too, that I've finished the *Terre Promise*, and sent it (not without some hesitation) to Père de Grandmaison, not so much for publication—I've no illusions about that—as in order to get his advice and let him see what definite line of thought I'm adopting. I've already begun, and got well into, the *Elément universel*, for which, as you know, my ideas were already matured. It won't be long,—but clear and substantial. It will, I think, be the most central exposition of my ideas that I've yet produced. And so I'll be able to make good use of it to let people know and assess my position, in a *private* way. I find it interesting to look back on the road I've travelled since three years ago (exactly), when I wrote *La Vie cosmique*. I find that I'm now concerned with just the same problems and see them in just the same way,—but I have them much straighter in my mind and have a better grip on them ... You know (I've told you, and anyway you can guess it) how much I feel, at the moment, that the future is *yawning* before me. I realize that now is the time when I must choose the *tangible point* on which to direct my effort;—but I can't see clearly where that point lies. —It's the time, you know, to have faith, to pray, and to remember that the road will become plain as we advance.

No answer yet, of course, from Père Chauvin, to my second

285

letter. I'm thinking of your lecture on Sunday. Kind regards to Mme Parion—and always yours in Christo.

PIERRE

Goldscheuer, 22nd February 1919

I'm sending you by this post a little notebook containing the *Elément universel*. You'll find that, basically, there's not much in it that you're not already familiar with. I'm sending it, in fact, chiefly in order to ask you to have it typed, when you can, with as many copies as possible (three, or five, or six—I don't know). I'm proposing to use this statement of my position, rather than others, for private circulation. (Tell me what it costs—I'm all right for money.)

Yesterday I had a favourable answer from Père Chauvin. He thinks it a good plan that I should go to Paris, even if it's not to the Institut Catholique, and says that he has decided to let me continue with geology. How much I'm longing now to get free, and to be finished with all the military and religious formalities of release, and so get back to work! I've come, these days, to realize one very elementary fact: that the best way to win some sort of recognition for my ideas would be for me myself to attain, in the truest possible sense of the word, to a ' sanctity ' that will be manifest to others—not only because of the particular force God would then give to whatever good is in my aspirations and influence,—but also because nothing can give me more authority over men than for them to see me as someone who speaks to them from close to God. With God's help, I must live my ' vision ' fully, logically, and without deviation. There's nothing more infectious than the example of a life governed by conviction and principle. And now I feel sufficiently drawn to and sufficiently equipped for, such a life. All this, of course, only so long as I am completely faithful to our Lord and his light.

I'm thinking of you giving your lecture on Benson tomorrow.

You must tell me about it. Who knows that you may not kindle the light invisible in some of your audience? I am so convinced, you know, that in spite of the rarity of those who can see it,—all of us, fundamentally, stand in need of it.

Still another ten days in the regiment! I really don't know how to occupy myself during this last spell. I expect there'll be odds and ends to pass the time. I still haven't been back to Strasbourg, although there are a number of people I should see there, apart from the pleasure it would give me to see the town again. I'll manage it, I expect, some time this week.

Goodbye. Remember me to Mme Parion.

Always yours in Christo.

PIERRE

Goldscheuer, 28th February 1919

Yesterday I received Mme Parion's letter of the 24th. I expect she'll have had mine of the 26th. Tell her, please, how grateful I am to her for the news she gave me, and how sorry I am for her for the death of her friend Trannoy: I said mass for him this morning. And you—you must try to get some rest, and make up for last week's sleepless nights. You know how glad I shall be to hear what you yourself thought about your Benson lecture. I expect that now, as soon as you have some leisure, you'll be writing your little essay on the Feminine and Feminism.—By now, I hope, you'll have received my last notebook and the letter with it.

So this, as far as I can see, will be my penultimate letter to you from the regiment. It's still the 5th that I'm to leave, for Haguenau at first—and then for the 13th area, by some slow train and roundabout route. As I told you, I hardly think I can be in Paris before the end of March. These last days in the army are going quite quickly and pleasantly enough. But I feel I'm rather (even too) acutely impatient and anxious about the new career that'll soon start for me. I've always been nervous about

287

the possibilities the future holds for me—and the war had got rid of that worry for me. I ought to be able to transform this irksome tendency into fuller union with God, since I feel that I'm being forced, if I am to master myself, to wait from day to day on the plans of Providence and to attach myself 'absolutely' only to the ambition to possess him. When I was writing the *Elément universel*, I remembered some things that Françoise said to me—when she was already a Little Sister—about the unique and beatifying importance that the *reality* of God had assumed in her life;—and I felt that I understood that we were fundamentally much more like one another than I had thought before. The only thing was that she was following a road where the realities of this world were much more effaced or left behind than happens with me.

I was in Strasbourg the day before yesterday, and it was a real joy to see its well-known streets again and its familiar shops. The evening before I had met Père de la Brière [1] at the seminary, and even the Superior, Baudrillart! I wouldn't have missed seeing, at the same time also (as in fact I did) the professor of geology at the university, Gignoux (a friend of Boussac, whom I'd seen in Grenoble in July 1914). As it happened, he had gone to Mulhouse to see the potassium deposits. I'm going back there tomorrow, which will make one more day go quickly. I paid a visit, of course, to the cathedral, which I found by chance silent and recollected. Not having been able to go there for two months made me appreciate it more than ever. I said a special prayer there for you.

Goodbye. I told you, didn't I, that Père Chauvin approves of my stay in Paris being prolonged?

Always yours in Christo.

PIERRE

---

[1] Père Yves de la Brière, s.j., a leading authority on international law, who for a long time edited the section of *Études* dealing with current religious affairs.

Goldscheuer, 5th March 1919

Thanks for your last letter, and for the details you give of your lecture. I very much hope that you'll manage to publish something about Benson. It will serve as a ready-made introduction to your own stories. As for me, I've had a long letter from Père de Grandmaison. *Terre Promise*, of course, will never be printed; —I expected that. At any rate, Père Léonce takes my views seriously,—and that's something achieved already. I realize that in this last essay I've attributed a considerable importance to human views of progress,—which obviously lays it open to a good many objections. I wrote back to Père de Gdm. at equal length; and I believe that my position in this matter remains pretty clear. I didn't tell you, I think, that I had a letter from my friend Père Charles[1], from Louvain,—who is on the road to becoming an important figure in his own country. He told me that, for his part, he has succeeded in defining some ideas that he believes to be 'liberalizing' and wishes that we could meet soon. I am just as anxious for the meeting to take place; Père Charles is more of a theologian than I am, and more practical; he could give me valuable advice and strong moral support.

So here I am on the eve of leaving the regiment. Tomorrow I'm off to Haguenau. The day after I leave for Clermont in a troop train. So I'll not be going through Paris. But that will come soon. I expect to stay two or three days at Clermont, go to Lyons, make a retreat as soon as possible,—and then get down to work in Paris. This return to peace would be much more attractive to me if it weren't for the prospect (rather restricting) of exams to pass. However, a man's strength and his faith in God are shown by his tenacity and patience in pressing on where duty lies, whatever one may feel about less important things.

I fear that I'll be rather a long time without news of you. You know that you can always write to me through Sarcenat. I'm counting on hearing from you there.

[1] Père Charles, a Belgian Jesuit, a professor at Louvain and author of a volume of meditations, *Prayer at all Times*.

And now, since this is my last letter from the 4th mixed, let me assure you again of all the depth and constancy of my affection. You have meant a great deal to me during these four years,—more, perhaps, than you imagine. I trust, more earnestly than ever, that in one form or another our Lord will unite us in an effort that brings us closer to him. All I want, you know, is to see you completely at peace and with your hopes resting on him.

Remember me to Mme Parion, and always yours.

PIERRE

Paris, *14th April 1919*

I'm writing to you from the museum lab., where I've come to spend the afternoon;—an afternoon of wind and rain, which makes me glad to think that none of it has reached you, in your blue radiance. It seems most odd to be writing to you again; just as when I was in the 4th mixed,—and yet so far from it. Basically, of course, you're quite right: it's good for friends to be separated sometimes; it makes them collect and clarify what they have to say to one another, and forces them to put it into words. I told you that, with you away, Paris rather gives me the impression of being empty. What makes up for this, I think, is that affection then becomes more concentrated and spiritualized. That's why letters have something that conversation can't be a substitute for.

Since Saturday, I've been on holiday, too. And even without getting away from the noisy streets, I am feeling the beneficial effect of a rest from my studies. I am really enjoying the quiet hours spent in my *Vieux-Colombier*[1]. To start off the holiday I went on Saturday to the Avenue de Madrid. It was a real clearing-up of all the ideas that came into my head that day. 'Serious' conversation began with the first dish, and I was hard at it until about six in the evening. On the whole I got

[1] Père Teilhard was living at this time in the Rue Vieux-Colombier.

as much as I gave, and I don't regret the time I spent. Mlle Z.'s [1] two young friends were there, and her nephew, the lieutenant who's convalescing. The youngest B. is still a *Bak fisch* [2], as the Germans say, and, seeing that he's only sixteen he's not unnaturally at the awkward age for philosophy. Still, he's amusing, but might well, I fear, go rather seriously astray. The elder is much more interesting. Although he's not yet quite certain of where he stands, he's a good example of one of those minds that are seduced by 'the other God' (by which I mean the great Universe) and who approaches that God in a spirit of religion. As you can imagine, I felt quite at home on that ground. I only pray that I didn't say too many silly things, and that some little grace found its way to him with my words. I feel we got on well with one another. We arranged to meet again some time at the museum, by the fossils and the man of the Chapelle-aux-Saints. After the disciples had left I stayed on for a good while talking to Mlle Z. She introduced me to some aspects of stoic pantheism that were quite new to me. And then we looked through Duhamel's *La Possession du Monde*. (I've heard elsewhere that it's making a great sensation.) So far as I could judge, the book is practically a presentation (vaguer and more longwinded) of what I tried to express in the section ' *Communion avec la Terre* ' of the *Vie cosmique*. I was glad in a way to realize this (for it showed me once again that it is indeed there, in the passion for some tangible absolute, that you touch the sensitive spot in the soul of today);—at the same time, it left me a little sad; while Duhamel has run through four editions, the *Vie cosmique*, and similar things, are tucked away among my papers or with some of my friends. And yet it's so much better put there (more precisely, more objectively) than in what the general public are going wild about. So we see that our Lord can still, more than ever, excite our generation! . . . However, there it is: half the success of a book like Duhamel's is due to its lack of precision. He makes his readers feel that they are in touch with the divine, and then he leaves them without pointing out

[1] Mademoiselle Zanta.   [2] i.e. *Back-fisch*, teenager, youngster.

to them the inexorable necessity of renunciation, the basic condemnation of selfishness and following the line of least resistance,
that are to be found in *La Possession du Monde*. And then, one
of these readers—his name, say, is Donnay,—writes from the
Côte d'Azur, where he's feasting his eyes on the sun, the green
vegetation, the sea, that he's really in the divine ambiance, but
that the Christian God, and grace, and the supernatural seem to
him more alien and distant than ever. Christianity has been
accused of sowing a seed of disquiet in the serenity of paganism.
I believe, on the contrary, that this disquiet is part of the very
essence of the world—I'd even go so far as to say of matter.
As you know, I've always been attracted by the idea of writing
a hymn to ' the spiritual power of matter'.

I should add that in spite of, or because of, this enthusiasm
I am rather sharply conscious, these days, of the ' limitations '
of life. The more I see that I'm in my own proper context, and
(apparently, at least) in a position to get into action, the more
I come up against obstacles that prevent me from ' producing '
and from giving myself,—which send me back to the school-
room,—and which will perhaps prevent me from ever having
a ' platform '. Indeed, although I've been thrown into the
world that suits me best, I'm cut off from it by a conjunction of
circumstances that prevent me from raising the cup to my lips
and from profiting by what I take hold of. It's really the time
when, as my dearest convictions tell me, I should be finding
unique joy in the divine that enters into me more fully I believe
through this road than through any other . . . Still, you know,
it's not always easy to master the impressions one feels.—Pray
that I may cling more closely than ever to ' the one thing that
is necessary ' now that I'm labouring under the limitations—in
fact, they're a blessing, too—that Providence imposes on me.

Forgive this scribble. I'm hurrying to finish this letter so
that I can send it off to bring you all the sooner my constant
thoughts of you in our Lord.

PIERRE

Paris Good Friday, 1919 [20th April]

I've had your card of Tuesday and I feel that I couldn't find a better day to answer it than today. In writing to you, I bring my own thought closer to yours, guided by the most vital influence to be found here below (that of our dying Lord),—and it may be, I hope, that this letter will reach you on Easter morning. I like to think that there will be sunshine and peace in your heart that morning, whatever may be your external circumstances— peace that is born from trust in him who conquered death, in him, that is, who can cause every diminution we suffer to be transformed into a growth of life in him. You well knew, of course, that I would share in your anxiety when I learnt that you found Robert going through not such a good spell. In that connexion, too, I very much hope that Easter may bring some improvement, and, so far as possible, dispel any distress Robert and you may be feeling. You see, Marg, the more I feel the depth of my affection for you, the more I want to see you firmly, deeply, centred on God alone. I see so clearly that you and I, of all people, cannot be happy in any other way. I am being less recollected during these holy days than I would wish. Paris is a bad place to find solitude in. All the same, I've been struck by the insistence with which the Church constantly repeats the final refrain ' *Christus factus est obediens usque ad mortem crucis* '. That's obviously the exact and profound significance of the cross: obedience, submission to the law of life. To work patiently until death,—and to accept everything, in a spirit of love, including death: there you have the essence of Christianity.—Believe me, you should cast away all vain regret for the past and all vague anxiety for the future. Concentrate on obedience to God, as, day by day, his will becomes manifest. In half an hour's time I'm off to hear some of the singing at St-Germain-l'Auxerrois. After that I'll make the stations of the cross. I'll be thinking, while I do so, that the two of us are before our Lord, and that once again we are surrendering ourselves to him so that he may lead us where he wills. No news to speak of since my letter on Monday. Even without lectures, I have more to do than I can fit into the day. For some mornings now I've been writing *Les Noms de la matière*.[1] I expect I'll finish it tomorrow. It makes quite a readable little essay, and could serve as an introduction to *The Spiritual Power of Matter*. I've begun reading —and rather enjoying—*Le Feu*.[2]—Transformation of matter! There's plenty of that problem in it!

[. . .]

Goodbye. Mind you benefit from the blue skies and sunshine.

Always yours,

PIERRE

[*Paris*] *24th April 1919*

You must be thinking that I'm being very slow in answering your long letter written on Holy Saturday.—It gave me, however, a great deal of pleasure,—a little pain, too, since in it you were obliged to speak again of things that cause you distress. It's quite true, the gayest and most tranquil exterior may hide a tortured soul; but surely that's only one more reason for finding that other blue sky and that other sun that shine on all things from within and leave no room for any internal shadow. I rather hope your next news may be happier, and in particular that you'll have been able to profit from a period of real silence and real rest. You know that my thoughts and prayers are constantly with you.

My life here isn't too unpleasant, except that time goes so quickly that I can't do half I plan to do,—except, also, that my Paris is not quite complete without you. I've finished the little essay I mentioned to you: there's nothing very brilliant in it

[1] This, written in Paris (Easter, 1919) introduces *The Spiritual Power of of Matter*, written in Jersey in the summer of the same year.

[2] Gabriel d'Annunzio's novel.

but it will serve to ' ram home ' the foundations of various other things. Besides this, I've been reading, very slowly, *Le Feu*, which interests me because I find in it a very definite pantheistic position, at once very akin to and very distinct from that which I am trying to analyse and bring into line. If I had read it during the war, it would I think have filled me with enthusiasm. At present, however, I'm too constricted by my scholastic life to be quite open to its influence. Even so, yesterday and today, when talking with some colleagues, I had occasion to notice that there's still a spark of fire hidden in the embers. This very morning, I fear I was rather too fiery (—we were talking about the failure of Wilson's blundering efforts—) in defending my optimistic views on the future of the world . . . Still, fundamentally I don't regret having now and again to proclaim the faith I profess. It's only through faith that one is strong, and only through faith that one can influence others.

Externally, I haven't done anything of interest. On Friday, looking for a quiet corner in which to make the stations of the cross, I went into the chapel in the Rue d'Ulm,—and passed by the former Carmelite house, too, in the Rue Denfert [. . .]

[. . .]

Goodbye. I'm writing from the Museum, where I'm spending the evening. When I leave I'm proposing to go to Uncle George's.[1]

Always devotedly yours. My love to Robert, and Marcel.

PIERRE

[*Paris*] *27th April 1919*

I must write to you once more before you get back,—the more so that yesterday I had your nice long letter of the 25th. I'm glad that you're feeling a relief from tension now (whatever form the relief may have taken),—pleased, too, that you have

---

[1] Their uncle, Georges Teillard d'Eyry.

come to attach less and less importance to the superficial ups and downs (and successes) of life. There's no doubt that there is a powerful educative force lodged in the world, which continually calls us to journey further into the deep layers of being: what attracts us in things is always withdrawing further from us, beyond every individual tangible reality, and finally beyond death: we're forced (by a necessity rooted in ourselves) to pass through the world,—and we're forced (by a necessity rooted in the world) to leave it.—While I've been finishing *Le Feu*, chance led me to buy at Alcan's a curious book translated from Baldwin, *Le Pancalisme* (*pan*= all, *calos*= beautiful). It's an obscure piece of work, written in startling style and language (startling because of its oddity and complexity). The author tries to show that the only possible unification of the universe must be sought in the ' aesthetic ' sphere. I haven't properly grasped the actual essence of his thought (which I suspect is fundamentally quite simple); but it's odd to find the same ' motif' treated so differently by the fiery d'Annunzio and the abstruse professor. Unlike W. James, Baldwin [1] seems to be utterly opposed to pluralism;—both of them, however, share a fundamental agreement in their respect for the universe and their faith in our power to build it. What you tell me of Froebel [2], and his possible usefulness, interests me, of course. You must tell me about this, and you must show me also your Benson in printed form. It's quite possible that, while your view of the subject is perfectly clear, you may feel that it hasn't been fully expressed in the lecture. (That's a good sign, anyway.) But I can assure you that taken as it stands your work certainly brings the subject into focus. I don't think anyone in France has properly criticized the English mystical novel. Nothing new in my external life. This holiday has certainly been a good rest for me. I went to the Georges yesterday. This afternoon, I'm to meet Joseph and Antoinette

[1] Possibly James Mark Baldwin (1861–1934) the American philosopher and psychologist, who in 1919 was teaching at the École des Hautes Études Sociales in Paris.

[2] Frederick Froebel, the German educationalist, 1782–1852.

at four, at your mother's. She'll give me news of you. Met, also, some of my friends in the 4th mixed.

Goodbye just for now. Always yours in Christo.

PIERRE

[. . .]

Jersey, 2nd August 1919

Yesterday, with real joy, I received your card from Arvant. I'm glad you were able to spend three quiet days at Sarcenat, with Guiguite;—but I see that my first letter to the family didn't arrive while you were there, so that you must have been a little puzzled by the news I sent you to Le Chambon. I imagined that you knew what I had written to Papa. In two words, it amounts to this—that my papers were fixed up without any trouble at Saint-Malo, and that, by a happy chance, there was a small sailing ship in the almost empty harbour just leaving for Jersey. We were able to get a passage;—we left at 2 o'clock in brilliant sunshine and arrived at Saint-Hélier at midnight on a most lovely night, romantically guided by the various lights on the island.

Since my last letter, my time has been fully and really rather pleasantly occupied. I've been twice down to the rocks at low tide to collect strange creatures of all shapes, and I've spent long hours watching how these beings, whose life is so far removed from ours, live and unfold. I've had several interesting conversations with the juniors here, and have noticed in them, I think, a salutary upsurge of vitality, the fruit of the war. I've begun to discuss things with Père Valensin[1], and, for a start, gave him *Mon Univers*. And finally I've settled down to a little writing.

To give you a bit more detail: I'm really expecting to get

---

[1] Père Auguste Valensin, s.j., author of numerous works, including some on Dante, whose correspondence with Blondel is of very great interest.

something useful out of my stay here. I feel that in Valensin I've indeed found a sure friend, all the more sure that, with all his warm personal and intellectual sympathy, he isn't quite at one with me. As it happened, I found him busily engaged in a study of pantheism he had been working on for an article in Alès' *Dictionnaire Apologétique*. As it happens, too, my friend Charles says that he is coming from Louvain, some time about the 15th. I couldn't hope for anything better. I feel sure that our individual views will react to fill one another out, and that a methodical movement for good will emerge from this little get-together. Say a prayer sometimes to our Lord that he may send me during these days some of his Spirit, so that I may be true to him in the light. I told you, I think, that Val. is a great friend of Blondel whom he sees frequently during the six months he's not in Jersey. It's very remarkable and very pronounced, this gulf between thought that lives and thought that doesn't! ...

At last I've got down to writing something—semi-poetical in style—allegorical in form. The allegory is the story of Elias [1]: ' And it came to pass, as they still went on, and talked, that, behold, there appeared a chariot of fire, and horses of fire, and parted them both asunder; and Elias went up by a whirlwind into heaven.' The whirlwind, as you'll have realized, is matter, which draws with it and liberates those who know how to grasp its spiritual power. It's quite a short piece, and it would call for Vigny's technical skill to express what's in my mind. Besides, I present my idea without any of the subtle qualifications and distinctions that my essay would include. So it'll again be something to be shown only to friends. At any rate, I'll have put down on paper the basic core of what I've been feeling these last four months,—that's always some satisfaction, isn't it?

A lovely feast of St Ignatius, the day before yesterday. For five years I'd quite forgotten these delights and used not to miss them. Even so it was a great joy to come back to them. I feel that I was able to offer our blessed father (as we say in the Society)

[1] The reference is to *The Spiritual Power of Matter*.

a better-prepared heart, for I've begun, at the age of thirty-five, to understand what it means to love something so much that you really don't give a damn for anything else compared with it . . .—Yesterday, I'm sure, we'll both have been praying to the heart of our Lord, in whom there is no separation.

My love to all of you.

Always yours,

PIERRE

[*Jersey*] *8th August 1919*

I received your most welcome letter of the first, three days ago. I'm glad to think that you're feeling at peace, in your own home, and I'm thinking of you enjoying the same wonderful weather that we're having here. Yesterday we went to pay a visit (—a goodbye visit, since the College—did I tell you?—is being closed) to the country house in the south of the island that the Bon-Secours nuns have rented for the last two years. I was surprised by the ' southern ' beauty of this corner which I hardly knew before, and that from the outside. This house, Italian in style and brightly painted, stands at the head of a little gully that runs down to the bay of St.-Hélier. The garden is planted with eucalyptus trees, cedars, cypresses, and holm-oaks. And it's through this warm, dark, foliage that yesterday we looked out on an almost dark-blue sea, dotted with red granite rocks. I think the Côte d'Azur must look much the same, though here, of course, the colours are rather soft and moist. In the summer, however, this loss of brilliance is an added charm. I find the sea here and the green in which everything is clothed, completely delightful. Last Monday, I spent a great part of the day on the water, again in a sailing boat and with Fr Bento. This time, we went out trawling for fish, with a man who knows the business. All we caught was a few plaice, and a sting-ray, which the fisherman threw back with disgust, as being evil and poisonous, though not without having first carefully removed the liver (the oil from which is said to be a universal remedy). But we had a delightful sail and I brought back some cuttlefish and a small dog-fish, which will give me a couple of days' work in the laboratory. So you see that I'm making the most of my open-air cure.—I still spend the best part of my time in dissecting and examining various things under the microscope. Even this I find quite a rest. However, when September comes, I must get down to systematizing a bit my hazy knowledge of botany.

I haven't yet had any really decisive talk with my friend V.[1] He's often tired, and I don't want to be a burden to him. However, he's already read two things, and I hope that on the essential point we'll be in agreement: he admits, in fact, that the universe forms one natural whole, which finally can subsist only by dependence from our Lord. That's the main thing: and I think that, following on from that, we'll be able to part company only on questions of emphasis or shading. I can tell you, I was most surprised to find my friend so categorical on this point, and with such a predominant interest, too, in pantheism. With him, I believe, it's primarily an intellectual problem: what impels him is more, I think, the need to formulate a philosophy than the urgency of venerating an omni-presence. Even that, however, has the advantage that each of us complements the other. He told me that Blondel has such strong views on the consistence of the universe in Christ that he doesn't dare to go all the way with him—even though, he added, Rousselot didn't hesitate to do so. I wasn't familiar with that side of Blondel's thought, and I'm going to try to learn more about it. I've had two or three interesting talks again with the juniors. The war has left its mark, and we'll see the result in ten years' time. Besides that, I've finished 'Elias' (don't worry—that's not the title). I'm fairly pleased with it, because I feel that in it I've got across what I was putting into words. But it'll hardly be intelligible to anyone who isn't already familiar from another source with my views of the role and nature of matter. Others, who haven't

[1] Père Valensin.

been prepared for it, will take me for some sort of rebel. I'll show it to you in October. If I write anything else meanwhile, it will be to readjust my ideas following on Val.'s remarks.—I'll be able to see the *Correspondant* here, and I'll read what you mention. Poor little S.!

Goodbye. You were specially in my thoughts on the 6th.— The Transfiguration has come to be a favourite feast of mine, because it expresses exactly what I love most in our Lord and what I most ardently seek from him.—I pray—don't you—that the blessed metamorphosis of all things may take place in us and our eyes be opened. Always yours. Kind messages to all of you.

PIERRE

Jersey, 21st August 1919

I haven't heard from you since my last letter,—but I can easily understand why. Time flies when you're on holiday, and you didn't leave for La Voûte [1] with any hope of greater leisure. I'm thinking of you now in your stately home, and hope that you're profitably enjoying the company of your friends, without letting yourself be worried by the little inconveniences you seemed rather to fear in July. Knowing that you're there makes me think of you still more, and pray for you, that there as elsewhere, you may do some good to those around you, and draw from it the utmost profit for your interior life. If any truth has come to assume greater importance for me during these peaceful days, it is the insignificance of all our cares, even those we take to be the most serious, once we shut our eyes to all but the inner, divine, element in them. How true it is that the vision of God—which is the only thing we should seek in anything that happens— should relieve us of many of our fears that we may not be happy enough or successful enough . . . You know that my dearest

[1] The Polignacs' château.

wish is that our Lord may become for you the only source of joy in everything: I would then be completely at ease in my mind for I would know that your peace is proof against every trial and every monotony and that, wherever you are, you are living in the light.

Nothing important this last week, so far as I'm concerned. My friend Ch.[1] left the day after I last wrote to you. We agreed to keep in touch regularly. And then, as I've long been thinking, we decided that the best way to spread our views was to start, first of all, from theology, from scripture, from the Church's mystical practice. That's the basic foundation, the firmest, that all the philosophies can do no more than illustrate, with more or less accuracy. While reaching a more precise definition of my points of contact with my friends, I have also come to realize the turn of my mind that divides me from them. I'm less concerned than they are with the metaphysical side of things, with what might have been or might not have been, with the abstract conditions of existence: all that seems to me inevitably misleading or shaky. I realize that, to the very marrow of my bones, I'm sensitive to the real, to what is made of it. My concern is to discover the conditions for such progress as is open to us, and not, starting from first principles, some theoretical development of the universe. This bias means that I'll always be a philistine to the professional philosophers: but I feel that my strength lies in the fidelity with which I obey it. So I'll continue to advance along those lines. Others can bring me into line with the principles, if they can. For the moment, I'd like to have enough time to straighten out some ideas on ' the attributes of the world ' (particularly according to St Paul). But I'm pretty well occupied—interestingly, too, I must say—with botany. I feel that I'm learning and systematizing a great deal —which is always a pleasant feeling.—Four-fifths of the house is in retreat. This gives me plenty of peace. I take some solitary walks along the sea shore, which I enjoy greatly. There have been days when the weather was so clear that you could see all

[1] Père Charles, S.J.

the details of the French coast from the cliffs of the Nord.—No
news at Sarcenat.—[. . .]

Goodbye. Remember me to Mlle Zanta.

Always yours,

PIERRE

Maison Saint-Louis, Jersey, C.I., 28th August 1919

Since my last letter, I've had yours of the 18th and your card of
the 21st. Robert's tiredness worried me a little;—and then
I was glad to know that you were at La Voûte, in an atmosphere
of faithful friendship. So it is that the Lord leads you, from day
to day, through worries and joys. Abandon yourself more and
more, with confidence,—and, as the *Imitation* says, love the divine
hand through all it gives you. As it happened, your letter of
the 18th came as an answer to the wish I expressed the day
before when writing to you: that peace might penetrate the
depth of your being, born of the conviction that whatever
happens can only increase within you the one Presence that
alone is worth seeking.—I was very glad to hear the news you
give me of your stay with your friends; but what I want more
than anything is for you to have a peaceful rest. I know that
all is well with you. And that's all I want.

There's not much to tell you about the week that's just gone
by. I haven't been out much, and I've made considerable progress
with my work. I've had a few short talks again with Val. I'm
becoming more and more convinced that my position is perfectly
tenable, and I'm not without hope of influencing my friend
sufficiently to induce him to undertake constructive work on the
lines that interest me. The long article *Pantheism* he has just
finished for the *Dictionnaire d'Apologétique*, is limited, he tells me,
to a *refutation of pantheistic incarnation* (= Spinoza's pantheism),
but he recognizes that that's only half what has to be done, and
the least fruitful half at that, and for that reason he is dissatisfied
with his article. There should also be, as he admitted to me
himself, a synthesis of the Christian faith to take the place of

303

what is rejected. To my mind, it's a great point that he realizes this need.

I'd very much like to write a few pages to be read by my friends who teach philosophy or theology. But botany takes my mind off it, and occupies the best part of my time. At any rate, I don't find it boring. I'm having no difficulty in giving precision to a great mass of rather vaguely apprehended knowledge; and that's considerable cause for satisfaction.

The good weather deserted us in the end. Rain and storm for the last four days: this is one of the typical aspects of Jersey. I hope you aren't being too much affected in your mountains by these disagreeable visitations. Since yesterday I go to say mass in one of the numerous Carmelite convents that have nested around our house. I really enjoy saying it in an atmosphere of such intense religious life. Sometimes I think of ' The Convent Chapel '—and I don't forget you.

Since nothing is so engrossing as work combined at the same time with rest, my correspondence is very much in arrears, and I have very little time for reading,—which I regret. However, I've borrowed from the library two old-fashioned novels, *Dominique* (by Fromentin) and Benjamin Constant's *Adolphe*. In each I've admired the analysis of souls, accurate in spite of some improbability in the plot. *Dominique* interested me also by its descriptions of the provincial and country life (the life of our grandparents, and even of our parents) which we saw something of and for which we still, I believe, retain a certain nostalgia. —It must be most restful, I think, to write a novel. You could put into it a number of things that are rather painful to keep shut up inside yourself. Daudet would say that you throw out the alien parts of your Ego. Unfortunately, I feel no better equipped for such work than for playing a musical instrument or writing verse . . .

Goodbye. Remember me to Mlle Zanta. You know how devotedly I am yours.

PIERRE

Jersey, 5th September 1919

Don't be horrified at this wretched format, by no means usual in our correspondence. I can't find any other paper on which to answer your excellent letter of the 25th, which I received yesterday. As you must have known, I was awaiting details of your life at La Voûte and read them with great interest. It really does me good to feel that you have some friends around you and that you're happy. And then, when I find myself beginning to wish that this situation (or its equivalent) may always last for you, I think, as you do, that all that is best in you has come about, no doubt, as a result of the ' ingratitudes ' of life, and that no environment can, for you, compare with that of our Lord—which, as a general rule, closely surrounds only those who have nothing in the world to rest upon but him. This thought makes up for the twinge of regret I feel when I realize that this letter will reach you almost at the end of your short holiday. You'll probably feel a shadow of melancholy pass over you during these last days at Le Chambon, between Polignac and the separations that are involved in your return. Maybe it's there that our Lord awaits you, to sanctify, in a fresh gift of yourself that you will make him, the new strength you have gained from your rest. In any case, don't be distressed if you feel the influence of a little sadness; but make use of this frame of mind to give even more consistence in your life to the divine. Everything is so precarious and so empty: we should have a sense of victory every time that life forces us to master it and to detach ourselves from it. As usual, I prayed most particularly for you on this first Friday, and on the 8th of this month I'll remember you with special care.

I didn't write to you yesterday, my usual day, because I was very busy in the afternoon,—agreeably, too. I don't know whether I ever told you that in 1914 a cave was discovered in the island, with numerous traces of Neanderthal (= Mousterian) man. The very extensive excavations were conducted by a Dr Marett, a Jersey man by birth and a professor at Oxford,—a friend of Breuil, Boule and all the others. I met Marett yesterday and visited the excavation site with him. In itself, it was a most interesting excursion; with Marett (a great big fellow, at least as strong and nimble as I, in spite of his fifty years) the interest was doubled. He told me lots of things about Oxford,—about Australia and its savages, whom he visited in 1914,—about Jersey, where his family has lived for centuries. Being a professor of anthropology, a number of his pupils follow him here. Thus I wasn't much surprised to find on the cliff, above the cave (not far from the place shown on the postcard I sent you) a tiny makeshift cottage, with a corrugated iron roof, tucked away in a hollow, in which two of the Hon. Marett's research students live snugly during their vacation. These ladies spend their leisure hours in reading, painting, bathing and neatly sorting out little jaw-bones of rodents found in the diggings. They offered us tea, with all the conventional formalities,—all very English, eh?—When we got back M. Marett did me the honours of his ' manor ', as they call it in Jersey—a very old house, restored under the first empire, hidden away in a luxuriantly green garden a hundred yards from the sea. Countless records of Jersey and Jersey artists have been collected in this manor with great taste: seascapes, costumes, admirals, governors. Surrounded by all this, you feel that you're one with the past right back to the fifteenth century. This is the ancient, hidden, Jersey that I've spent several years without even suspecting. It's one more of those things that it's rather distressing to feel threatened by the social changes we're involved in. The future, however, is finer than any past. That, as you know, is what I firmly believe.

Apart from this little expedition, my life is still the same, hardworking but easy. I've had some interesting walks all by myself along the coast. I've got on well with my botany. Finally, I've recently written eight pages on the way in which one should understand the limits of the human body. I tell you this because Val. told me he was delighted with what I wrote and wants to send it to Blondel,—with my ' Stories after Benson ',

too. I'll tell you if this comes off, and what impression it makes.
Goodbye. Always yours,

PIERRE

Maison Saint-Louis, Jersey, C.I., 17th September 1919

I've had your card of the 11th, which seemed to me extremely
symbolic of what true feminism should always be. I'm sure you
chose it purposely. I was glad to hear that you're in good spirits.
I'm praying now that you may not be dismayed at having to
face another new year—which is always a nasty shock—but
that you may master it through the strength of the ' new spirit '
in you. I must tell you how much I've been moved today by what
I feel I've come to see in the feast of the stigmata of St Francis.
Hitherto, this hasn't meant much to me. This time, however,
when I was reading in the breviary St Bonaventure's account of
the vision, I was very much struck by the symbolism of the
ardent crucified spirit that appeared to St Francis and filled him
with a mixture of pain and joy. I don't know whether it's what
the miracle really means: but in it I saw one of the most perfect
representations and revelations that the Church has ever received
of the universal, transforming Christ who showed himself, I
believe, to St. Paul and whom our own generation so undeniably
needs. On this occasion I felt once again the longing to live
only as a force or a living idea, so completely would the influence
of the *unum necessarium* animate me—to live completely depersonalized—' in him seen in all things '. What makes me feel
sure that this is a good desire is the deep conviction I'm carried
along by, that the flame can come only from above and that
we'll be able to keep it burning only through purity and humility.

Yes, we'll have a great deal to say to one another in a fortnight's time: the fruits of absence. These last days at Jersey
seem to me even better than the first—no doubt because I've
become accustomed again to the house and the country;—no
doubt, too, because the island is beginning to take on the autumn

tints and provide the autumn weather that I've always liked best. All that's waiting for me in Paris will stop me from being tempted to have any regrets at leaving. As there's no fixed time-table for the boats, I can't yet make any exact plans for my return: I'd like to be back by October 1st. You'll be pleased to know that I showed Val. the paper I wrote in August, the ' hymn to matter '[1]. He was absolutely delighted with it, had two copies made on the spot, and took them with him. He'd like it to be published. If it should ever get by the censors I'd like it to come out anonymously: it wasn't written as a personal discovery, but rather as the expression of a truth. To sign it would, as I see it, only detract from its importance—' *Vox clamantis in deserto* ', if I may put it so.

Remember me kindly to Mme Parion. Always yours.

PIERRE

[1] Included in *The Spiritual Power of Matter*.

Index

INDEX

action: and discussion, 157-8; God and appetite for, 210; passive, 149; and sanctification, 58

Action Française, 122, 143, 253

adoration, 68, 79

affective and apprehensive powers, 106

Agadir incident, 25n

Agoult, Marie, Comtesse d', 18

agrégation, 15

Alès, M. d', 280

all, God as, 84

Aloysius Gonzaga, St, 278

Alsace, 254ff

Americans, as soldiers, 218

Amiens, 228

angels, 94

Annamites, 125, 126

Aragonnès, Claude (Marguerite Teillard-Chambon), writings: *Lincoln, héros d'un peuple*, 19, 21; *La Loi du faible*, 17; on Marie d'Agoult, 18; *Mlle de Scudéry*, 18; *Prises de vues américaines*, 19; *Véroniques*, 227, 243

armistice (1918), 250

Auffray, M., 97, 99

Augustine, St, 62

Ave Maria, 246-7

baccalauréat, 17

Baldwin, James Mark, 296

Balzac, Honoré de, 36, 234

Barbusse, Henri, 28, 186

Bar-le-Duc, 118

Baudelaire, Charles, 214

Baudrillart, Mgr, 63, 270, 272, 288

Beaugeard (Baugeard), Abbé, 178, 179, 206, 207, 224, 238, 244, 270

Bégouën, Count, 208

Bégouën, Max and Jacques, 208

Bélinay, Capt. de, 135-6

Benson, Robert Hugh, 130, 134, 135, 236, 271, 276, 277-9, 286, 289, 296

Bento, Fr., 299

Bergson, Henri, 16, 62, 96, 103, 111, 170

Berkaire, St, 172, 173

Black Forest, 281, 283, 285

Blondel, Maurice, 158, 173, 176, 210, 298, 300, 306

Bordeaux, Henry, 208

Boule, Marcellin, 98

Bourget, Paul, 76, 78, 79, 95, 96

Boussac, Jean, 91, 103, 110, 116, 123, 124

Boútroux, Émile, 121

Breuil, Henri, 66, 91, 103

Brie, 179

Brière, Yves de la, 288

CAPES, 15

Cathelineau, Anne-Marie de, 94

cathedrals, 188

Chambon, Le, 48, 198, 243

Chanteur, Père, 243, 247

chaplaincy, Teilhard de Chardin's, 169, 170

charity, 117, 133, 134, 137, 146

Charles, Pierre, 289, 298, 302

INDEX

313